The Blues Line

The Blues Line

A Collection of Blues Lyrics

Compiled by Eric Sackheim

with Illustrations by Jonathan Shahn

A MUSHINSHA BOOK

Published by GROSSMAN PUBLISHERS

Some of the song versions in this book were previously printed in *Origin* magazine. The illustrations were completed under a grant from the Center for Advanced Study at the University of Illinois.

Distributed in Japan by
CHARLES E. TUTTLE CO., Inc.
Suido 1-chome, 2-6, Bunkyo-ku
Tokyo, Japan

First Published in the United States of America
in 1969 by
GROSSMAN PUBLISHERS, Inc.
125 A East 19th Street
New York, N. Y. 10003

Designed and produced by Mushinsha Limited, IRM/Rosei Bldg., 4, Higashi Azabu 1-chome, Minato-ku, Tokyo, Japan. Copyright in Japan, 1969, by Eric Sackheim. All rights reserved. Printed in Japan.
First edition, 1969.
Library of Congress Catalogue Card No. 78-87912

To the Memory of Go-Toba-In (1180-1239),
Who Had a Vision of What an Anthology Might Be

Preface

A COLLECTION such as this might have been compiled out of an interest in politics or anthropology or sociology or history or musicology or literary criticism or biography or psychology; in fact it was motivated simply by a belief that a man who makes a song has accomplished something of consequence.

"A man . . . makes a song:" that is, he *sings* it on a particular occasion, confronts his universe with a structure of sound and meaning in a way appropriate only to himself and relevant to a specific point in time. That another singer, or the same, could have sung (or written) that song on a previous occasion, or later, is inconceivable; though similar songs certainly can and do result from other occasions, there is an unfortunate tendency on the part of the disciplines, academic and politic, to lose contact with the uniqueness and particularity of a given achievement, to be over-ready to sacrifice that to the desire for security offered by a facile "comprehension" based on the similarities, and similarities of similarities. "The ephemeral blues must merge for them in one; / The basic slate, the universal hue."[1]

As the particular man is a unique phenomenon, his song is a unique event.

The universe from which the collection in this volume was made consists of songs sung by black singers, recorded (with few exceptions) on 78 rpm records for black audiences from the mid 1920's through the mid '50's—which is hardly exclusive enough to constitute a definition: most of the singers, however, would be willing to have most of the songs called "blues." And that will *have* to serve to define the territory.

As for selection, these 270 songs were included after listening to some six thousand.[2] That individual readers will object to the inclusion or exclusion of particular songs is, I suppose, inevitable. Regarding broader categories, some may argue that the female "city blues" singers of the late '20's do not "belong" in this essentially "country blues" anthology. But, even admitting the validity of the distinction, the reciprocal influences of the two groups of singers is certainly sufficient justification for the inclusion. On the other hand, the bulk of the most popular post-war blues material has been left out, as it was felt that those songs and singers could be better treated separately.[3]

Grouping of the songs is primarily geographical and historical, with women singers and piano-player singers being presented in separate sections of their own. A glance at the table of contents will reveal the inadequacy of the system: consider a woman piano-player from the Mississippi delta who played, sang and made records successively in Jackson, Memphis, St. Louis, and Chicago from 1927 to 1950. Nevertheless, in that it serves to break up the whole into smaller relatively coherent units, and brings singers close to others (though certainly not all others) with whom they may have something in common, the system is probably not much worse than some other system that could have been devised.[4]

The arrangement of the songs on the page may appear at first an arbitrary and gratuitous playing with spatial effects in imitation of some seventeenth or twentieth century poet. That is not the intent:

Even if a case can be made for the presentation of these songs as poetry, without including musical notation[5] (and such a case should not be overly difficult to develop), the one who sets the songs down, who translates them from sound to print, surely has the responsibility of making his typography tell as much as it can about the songs as vocal performance: breath, pause, break; spacing, weight. And his inability to render such elusive factors as tone and color merely makes it more imperative that he do what he can with what he can. And that has been the attempt here—admittedly, in all too many cases, not as successful as one might wish.

As it was felt to be important to abandon the confining yet more or less ubiquitous notion that the blues constitute essentially a single form, so it was considered to be worth the effort to try to avoid the all-too-common sloppiness in the hearing and setting down of words: if a song has value its value is certainly in the words as they are and not as filtered through a careless ear or hasty hand that is satisfied to write "repeat" in place of a line that is only approximately similar to the line that went before.

But, the objective stated, it must be followed immediately by apologies for failing to live up to it. Particularities of diction and pronunciation, parochial vocabulary,[6] primitive recording techniques, and poor preservation of records, in some cases, render impossible the certainty with which one would like to be able to offer the printed versions. Charlie Patton, Blind Willie Johnson, King Solomon Hill, Buddy Boy Hawkins, Son House —all present problems to the listener that sometimes appear insurmountable, but, these being some of the greatest of the blues singers, it was felt to be worth the trouble to struggle through to a version as closely approximating the original as possible, and not to accede to the dictates of an embarrassment that would rather repress a good song entirely than reveal an inadequacy in handling some of its difficulties.

The most doubtful words or passages are printed in italics; in the few cases where what the ear heard could not be converted by the mind into anything plausible in print, a ". . ." has been inserted (all other typographical indications—spaces, dashes, etc. —are intended to represent something that actually happens in the song itself; words in parentheses are spoken, rather than sung, either by the singer or someone else). In all cases of doubt, ear was given precedence over mind.

There is much to be said for attempting to reproduce a man's phonetics as faithfully as possible. There is also, from other points of view, much to be said against it. Here, "standard" spellings were adhered to except where a more precise indication seemed required by the workings of the whole of any particular song.

I believe that this volume contains a number of improvements on other versions that have been previously printed elsewhere; and some songs have been included which others had given up as utterly undecipherable. As for the mistakes, which I am sure abound, I hope that they will be corrected by listeners with better ears than mine.[7]

At the end of the volume is an afterword, "A Survey of Sorts: Various Voices," containing some 50 pages of quotations from a wide variety of different sources. The biographical and autobiographical quotes from the singers, their friends, relations, and acquaintances are not included out of a belief that it is necessary, or even useful, to know something of a man's history in order to appreciate his creative achievement. And the passages from other literatures are not there because they are felt to shed any more light on the blues they follow than any other quotations might have done, nor are they intended to affirm any notion of universality in the needs, motivations, and expressions of men. Their inclusion is predicated on the conviction that constructive dialogue can be established between almost any two points, and that dialogue is generally to be preferred to its absence.

ERIC SACKHEIM
Tokyo, 1969

1. Wallace Stevens. This should not be confused with the common assumption that these songs are necessarily an expression of personally felt grief, pain, anger, joy, etc.

2. For what it's worth, compare Confucius who is supposed to have selected the 300-odd songs of the present *Book of Odes* from an original collection of 3000.

3. Cf. *Urban Blues,* Charles Keil, Chicago, 1966.

4. Occasionally, however, the decision to include a singer in any particular category may be quite arbitrary, and readers might prefer to have certain singers classified differently: my own feelings on the matter are not very strong. ("Although our information is inaccurate we do not guarantee it." (Erik Satie))

5. Representing the music of one culture with the notation of another is never satisfactory: either it fudges and fakes or becomes too complex to be very widely useful. Wherever possible, the reader should, of course, listen to the songs, which are available on a number of reissue labels—such as Origin Jazz Library (OJL), Blues Classics, Belzona/Yazoo, RBF, Historical, Roots, Riverside, Victor, Columbia, and others.

6. Local place-names is an area where a great deal of progress has been made in recent years in deciphering the records of a number of singers; sometimes I feel the method has been overly relied on to fill in problem passages: one listener of King Solomon Hill's "Gone Dead Train," for example, has used a great deal of ingenuity in loading up the song with names of small towns, which I must confess not to hear in it at all—which is not to say that I'm satisfied with my own version.

7. One such listener, Clay Jackson, is responsible for most of the versions included here of the songs of Blind Lemon Jefferson and Robert Johnson. Others whose ear-help was invaluable include Dave Evans, Bernard Klatzko, Bill Givens, Pete Welding, Nick Perls, Ron Foreman, and Goddard Greaves. Published work of Paul Oliver, Samuel Charters, and Dick Spottswood was also useful.

Contents

PREFACE   *page 7*

SOMEWHERE TO BEGIN
    Doc Read and Vera Hall   Death is Awful   25
    Doc Reese   Ol' Hannah   26
    Blind Blake   Diddie Wa Diddie   29

SOME WOMEN
    Lottie Kimbrough (Beaman)   Rolling Log Blues   33
          Going Away Blues   34
    Louise Johnson   On the Wall   35
    Bertha Lee   Mind Reader Blues   36
    Geechie Wiley   Eagles on a Half   37
    Elvie Thomas   Motherless Child Blues   38
    Lillian Miller   Dead Drunk Blues   39
    Nellie Florence   Jacksonville Blues   40
    Jenny Pope   Doggin' Me Around Blues   41
    Iva Smith   Third Alley Blues   42
    Lil Johnson   Never Let Your Left Hand Know   43
          You'll Never Miss Your Jelly   44
    Bessie Jackson (Lucille Bogan)   Tired As I Can Be   45
          Stew Meat Blues   46

Ma Rainey	Don't Fish in My Sea	47
	Southern Blues	49
Bessie Smith	Back Water Blues	50
	Black Mountain Blues	51
	Jailhouse Blues	52
Bessie Tucker	Frying Pan Skillet Blues	54
Sara Martin	Death Sting Me Blues	55
Victoria Spivey	Blood Hound Blues	56
Memphis Minnie	Nothing in Rambling	57
	Me and My Chauffeur Blues	58
	Killer Diller	59
	'Frisco Town	60
	Memphis Minnie-Jitis Blues	62
Alice Moore	Three Men	63
Ma Yancey	Make Me a Pallet on Your Floor	65
Chippie Hill	Charleston Blues	66

TEXAS

Henry Thomas	Fishing Blues	69
	Bob McKinney	70
Blind Lemon Jefferson	Pneumonia Blues	72
	Rabbit Foot Blues	73
	Prison Cell Blues	74
	Rising High Water Blues	75
	Bad Luck Blues	76
	Big Night Blues	77
	Peach Orchard Mama	78
	Tin Cup Blues	79
	That Black Snake Moan	80
	Stocking Feet Blues	81
	Chock House Blues	83
	Broke and Hungry	84
	Deceitful Brownskin Blues	85
	Long Distance Moan	86
	That Crawling Baby Blues	87
	Piney Woods Money Mama	88
	Wartime Blues	89
	Black Horse Blues	90
	Easy Rider Blues	91
Buddy Boy Hawkins	Awful Fix	92
Ramblin' (Willard) Thomas	Poor Boy Blues	93
	No Job Blues	94
	Back Gnawing Blues	95
Blind Willie Johnson	I'm Gonna Run to the City of Refuge	96
	God Don't Never Change	98
	If I Had My Way	100
	Jesus Make Up My Dying Bed	102
	Jesus Is Coming Soon	104
	Motherless Children	106

Leadbelly	T. B. Blues	108
	Roberta—Part 1.	110
	Roberta—Part 2.	111
	Pigmeat	113
	Becky Deem	114
	Packin' Trunk Blues	116
	All Out and Down	117
Little Hat Jones	Kentucky Blues	119
"Funny Paper" Smith	Fool's Blues	120
Texas Alexander	No More Women Blues	121
	98 Degree Blues	122
	Levee Camp Moan	124
Gene Campbell	Robbing and Stealing Blues	125
L. C. Williams	You Never Miss the Water	126
Lightning Hopkins	Katie May	127
	Highway Blues	128
	Short Haired Woman	130
	She's Mine	131
	Mister Charlie	132
	Death Bells	134
Mance Lipscomb	Captain Captain	135
	Alabama Bound	136
Lil' Son Jackson	Charlie Cherry	138
	Homeless Blues	139

NEW ORLEANS TO JACKSON

Rabbit Brown	James Alley	143
Sam Collins	The Jailhouse Blues	145
	Slow Mama Slow	146
King Solomon Hill	Whoopee Blues	147
	The Gone Dead Train	148
Arthur Pettis (Petties)	Out on Santa-fe Blues	149
Blind Willie (Joe) Reynolds	Married Man Blues	150
	Nehi Blues	152
Tommy Johnson	Maggie Campbell Blues	154
	Canned Heat Blues	156
	Big Road Blues	158
Ishman (Ishmon) Bracey	Leaving Town Blues	161
	Saturday Blues	162
Willie Lofton	Dark Road Blues	164
Rube Lacy	Ham Hound Crave	166
Charlie McCoy	That Lonesome Train Took My Baby Away	167
(Kansas) Joe McCoy	Evil Devil Woman	168
Bo Carter	All Around Man	170
	Old Devil	172
John Byrd	Old Timbrook Blues	173
Skip James	Devil Got My Woman	175
	Hard Time Killin, Floor Blues	176
	Cypress Grove Blues	177

Tommy McClennan	Brown Skin Girl	*179*
Arthur "Big Boy" Crudup	Death Valley Blues	*180*

MISSISSIPPI: THE DELTA

William Harris	Bullfrog Blues	*183*
Bo Weavil Jackson	You Can't Keep No Brown	*185*
Charlie Patton	34 Blues	*187*
	Bird Nest Bound	*188*
	High Sheriff Blues	*190*
	Moon Going Down	*192*
	High Water Everywhere—1.	*193*
	High Water Everywhere—2.	*194*
	Revenue Man Blues	*196*
	Hang It on the Wall	*198*
Willie Brown	Future Blues	*201*
	M & O Blues	*202*
Henry Sims	Tell Me Man Blues	*203*
Son House	My Black Mama	*204*
	The Jinx Blues	*208*
	The Pony Blues	*210*
	Preaching the Blues	*212*
Bobby Grant	Nappy Head Blues	*214*
Robert Johnson	Come On in My Kitchen	*215*
	Walking Blues	*216*
	Terraplane Blues	*218*
	Stones in My Passway	*219*
	Traveling Riverside Blues	*220*
	I Believe I'll Dust My Broom	*221*
	Milkcow's Calf Blues	*222*
	Hellhound on My Trail	*223*
	Me and the Devil Blues	*224*
	Preachin' Blues	*225*
Mississippi John Hurt	Spike Driver Blues	*226*
	Candy Man Blues	*229*
	Got the Blues, Can't Be Satisfied	*230*
	Frankie	*231*
	Ain't No Tellin'	*232*
Garfield Akers	Dough Roller Blues	*233*
Joe Calicott	Fare Thee Well Blues	*234*
Booker (Bukka) White	Aberdeen, Mississippi Blues	*235*
	Parchman Farm Blues	*236*
	Sleepy Man Blues	*238*
	Sic 'Em Dogs On	*239*
	The Panama Limited	*240*
	Fixing to Die	*242*
Isaiah Nettles	It's Cold in China Blues	*243*

MEMPHIS

Jim Jackson	Old Dog Blue	*247*

Frank Stokes	'Tain't Nobody's Business	249
	You Shall	251
Furry Lewis	Big Chief Blues	253
	Judge Harsh Blues	254
	Billy Lyons and Stack O'Lee	255
	Dry Land Blues	256
	Kassie Jones	258
	I Will Turn Your Money Green	260
Robert (Tim) Wilkins	Nashville Stonewall Blues	261
	That's No Way to Get Along	262
	I'll Go With Her Blues	264
Sleepy John Estes	Stack o' Dollars	265
	My Black Gal Blues	266
	Milkcow Blues	268
	Everybody Ought to Make a Change	269
	Street Car Blues	270
	Brownsville Blues	271
	Lawyer Clark Blues	272
	Floating Bridge	274
	Working Man Blues	276
(James) Yank Rachel	T-bone Steak Blues	277
	Lake Michigan Blues	278
Memphis Jug Band	Oh Ambulance Man	279
Noah Lewis's Jug Band	New Minglewood Blues	282
Cannon's Jug Stompers	Going to Germany	283
Bill Wilber	My Babe My Babe	286
Memphis Willie B. (Borum)	Bad Girl Blues	288

ALABAMA

Ed Bell	Frisco Whistle Blues	293
	Hambone Blues	294
"Slue Foot Joe"	Tooten Out Blues	296
Barefoot Bill	From Now On	297
	Squabbling Blues	298
	My Crime	300
	Big Rock Jail	302
Edward Thompson	Seven Sister Blues	303
Clifford Gibson	Keep Your Windows Pinned	304
Sunny Boy & His Pals	France Blues	306
Two Poor Boys	Two White Horses in a Line	308
Jaybird Coleman	No More Good Water	309

GEORGIA

Charlie Lincoln (Hicks)	If It Looks Like Jelly, Shakes Like Jelly	313
	Chain Gang Trouble	314
	Depot Blues	316
Barbecue Bob (Hicks)	Barbecue Blues	318
	She's Gone Blues	320
	Cold Wave Blues	322

	Ease It to Me Blues	324
Peg Leg Howell	Lowdown Rounder's Blues	327
Willie Baker	No No Blues	328
Bumble Bee Slim	No Woman No Nickel	329
Blind Willie McTell (Blind Samuel)	Savannah Mama	331
	Three Women Blues	332
	Statesboro Blues	333
	Searching the Desert for the Blues	334
	Talking to Myself	336
	Drive Away Blues	338
	Travelin' Blues	340

NORTH CAROLINA/VIRGINIA

Blind Boy Fuller	Mojo Hiding Woman	345
	Pistol Slapper Blues	346
	Lost Lover Blues	348
	Bye Bye Baby Blues	349
Blind Gary Davis	You Got to Go Down	350
	Blow Gabriel	352
William Moore	One Way Gal	353

ST. LOUIS

Lonnie Johnson	Jersey Belle Blues	357
	Careless Love	358
Charlie Jordan	Keep It Clean	359
	Hunkie Tunkie	361
Hi Henry Brown	Skin Man	365
	Titanic Blues	366
Henry Townsend	Poor Man Blues	367
J. D. (Jelly Jaw) Short	Telephone Arguin' Blues	368
	Snake Doctor Blues	370
Big Joe Williams	Someday Baby	372
	Stepfather Blues	374
	President Roosevelt	376

SOME PIANOS

Wesley Wallace	Number 29	381
Bert Mays	Oh Oh Blues	382
Leroy Carr	Mean Mistreater Mama	383
	Take a Walk Around the Corner	384
Walter Roland	45 Pistol Blues	386
Black Ivory King	Flying Crow	387
Roosevelt Sykes	West Helena Blues	388
	High Price Blues	389
Little Brother Montgomery	The First Time I Met You	391
Lost John Hunter	Y M & V Blues	392
Jesse James	Sweet Patuni	393
Peetie Wheatstraw	More Good Whiskey Blues	394
Walter Davis	I Can Tell By the Way You Smell	396

Speckled Red   The Dirty Dozens   397

Cripple Clarence Lofton   I Don't Know   399

CHICAGO

Big Bill Broonzy   I'm Gonna Move to the Outskirts of Town 404

                              Looking Up at Dawn   405

Hokum Boys:Georgia Tom

        (with Jane Lucas)   Hip Shakin' Strut   406

Washboard Sam   Big Woman   409

                              I Been Treated Wrong   411

Tampa Red   You Got to Love Her with a Feeling   412

Jazz Gillum   Go Back to the Country   414

Sonny Boy Williamson   Big Apple Blues   415

                              Moonshine   416

                              Bad Luck Blues   418

                              Welfare Store   419

Kokomo Arnold   Mean Old Twister   420

Floyd Council   Don't Want No Hungry Woman   421

THE '40's AND '50's

Robert Lockwood   Little Boy Blue   425

Tony Hollins   Stamp Blues   426

Wright Holmes   Alley Blues   428

John Henry Barbee   Six Week Old Blues   430

L. C. Green   Remember Way Back   431

Muddy Waters   Hoochie Coochie   432

Howlin' Wolf   Smokestack Lightning   434

John Lee Hooker   Black Snake   437

SOMEWHERE TO END

Smoky Babe   Hottest Brand Goin'   441

Brother Will Hairston   Alabama Bus   443

Robert Pete Williams   I Got So Old   445

A SURVEY OF SORTS: VARIOUS VOICES   449

List of Illustrations

Blind Blake	page 30
Ma Rainey	48
Bessie Smith	53
Memphis Minnie	61
Ma Yancey	64
Henry Thomas	70
Blind Lemon Jefferson	82
Ramblin' (Willard) Thomas	93
Blind Willie Johnson	103
Leadbelly	109
Texas Alexander	123
Lightning Hopkins	128
Mance Lipscomb	137
Lil' Son Jackson	140
Tommy Johnson	156
Ishman Bracey	160
Bo Carter	171
Skip James	174
Tommy McClennan	178
Charlie Patton	189
Son House	209

Mississippi John Hurt	228
Booker White	237
Jim Jackson	247
Frank Stokes	250
Furry Lewis	253
Furry Lewis	256
Robert Wilkins	262
Sleepy John Estes	267
Sleepy John Estes	273
Memphis Jug Band	280–1
Cannon's Jug Stompers	284–5
Memphis Willie B.	289
Barefoot Bill	299
Clifford Gibson	305
Jaybird Coleman	310
Barbecue Bob	319
Peg Leg Howell	326
Blind Willie McTell	330
Blind Boy Fuller	347
Blind Gary Davis	351
Lonnie Johnson	358
Charlie Jordan	362–3
Henry Townsend	367
J. D. (Jelly Jaw) Short	370
Big Joe Williams	378
Leroy Carr	385
Roosevelt Sykes	388
Roosevelt Sykes/Little Brother Montgomery	390
Peetie Wheatstraw	395
Big Bill Broonzy	403
Georgia Tom	407
Washboard Sam	410
Tampa Red	413
Sonny Boy Williamson	417
Muddy Waters	433
John Lee Hooker	436
Robert Pete Williams	447
Will Shade	478
Gus Cannon	480
Peg Leg Howell	483
Big Joe Williams	487
Leroy Carr	488
Scrapper Blackwell	489
Big Bill Broonzy	493
Muddy Waters	497

The Blues Line

That man walks along weeping
no one knows why
sometimes they think he's weeping for lost loves
like those that torture us so much . . .

Somewhere to Begin

Death Is Awful

        Oh-oh: death is awful
        Oh-oh: death is awful
        Oh-oh: death is awful
        Spare me over
                  another year

If I was a flower
            in my bloom, and
Make death cut me
            down so soon

        Oh-oh: death is awful
        Mm-mm: death is awful
        Mm-mm: death is awful
        Spare me over
                  another year

Oh what is this that
            I can't see, well
Call that the angel
            over me

        Oh-oh: death is awful
        Ah-ah: death is awful
        Oh-oh: death is awful
        Spare me over
                  another year

This is the way that
            death begin, you
Stretch your limbs and
            close your eyes

        Oh-oh: death is awful
        Mm-mm: death is awful
        Mm-mm: death: :
        Just spare me over
                  another year

DOC REED AND VERA HALL

Ol' Hannah

Why don't you
        go down Old Hannah
                well well well
                don't you rise no more
                don't you rise no more
Why don't
      you
        go down Old
            Hannaaaaaah
Don't you
      rise no-o more

If you
    rise in the morning
             well well well
             bring judgement sure
             bring judgement sure
If you
    rise
      in the
         morniiiiiing
Bring judge-
      me-ent sure

Well I
    looked at Old Hannah
             well well well
             and she was turning red
             she was turning red
Well I
    looked at
        my
          partneeeeeer
And he was
      al-
        mo-ost dead

Well you
    oughta been on this old river
             well well well
             19 and 4
             19 and 4
You oughta
    been on
        this old
          riveeeeeer
19
  a-and 4

You could
   find a dead man
       well well well
       right a cross your row
       right a cross your row
You could
   find
     a-a
      dead maaaaaan
Right a-
   cross your row

Why don't you
    get up old dead man
        well well well
        help me carry my row
        help me carry my row
Why don't you
    get up
      old
       dead maaaaaan
Help me
   carry my-y-y row

Well you
    oughta been on this old river
         well well well
         19 and 5
         19 and 5
You oughta
    been on
      this old
        riveeeeeer
19
  a-and 5

You couldn't hardly find a
       a man alive
       a man alive
You couldn't hardly
      find
       aaaaaa
A man
   alive

You oughta been on this old river
        well well well
        in 1910
        19 and 10
You oughta been on
      this old
       riveeeeeer

DOC REESE

a-and 10

When they were working all the women

well well well
right along with the men
right along with the men

When they was working

all the

womeeeeeen

Right a-

long

with the men

Well I been on this old river

well well well
so jumping long
so jumping long

I don't know

which side of the

brazaaaaaas

My ma-

ma's on

Run and call the major
O run and call major
Well run and call the major

. . .

Well tell him I'm worried
O my lord god
Well tell him I'm worried

. . .

Well look-a look-a yonder
O my lord god
Well look-a look-a yonder

. . .

I b'lieve I'll find the major
O my lord god
I b'lieve I'll find the major

. . .

Well you talk about

your troubles:

Take a look at mine

Ohhhhhhhhh, my lord
You say you got a hundred:

I got 99

Oh my lord
Well it don't

make no difference:

They both life time

Ohhhhhhhhh, my lord
I say it don't make no difference

'cause they both life time

DOC REESE

Diddie Wa Diddie

There's a great big mystery
And it surely is worrying me
   This diddie wa diddie
   This diddie wa diddie
  I wish somebody would tell me what diddie wa diddie means

The little girl about four feet four:
"Come on papa and give me some more
   Of your diddie wa diddie
   Your diddie wa diddie"
  I wish somebody would tell me what diddie wa diddie means

I went out and walked around
Somebody yelled, said: "Look who's in town—
   Mister diddie wa diddie
   Mister diddie wa diddie"
  I wish somebody would tell me what diddie wa diddie means

Went to church, put my hand on the seat
Lady sat on it, said: "Daddy you sure is sweet,
   Mister diddie wa diddie
   Mister diddie wa diddie"
  I wish somebody would tell me what diddie wa diddie means

I said: "Sister I'll soon be gone
Just gimme that thing you setting on
   My diddie wa diddie
   My diddie wa diddie"
  I wish somebody would tell me what diddie wa diddie means

Then I got put out of church
'Cause I talk about diddie wa diddie too much
   Mister diddie wa diddie
   Mister diddie wa diddie
  I wish somebody would tell me what diddie wa diddie means

BLIND BLAKE

BLIND BLAKE

Some Women

Rolling Log Blues

I been drifting and
          rolling along
                  the road
Looking
     for my room and board

Like a log I've
        been jammed on
               the bank
So hungry
      I've grew lean and lank

Get me a pick and
        shovel, dig down
                in the ground
Gonna keep on
       digging till the blues come down

Mmmmmmmmmm mmmmmm mmmm
Mmmmmm mmmmmm
Mmmm mmmm mmmm mmmm

I've got the blues
        for my sweet man
             in jail
Now and the judge
       won't let me go his bail

I've been rolling and
        drifting from shore
              to shore
Gonna fix it
      so I won't have to drift no more

Mmmmmmmmmm mmmmmm mmmm
Mmmmmmm mmmmmm
Mmmm mmmm mmmm mmmm

Going Away Blues

I'm going away
It won't be long
I know you'll miss me from singing this
Lonesome song
I'm going away
Mmmm won't be long
And then you know
You must have done me wrong

My daddy got ways
Like a baby child
Those doggone ways are
Driving me wild
Those doggone ways
Are driving me wild
And that is why
You never see poor Lottie smile

My heart aches so
I can't be satisfied
I believe I'll take a
Train and ride
I believe I'll take
A train and ride
'Cause I miss my cruel
Daddy from my side

I've got Cadillac ways
Got some Super ideas
I can't see what
Brought me here
I can't see
What brought me here
It must have been this
New canned city beer

Eeeeee eeeeee
Eeeeee eeeeee
Eeeeeeeeee
Eeee eeee eeee eeee

I'm lame and blind
Can't hardly see
My doggone daddy turned his
Back on me
'Cause I'm lame
I can't hardly see
I ain't got nobody to
Really comfort me

LOTTIE KIMBROUGH

On the Wall

Well I'm
      going to Memphis, come to stop at
                Cincinnat'
I'm gonna
      tell you women how to treat a man
I said
     I'm going to Memphis
          stop at Cincinnatti
I'll tell you women
       honey, how to treat a man

Now then, now you
        ain't good looking and you
               don't dress fine
Just kind treatment make me *buddy* you
           'most any old time
Say you
     ain't good looking
         you don't dress so fine
And just kind treatment
        make me *buddy* you 'most any time
           (...)

Well I'm
      going to Memphis, stop at
           Satch's Hall
Gonna
     tell you women how to cock it
          on the wall
Oh
   going to Memphis
        stop at *Satch's Hall*
         (...)
I'm going to show you women
        honey, how to cock it on the wall

Now you can snatch it, you can break it, you can
             hang it on the wall
Throw it out the window, see if you
        can catch it 'fore it fall
I mean, you can
      snatch it, you can break it
          hang it on the stinkin' wall
Don't throw it out the window, women
         'less you catch it 'fore it fall
         (...)

        (Do it a long time, honey)

Well I'm gon' leave here

                                                LOUISE JOHNSON

Mind Reader Blues

Baby I
    can see
        just what's on your mind
Baby I
    can see
        just what's on your mind
You got a long black woman with *her* gold teeth in her face

I take a long
        look
            right smack down in your mind
I take a long
        look
            right smack down in your mind
And I don't see but one woman rambling up and down the line

Don't kid
        your mama
                you ain't fooling nobody but your self
Oh don't kid
        your mama
                you ain't fooling nobody but yourself
And what I see on your mind you would not have no friend

I remem-
        ber the day
                when I was living at Lula town
I remem-
        ber the day
                when I was living at Lula town
My man did so many wrong things that I had to leave the town

I caught the ri-
        verside
                my man caught the transfer boat
I caught the ri-
        verside
                my man caught the transfer boat
And the last time I seed him he had a gal way up the road

Well I'm wo-
        rried now
                and I won't be worried long
Well I'm wo-
        rried now
                and I won't be worried long
Well I'm worried now and I won't be worried long

Eagles on a Half

It's a low it's a low low
                low down dirty shame
It's a low it's a low low
                low down dirty shame
I've got a brown skin man but I've
                      yet to call his name

I just swear old papa
                let your mama see
I just swear old papa
                let your mama see
I want to see that old business
                  keeps on worrying me

I twisted and I tumbled
                I rolled the whole night long
I twisted and I tumbled
                I rolled the whole night long
I didn't have no daddy to
                hold me in his arms

I say get back rider
                don't care how you lay
I say get back rider
                don't care how you lay
I wanna tell you
                can't stay here till day

I say eagle's on a half, lord
                baby, in God we trust
I saw the eagle's on a half and
                oh, in God we trust
I love you daddy
                what you done it for

GEECHIE WILEY

Motherless Child Blues

My mother told me just before she died
My mother told me just before she died
My mother told me just before she died
My mother told me just before she died

Oh daughter daughter please don't be like me
Oh daughter oh daughter please don't be like me
Oh daughter oh daughter please don't be like me
To fall in love with every man you see

But I did not listen to what my mother said
But I did not listen what my mother said
But I did not listen what my mother said
That's the reason why I'm sitting here in Hattiesburg

Baby now she's dead and six feet in the ground
Baby now she's dead, she's six feet in the ground
Baby now she's dead, she's six feet in the ground
And I'm her child and I am drifting 'round

Do you remember the day, baby, you drove me from your door
Do you remember the day, baby, you drove me from your door
Do you remember the day you drove me from your door
Go away from here woman and don't come here no more

I walked away and I wrang my hands and cried
I walked away and I wrang my hands and cried
I walked away and I wrang my hands and cried
Didn't have no blues, I couldn't be satisfied

ELVIE THOMAS

Dead Drunk Blues

                                        (I'm dead drunk this morning, daddy,
                                        behave yourself)

You knowed I was drunk when I lay down across your bed
You knowed I was drunk when I lay down across your bed
All the whiskey I drank, it's gone right to my head

Oh give me Houston, that's the place I crave
Oh give me Houston, that's the place I crave
                                        (Oh play it Papa Charlie Hill)
So when I'm dry I can get whiskey *some place*

Whiskey whiskey is some folks' down / fall
                                (Ain't none a my downfall,
                                don't put that washing out)
Oh whiskey whiskey is some folks' down / fall
But if I don't get whiskey I ain't no good at all
                                (You ain't by your self, neither)

When I was in Houston, drunk most every day
When I was in Houston, drunk most every day
I drank so much whiskey I thought I'd pass away

Have you ever been drunk and slept in all your clothes
                                (No sir, I ain't never did that,
                                no sir)
Have you ever been drunk and slept in all your clothes
And when you wake up, feel like you want a dose

I'm gonna get drunk, daddy, just one more time
                                (Go ahead, get drunk,
                                and stay drunk)
I'm gonna get drunk, daddy, just one more time
                                (Yes, stay drunk; I don't care)
'Cause when I'm drunk, nothing don't worry my mind

LILLIAN MILLER

Jacksonville Blues

Let me be your wiggler
                    until your wobbler come
Let me be your wiggler
                    until your wobbler come
If she *be seen with 'em*
                    she got to wobble some

Women crying danger
                    but I ain't risen my hand
Women crying danger
                    but I ain't risen my hand
I got a way of loving they
                    just can't understand

Men, they call me oven, they
                    say that I'm red hot
Men, they call me oven, they
                    say that I'm red hot
They say I got something
                    the other gals ain't got
                         (Ha ha ha ha ha ha ha
                         ha ha ha ha ha ha ha.)

I can strut my pudding
                    spread my grease with ease
I can strut my pudding
                    spread my grease with ease
'Cause I know my onions
                    that's why I always please

Wild about coffee
                    but I'm crazy 'bout China tea
Wild about my coffee
                    but I'm crazy 'bout my China tea
But this sugar daddy is
                    sweet enough for me

Men, they call me oven
                    they say I am red hot
Men, they call me oven
                    they say that I'm red hot
They say I got something
                    the other gals ain't got
                         (Ha ha ha ha ha ha.)

One John in the city
                    one lives up on the hill
One John 's in the city
                    one lives up on the hill
But the man I'm loving lives
                    down in Jacksonville

NELLIE FLORENCE

Doggin' Me Around Blues

I'm a stranger here
          just blowed in your town
I'm a stranger here
          just blowed in your town
Just because I'm a stranger
          I won't be dogged around

It's raining here
          storming all over the sea
It's raining here
          storming all over the sea
I ain't got no body
          care to take care of me

I wonder do my
          good man know I'm here
I wonder do my
          good man know I'm here
If he do
          he sure don't feel my care

I been your dog
          every since I entered your door
I been your dog
          ever since I entered your door
I'm gonna leave this town
          I won't be dogged around no more

I been your dog
          been your dog all of my days
I been your dog
          been your dog all of my days
The reason I'm leaving you
          I don't like your dogging ways

JENNY POPE

Third Alley Blues

I just want to get back
                    to Birmingham
I just want to get back
                    to Birmingham
I got a gang in Third Alley
                        don't know where I am

I'd rather be in Third Alley
                    without a dime
I'd rather be in Third Alley
                    without a dime
Than to be in Chicago
                simply wasting my time

I'm going in Third Alley
                    and bring my rider home
I'm going in Third Alley
                    and bring my rider home
All these women in Third Alley
                        won't let my rider alone

IVA SMITH

Never Let Your Left Hand Know

I had the blues
  Last night
I've got 'em again today
My man told me he was
  Going away

Trouble
  Trouble
Is all I can see
Looks like my man has turned his
  Back on me

Just let
  Me tell you
What your friends will do
Grin in your face and then they'll
  Talk about you

Me and my
  Girl friend
Went out for a little run
When she seen my man she told him what
  I had done

Bring me
  A pint of whiskey
And a bottle of beer
If I get drunk
  I sure don't care

Eeeeeeeeee
  Eeeeee
Eeeeeeeee eeeeee
Eeeeeeeeeeee eeee
  Eeee eeee eeee

    (Harmonize me daddy)
    (Oh run into me, but don't hurt me.)

Take me
  Back baby
Try me one more time
I'll do every thing to
  Satisfy your mind

Listen
  People
Hear what I'm telling you
Don't let your left hand
  Know what your right hand do

43   *LIL JOHNSON*

You'll Never Miss Your Jelly

I woke up this morning with the blues all 'round my bed
I woke up this morning with the blues all 'round my bed
I felt just like
                somebody in my family was dead

I began to moan
           and I began to cry
I began to moan
           and I began to cry
My sweet man went away
              didn't know the reason why

If you don't like my sweet potato
                    what made you dig so deep
If you don't like my sweet potato
                    what made you dig so deep
Dig my potato field
           three, four times a week

Whoopin', I been whoopin'
              whoopin' all night long
Whoopin', I been whoopin'
              whoopin' all night long
Whoopin', I been whoopin'
              ever since my man been gone

(Oh shake that thing, Mr. Avery. You play it so good.)

(Mmmm, the blues sure sound good this morning.)

(Don't kill that half pint.)

My dog jumped a rabbit
              the rabbit fell down on his knees
My dog jumped a rabbit
              the rabbit fell down on his knees
He looked up at the dog
              he said, Won't you have mercy on me please

Just as sure as you
          hear me sing this song
Just as sure as you
          hear me sing this song
You sure won't miss your jelly
              till your jelly roller's gone

Tired As I Can Be

I worked all the winter
    And I worked all fall
I got to wait till spring
    To get my ashes hauled
        And now I'm tired
            Tired as I can be
        And I'm going back home
            Where these blues don't worry me

I'm a free-hearted woman
    I let you spend my dough
And you never did win
    You kept on asking for more
        And now I'm tired
            I ain't gonna do it no more
        And when I leave you this time
            You won't know where I go

My house rent's due
    They done put me out doors
And here you riding 'round here
    In a V-8 Ford
        I done got tired
            Of your low-down dirty ways
        And your sister say you been dirty
            Dirty all a your days

I never will forget
    When the times was good
I caught you standing out yonder
    In the piney wood
        And now I'm tired
            Tired as I can be
        And I'm going back south
            To my used to be

BESSIE JACKSON (LUCILLE BOGAN)

Stew Meat Blues

A man say I had something
                    look like new
He wanted me to credit him
                         for some of my stew
Say he's going up the river
                    try to sell his sack
He would pay me for my stuff
                         when the boat get back
        Now you can go on up the river
        Man and sell your sack
        You can pay me for my stew
        When the boat get back

I got good stew
            and it's got to be sold
The price ain't high
                I want to get you told
        Go on up the river
        Man and sell your sack
        There'll be stew meat here
        Baby when the boat get back

Now look here man
                    what you want me to do
Give you my stew meat
                    and credit you too
        You go on up the river
        Try and sell your sack
        'Cause I have my stew meat here
        When that boat get back

I credit one man
                it was to my sorrow
It's cash today
            credit tomorrow
        So hurry up the river
        Baby and try to sell your sack
        It's gonna be meat here
        When that boat get back

Now it's ashes to ashes
                    dust to dust
You try my stuff one time
                         you can't get enough
        So go on up the river
        Man and sell your sack
        'Cause the stuff'll be here
        Baby when the boat get back

BESSIE JACKSON (LUCILLE BOGAN)

Don't Fish In My Sea

My daddy come home this morning
                              drunk as he could be
My daddy come home this morning
                              drunk as he could be
I knowed by that, he's
                  done got bad on me

He used to stay out late, now
                      he don't come home at all
He used to stay out late, now
                    he don't come home at all
                              (No kidding, either.)
I know there's another mule
                been kicking in my stall

If you don't like my ocean
                don't fish in my sea
Don't like my ocean
              don't fish in my sea
Stay out of my valley
              and let my mountain be

I ain't had no loving
              since god knows when
I ain't had no loving
              since god knows when
That's the reason I'm through with these
                      no good trifling men

You'll never miss the sunshine
                  till the rain begin to fall
Never miss the sunshine
                till the rain begin to fall
You'll never miss your ham till a-
                  nother mule be in your stall

MA RAINEY

MA RAINEY

Southern Blues

House catch on fire
                    and ain't no water 'round
If your house catch on fire
                          ain't no water 'round
Throw your trunk out the window
                                building burn on down

I went to the Gypsy
                    to have my fortune told
I went to the Gypsy
                    to have my fortune told
He said, Doggone you, girlie
                          doggone your bad luck soul

I turned around
                went to the Gypsy next door
I turned around
                went to the Gypsy next door
He said, You'll get a man
                      any where you go

Let me be your rag-doll
                        until your chiny come
Let me be your rag-doll
                      till your chiny come
If he beats me ragged
                      he's got to rag it some

MA RAINEY

Back Water Blues

When it rained five days and the skies turned dark as night
When it rained five days and the skies turned dark as night
Then trouble taken place, in the lowlands at night

I woke up this morning, can't even get outa my door
I woke up this morning, can't even get outa my door
There's enough trouble to make a poor girl wonder where she want to go

Then they rolled a little boat about five miles 'cross the pond
Then they rowed a little boat about five miles 'cross the pond
I packed all my clothes, throwed 'em in, and they rolled me along

When it thunders and lightning, and the wind begin to blow
When it thunders and lightning, and the wind begin to blow
There's thousands of people, ain't got noplace to go

Then I went and stood up on some high old lonesome hill
Then I went and stood up on some high old lonesome hill
And looked down on the house, where I used to live

Backwater blues done caused me to pack my things and go
Backwater blues done caused me to pack my things and go
'Cause my house fell down and I can't live there no more

Mmmmmmmmmmm, I can't move no more
Mmmmmmmmmmm, I can't move no more
They ain't no place for a poor old girl to go

Black Mountain Blues

Back in Black Mountain
                    a child will smack your face
Back in Black Mountain
                    a child will smack your face
Babies crying for liquor
                    and all the birds sing base

Black Mountain people
                    are bad as they can be
Black Mountain people
                    are bad as they can be
They uses gun powder
                    just to sweeten their tea

On the Black Mountain
                    can't keep a man in jail
On the Black Mountain
                    can't keep a man in jail
If the jury finds them guilty
                    the judge'll go their bail

Had a man in Black Mountain
                    sweetest man in town
Had a man in Black Mountain
                    the sweetest man in town
He met a city gal
                    and he throwed me down

I'm bound for Black Mountain
                    me and my razor and my gun
Lord, I'm bound for Black Mountain
                    me and my razor and gun
I'm gonna shoot him if he stands still
                    and cut him if he run

Down in Black Mountain
                    they all shoots quick and straight
Down in Black Mountain
                    they all shoots quick and straight
The bullet 'll get you
                    if you starts a-dodging too late

Got the devil in my soul
                    and I'm fulla bad booze
Got the devil in my soul
                    and I'm fulla bad booze
I'm out here for trouble
                    and I've got the Black Mountain Blues

BESSIE SMITH

Jailhouse Blues

(Lord, this house is gonna get raided—yes sir.)

Thirty days in jail with my back turned to the wall
                turned
                    to the wall
Thirty days in jail with my back turned to the wall
Look here Mr. Jail Keeper
                put another gal in my stall

I don't mind being in jail
                but I got to stay there so long
                    so long
I don't mind being in jail
                but I got to stay there so long
                    so long
When every friend I had
                is done shook hands
                    and gone

You better stop your man
                from tickling me under my chin
                    under my chin
You better stop your man
                from tickling me under my chin
'Cause if he keeps on tickling
                I'm sure gonna
                    take him on in

Good morning, blues
                blues, how do you do
                how
                    do you do
Good morning, blues
                blues, how do you do
Well I just come here
                to have a few
                    words with you

BESSIE SMITH

BESSIE SMITH

Frying Pan Skillet Blues

(Bring me some black-eyed peas.)

I done lose all-a my money
        ahhhhhhhhh-ha
             and now losing my mind
I done lose all-a my money
        ahhhhhhhhh-ha
             and now losing my mind
He at home with that woman
        but he's on my mind

If you and your woman
        you all can't agree
If you and your woman
        ahhhhhhhhh
           you all can't agree
Get your frying pan and skillet
        come and
           live with me

Ahhhhhhhhh hahhhh hahhhh
        Oh lord: my lord
Ahhhhhhhhh hahhhh hahhhh
        Oh lord: my lord
Lord, lordy lord

(Oh lord).

Death Sting Me Blues

I want all you women
                  to listen to my tale of woe
I want all you women
                  to listen to my tale of woe
I've got consumption of the heart
                      I feel myself sinking so

Oh my heart is aching
                  and the blues are all around my room
Oh my heart is aching
                  and the blues are all around my room
Blues is like the devil
              they'll have me hell-bound soon

Blues, you made me roll and tumble
                      you made me weep and sigh
Lordy lordy lordy
            blues you roll and tumble
                        you made me weep and sigh
Made me use cocaine and whiskey
                  but you wouldn't let me die

Blues: blues: blues
              why did you bring trouble to me?
Blues: blues: blues
              why did you bring trouble to me?
Oh death please sting me,
                and take me out of my misery

SARA MARTIN

Blood Hound Blues

Well I poisoned my man
        I put it in his drinking
        now I'm in jail
        and I can't keep from thinking
I poisoned my man
        I put it in his drinking cup
Well it's easy to go to jail
        but lord, they sent me up

Well I broke out of my cell
        when the jailer turned his back
I broke out of my cell
        when the jailer turned his back
But now I'm so sorry
        blood hounds are on my track

Blood hounds, blood hounds
        blood hounds are on my trail
Blood hounds, blood hounds
        blood hounds are on my trail
They want to take me back
        to that cold cold lonesome jail

Ohhhhh
        blood hounds are on my trail
Mmmmmm
        blood hounds are on my trail
They want to take me back
        to that cold old lonesome jail

Well I know I done wrong
        but he kicked me and blacked my
        I done it in a passion
        I thought it was a fashion
I know I've done wrong
        but he kicked me and blacked my eye
But if the blood hounds ever catch me
        in the 'lectric chair I'll die

Nothing in Rambling

I's born in Louisiana
I raised in Algiers
And everywhere I been
The peoples all say

Ain't nothing in rambling
Either running around
Well I believe I'll marry
Oooooo oooo, lord, and settle down

I first left home
I stopped in Tennessee
The peoples all begging
Come and stay with me

'Cause ain't nothing in rambling
Either running around
Well I believe I'll get me a good man
Oooooo oooo, lord, and settle down

I walked through the alley
With my hand in my coat
The po-lice start to shoot me
Thought it was something I stole

You know it ain't nothing in rambling
Either running around
Well I believe I'll marry
Oooooo oooo, lord, and settle down

The peoples on the highway
Is walking and crying
Some is starving
Some is dying

You know it ain't nothing in rambling
Either running around
Well I believe I'll get me a good man
Oooooo oooo, lord, and settle down

You may go to Hollywood
And try to get on the screen
But I'm gonna stay right here
And eat these old charity beans

'Cause it ain't nothing in rambling
Either running around
Well I believe I'll marry
Oooooo oooo, lord, and settle down

Me and My Chauffeur Blues

Won't you be my chauffeur
Won't you be my chauffeur
      I want someone to drive me
      I want someone to drive me
            Down town
Baby drives so easy
      I can't turn him down

But I don't want him
But I don't want him
      To be riding these girls
      To be riding these girls
          A-round
You know I'm gonna steal me a pistol
         Shoot my chauffeur down

Well I must buy him
Well I must buy him
      A brand new V-8
      A brand new V-8
        Ford
And he won't need no passengers
        I will be his load

        (Yeah, take it away)

Going to let my chauffeur
Going to let my chauffeur
      Drive me around the
      Drive me around the
        World
Then he can be my little boy
        Yes I'll treat him good

Killer Diller

Well the ugliest little thing
I ever seed before
He *gives me the cramps*
                    he's a hobo

    But he's a ugly little something on a scout
    He's a terrible little something, hush your mouth
    He's a awful little creature
    He's a killer diller from the South

Well he walks up to *the store*
Where I was at
And in his face
               looked like a crying cat

    'Cause he's a ugly little something on a scout
    He's a terrible little creature, hush your mouth
    He's a awful little thing
    He's a killer diller from the South

Well he walks down the street
Looking in the showcase
The statue walks out
              and say, You can take my place

    'Cause you're an ugly little figure on a scout
    You's a terrible little something, hush your mouth
    You's a awful little creature
    You's a killer diller from the South

Well he walked into the hotel
Everybody left
He looked in the glass
            and he smiled at himself

    Saying, I'm an ugly little figure on a scout
    I'm a terrible little something, hush your mouth
    I'm an awful little creature
    I'm a killer diller from the South

'Frisco Town

That old 'Frisco train left a mile a minute
That old 'Frisco train left a mile a minute
Well it's that old coach, I'm gonna sit right in it
I'm on my way
        to 'Frisco town

You can toot your whistle, you can ring your bell
You can toot your whistle, you can ring your bell
Well I know you been want' it by the way you smell
I'm on my way
        to 'Frisco town

Oh there's a boa constrictor and a lemon stick
There's a boa constrictor and a lemon stick
I don't mind being with you but my mama's sick
I'm on my way
        to 'Frisco town

I would tell you what's the matter but I done got scared
I would tell you what's the matter but I done got scared
You have to wait now until we go to bed
I'm on my way
        to 'Frisco town

If you was sick I wouldn't worry you
If you was sick I wouldn't worry you
I wouldn't want you to do something that you couldn't do
I'm on my way
        to 'Frisco town

Well if you want it you can get it and I ain't mad
If you want it you can get it and I ain't mad
If you tell me this is something that you ain't never had
I'm on my way
        to 'Frisco town

Lookee here, you get mad every time I call your name
Lookee here, you get mad every time I call your name
I ain't never told you that you couldn't get that thing
I'm on my way
        to 'Frisco town

I woke up this morning about half past five
Woke up this morning about half past five
My baby turned over, cried just like a child
I'm on my way
        to 'Frisco town

I got something to tell you, I don't want to make you mad
Got something to tell you, don't want to make you mad
I got something for you, make you feel glad
I'm on my way
            to 'Frisco town

Look-a here, look-a here, what you want me to do
Look-a here, look-a here, what you want me to do
Give you my jelly then die for you
I'm on my way
            to 'Frisco town

I got something to tell you, gonna break your heart
Got something to tell you, gonna break your heart
We been together so far, we gotta get *smart*
I'm on my way
            to 'Frisco town

MEMPHIS MINNIE

Memphis Minnie-Jitis Blues

Mmmmmmmmmmmmmmmm
                      the meningitis killing me
Mmmmmmmmmmmmmmmm
                      the meningitis killing me
I'm sitting, I'm standing, baby,
                      my head is nearly down to my knee

I come in home one Saturday night
                      pull off my clothes and I lie down
I come in home one Saturday night
                      pull off my clothes and I lie down
And that morning just about day
                      the meningitis begin to creep around

My head and neck was paining me
                      feel like my back would break in two
My head and neck was paining me
                      feel like my back would break in two
Lord I had such a *mood* that morning
                      I didn't know what else there was to do

My companion take me to the doctor:
                      Doctor, please tell me my wife's complaint
My companion take me to the doctor:
                      Doctor, please tell me my wife's complaint
The doctor looked down on me, shook his head,
                      said, I would lie to you, son, but I can't

You take her round to the city hospital
                      just as quick quick as you possible can
Take her round to the city hospital
                      just as quick quick as you possible can
Because the condition she's in now
                      you never will get her back home 'live again

He drove me round to the city hospital
                      the clock was striking ten
Drove me round to the city hospital
                      the clock was striking ten
I heard my companion say
                      I won't see your smiling face again

Three Men

There ain't but three men
                    who really can spend my dough
There ain't but three men
                    who really can spend my dough
There's the rent man, the grocery man
                              and the man that owns the clothing store

There's only three men
                    that can flag this train of mine
There's only three men
                    that can flag this train of mine
There's the working man and the gambler
                              and the one that loves me all the time

There ain't but three men
                    that I really won't treat wrong
There ain't but three men
                    that I really won't treat wrong
That's my father and my brother
                    and the one that lays on my arm

There ain't but three men
                    who can make a clown out of me
There ain't but three men
                    who can make a clown out of me
That's my husband and my sweetheart
                              and my old-time used-to-be

There ain't but three men
                    who really can make me fall
There ain't but three men
                    who really can make me fall
That's my *best* friend, my kid man,
                         the one that's kicking in my stall

ALICE MOORE

MA YANCEY

Make Me a Pallet on Your Floor

Make me a pallet on your floor
Make me a pallet on your floor
      Just make me a, a pallet
      Baby, down upon your floor
      When your main girl come
      I swear, she will never know

Just make it, baby, make it very soft and low
If you will make it, baby, make it very soft and low
      If you feel like—lying down
      With me on the pallet on the floor
      When your main girl come
      I swear, she will never know

I'll get up in the morning, and I'll make you a red hot meal
I'll get up in the morning, and I'll make you a red hot meal
      Just to show you I—appreciated
      Baby, baby, what you done for me
      When you made me that pallet
      Down upon your floor

Won't you make it, baby, make it very soft and low
Make it, baby, make it near the kitchen door
      If she comes in the front door
      I swear, I swear she will never know
      That you made me that pallet
      Down upon your floor

MA (AND JIMMY) YANCEY

Charleston Blues

Charleston, South Carolina, baby
                                        is where I was born
Charleston, South Carolina, baby
                                        is where I was born
Now if you get *there,* baby
                                        them *Geechies* put your water wrong

I don't want no gravy
                                        spread over my rice
I don't want no gravy, baby
                                        spread over my rice
'Cause the man that gets me, baby
                                        sure got to treat me nice

I'm going to Charleston
                                        buddy, but I can't take you
I'm going down on King Street, baby
                                        honey, 'cause I can't take you
Now it ain't nothing on King Street, baby
                                        that a crazy gal like you can do

I'm going back to the fish-house, baby
                                        and get me some shrimps
I'm going back, baby
                                        and get me some good shrimps
I've gotta feed, baby
                                        two or three hungry old pimps

Now I knowed you, baby
                                        when you did not even know yourself
And I knowed you, baby, when
                                        you did not even know yourself
Now you trying to give me the jive, baby, but you
                                        you got to help yourself

Texas

Fishing Blues

Went up on the hill, 'bout 12 o'clock
Reached right back and got me a pole
Went to the hardware, got me a hook
'Tached that line right on that hook
Tell you been a-fishin', all the time
I'm a-goin' to fishin' too
        I bet your life
        Your lovin' wife
        Catch more fish 'n you
        Any fish bite
        Got good bait
        Here's a little somethin' I would like to relate
        Any fish bite
        Got good bait
        I'm a-goin' to fishin'
        Yes I'm goin' to fishin'
I'm a-goin' to fishin' too

Looked down the river 'bout 1 o'clock
Spied those catfish swimmin' around
I got so hungry, didn't know what to do
I'm gonna get me a catfish too
Tell you been a-fishin', all the time
I'm a-goin' to fishin' too
        I bet your life
        Your lovin' wife
        Catch more fish 'n you
        Any fish bite
        Got good bait
        Here's a little somethin' I would like to relate
        Any fish bite
        Got good bait
        I'm a-goin' to fishin'
        Yes I'm goin' to fishin'
I'm a-goin' to fishin' too

Put on the skillet, lay by the lid
Mama's gonna cook a little shortnin' bread
Tell you been a-fishin', all the time
I'm a-goin' to fishin' too
        I bet your life
        Your lovin' wife
        Catch more fish 'n you
        Any fish bite
        Got good bait
        Here's a little somethin' I would like to relate
        Any fish bite
        Got good bait
        I'm a-goin' to fishin'
        Yes I'm goin' to fishin'
I'm a-goin' to fishin' too

Bob McKinney

Went down on Johnson Street
Bob McKinney came passing by
Going down that Johnson Street
Make trouble in their lives
       Wasn't he bad
       Yes wasn't he bad

Bobby said to *Marg'et*
Come to me I said
If you don't come in a hurry
I put a 38 through your head
       Wasn't he bad
       Yes wasn't he bad

Bobby said to *Ben Cass*
I'm bound to take your life
You caused trouble
Between me and my wife
      Wasn't he bad
      Yes wasn't he bad

Bobby said to the high sheriff
Maybe you think I'm going to run
If I had another load
Me and you have some fun
      Wasn't he bad
      Yes wasn't he bad

     Oh my babe
     Take me back
     I ain't no bird dog
     Take me back
     One of these mornings
     Won't be long
     You gonna call me
     I'll be gone
     She turned 'round
     Two or three times
     Take my *bag*
     Take me back
     Take me back
     Take me back
     Take my *bag*
     Take me back

Oh make me a pallet on your floor
Hey make me one pallet on your
Oh make a pallet on your floor
Won't you make it so your man'll never know

Yes make it so your man'll never know
And make it so your man'll never know
Oh make a pallet on your—
Won't you make it so your man'll never know

Yes I'm looking for that bully to lay me down
Hey I'm looking for that bully to lay me down
I'm looking for that bully and that bully can't be—
Yes I'm looking for that bully to lay me down

Hey looking for that bully to lay me down
Hey I'm looking for that bully to lay me down
I'm looking for that bully and that bully can't be found
I'm looking for that bully to lay me down

                    HENRY THOMAS

Pneumonia Blues

Aching all over
          I believe I've got the pneumonia this time
I'm aching all over
          believe I got the pneumonia this time
And it's all on account of
          that low down gal of mine

Slipping 'round the corner
          running up alleys too
I went slipping 'round corners
          running up alleys too
Watching my woman
          trying to see what she goin' do

Sit down in the street
          one cold dark stormy night
I sit down in the street
          one dark and stormy night
Trying to see if my good gal
          goin' make it home all right

I believe she's found something
          that prob'ly made her fall
She must did found something
          and I believe it made her fall
I stood out in the cold all night
          and she didn't come home at all

Well it's BVD's in the winter
          traveling 'round in the rain
Wear BVD's in the winter
          traveling 'round in the rain
Last night my baby
          give me this pneumonia pain

Now when I die
          bury me in a Stetson hat
Oh I say, when I die bury
          me in a Stetson hat
Tell my good gal I'm going, but I'm
          still a-standing pat

BLIND LEMON JEFFERSON

Rabbit Foot Blues

Blue jumped a rabbit, run him one solid mile
Blue jumped a rabbit, run him one solid mile
This rabbit sat down, crying like *a natural child*

Well it seem like you hungry, honey come and lunch with me
Seem like you hungry, honey come and lunch with me
I wanna stop these married looking women from worrying me

I have Uneeda biscuits here and a half a pint of gin
I have Uneeda biscuits here and a half a pint of gin
The gin is mighty fine but them biscuits are a little too thin

Baby tell me something about those meatless and wheatless days
I want to know about those meatless and wheatless days
This not being my home I don't think I should stay

I cried for flour and the meat I declare it was gone
Well I cried 'bout flour and the meat I declare it was gone
Keeps a-feeding me corn bread, I just can't stick around long

Got an air plane, baby, and I'm gonna get a submarine
An air plane, and I'm a-gonna get a submarine
Gonna get that Kaiser, *and will be seldom seen*

Mmmm mm hitch me to your buggy, mama, drive me like a mule
Hitch me to your buggy and drive me like a mule
Reason I'm going home with you, sugar, *I ain't much hard to be fooled*

BLIND LEMON JEFFERSON

Prison Cell Blues

Getting tired of sleeping in this: : low down lonesome cE-Ell
Lord I wouldn't of been here if it: : hadn't of been for Nell

Lay awake at night and: : just can't eat a bI-Ite
Used to be my rider but she: : just won't treat me right

Got a red-eyed captain: : and a squabbling bO-Oss
Got a mad-dog sergeant: : honey, and he won't knock off

I'm getting tired of sleeping in this: : low down lonesome cE-Ell
Lord I wouldn't of been here if it: : hadn't of been for Nell

I asked the gov'ment to knock: : some days off my tI-Ime
Well the way I'm treated I'm: : 'bout to lose my mind

I wrote to the governor: : to please turn me a-lOO-OOse
Since I didn't get no answer: : I know it ain't no use

I'm getting tired of sleeping in this: : low down lonesome cE-Ell
Lord I wouldn't of been here if it: : hadn't of been for Nell

I hate to turn over and: : find my rider gO-One
Walks across the floor: : lordy how I moan

Lord I wouldn't of been here if it: : hadn't of been for NE-Ell
I'm getting tired of sleeping in this: : low down lonesome cell

Rising High Water Blues

Black water rising:
                    southern people can't make no time
I said black water rising:
                            southern people can't make no time
And I can't get no hearing
                        from that Memphis gal of mine

Water all in Arkansas:
                            people screaming in Tennessee
Ohhhhhhhhhhhhhhh:
                        people screaming in Tennessee
If I don't leave Memphis
                    black water been all over poor me

People, cinch it's raining:
                        it has been for nine ten days
People, it's a cinch it's raining:
                            has been for nine ten days
Thousand people stands on the hill
                        looking down where they used to stay

Children standing and pleading:
                            mama we ain't got no home
Ohhhhhhhhhhhhhhhhhhhhh:
                        mama we ain't got no home
Papa says to children:
                    black water left us all alone

Black water rising,
                    coming in my windows and doors
The black water rising,
                        coming in my windows and doors
I leave with a prayer in my heart:
                        black water won't rise no more

Bad Luck Blues

I want to go home and I ain't got sufficient
                    clothes doggone my bad luck soul
I want to go home and I ain't got sufficient clothes
        I mean sufficient—talking 'bout clothes—well I want to go
                            home and I ain't got
                                sufficient clothes

I bet my money and I lost it lord it's
                    oh doggone my bad luck soul
Mmmmmmmmmmmmmmmm lost a great big roll
        I mean lost it—speaking about dough—now
                    I'll never bet on
                        this old trey game no more

Oh my big gal has gone why don't you quit crying
                        doggone my bad luck soul
Mmmmmmmmmmmmmmmmmmmmmmmmmmm why don't you quit crying
        Why don't you quit—I mean crying—
                    that joker stole off
                        with that long-haired brown of mine

Sister you catch the Katy, I'll catch that Santy Fee
                        doggone my bad luck soul
Sister you catch that Katy and I'll: catch that Santy Fee
        I mean Santy—speaking about Fee—when you
                    get in Denver
                        pretty mama look around for me

The woman I love why she's five feet from the ground
                        doggone my bad luck soul
Hehhhhhhhhhhhhhhhhhhhh five feet from the ground
        Five feet from the—I mean ground—
                    she's a tailor made woman
                            she ain't no hand me down

I ain't seen my sugar in two long weeks today
                        doggone my bad luck soul, I ain't
Seen my sugar in two long weeks today
        Two long weeks to—I mean day—
                    girl it's been so long seems like my
                        heart gonna break

I'm gonna run 'cross town catch that southbound Santy Fee
                        doggone my bad luck soul
Mmmmmmmmmmmmmmmmmmmmmmmmmm lord that Santy Fee
        I mean Santy—singing about Fee—
                    be on my way to what you call
                        loving Tennessee

BLIND LEMON JEFFERSON

Big Night Blues

My feets is so cold
             can't hardly wear my shoes
Well my feet so cold can't
             hardly wear my shoes
Out last night with wild women and it
             give me the big night blues

I grabbed my baby
             I danced till the clock struck twelve
I grabbed my baby and I
             danced till the clock struck twelve
I had to wrestle so hard with my good gal, I
             just ain't feeling so well

I'm going back to that party
             get with them wild women again
I'm going back to that party
             get with them wild women again
Well I ain't gonna leave my home till I
             order me a quart of gin

Wild women like their liquor
             their gin and their rock and rye
Wild women like their liquor
             their gin and their rock and rye
My gal wouldn't let me go home last night
             wouldn't tell me the reason why

Turned my face to the wall and my
             baby made an awful moan
Mmmmmmmmmmmmmmmmmmmm
             my baby made an awful moan
Well I needs my daddy 'cause my
             clock is run down at home

Peach Orchard Mama

Peach orchard mama, you swore
                          nobody'd pick your fruit but me
Peach orchard mama, you swore that
                           no one picked your fruit but me
I found three kid men
               shaking down your peach-a tree

One man bought your groceries
                       another joker paid your rent
One man bought your groceries
                       another joker paid your rent
While I work in your orchard and
                   giving you every cent

Went to the police station, begged the
                         police to put me in jail
Went to the police station
                 begged him to put me in jail
I didn't want to kill you, mama, but I
                     hate to see your peach-a tree fail

Peach orchard mama, don't
               treat your papa so mean
Peach orchard mama, don't
               treat your papa so mean
Chase out all those kid men
               and let me keep your orchard clean

Peach orchard mama, don't
               turn your papa down
Peach orchard mama, don't
               turn your papa down
Because when I gets mad I
               acts just like *I sound*

Tin Cup Blues

I was down and I cried
                              my suitcase was down the line
I was down and I cried, *my suitcase*
                              was down the line
Ain't it tough to see a man go to wreck and
                              almost fall and die

I stood on the corner
                              and almost bust my head
I stood on the corner
                              almost bust my head
I couldn't earn enough money
                              to buy me a loaf of bread

Baby, times is so hard
                              I almost call it tough
I said baby, times is so hard
                              I almost call it tough
I can't earn money to buy no bread
                              and you know I can't buy my snuff

My gal's a house maid
                              and she earns a dollar a week
I said my gal's a house maid
                              and she earns a dollar a week
I'm so hungry on payday
                              I can't hardly speak

Now gather 'round me people
                              let me tell you a true fact
I said gather 'round me people and
                              let me tell you a true fact
That tough luck has sunk me
                              and the rats is getting in my hat

BLIND LEMON JEFFERSON

That Black Snake Moan

Ummmmh oh
                    ain't got no mama now
Ummmmh oh
                    ain't got no mama now
She told me late last night
                              you don't need no mama no how

Mmmmmm mmmm
                              black snake crawling in my room
Mmmmmm mmmm
                              black snake crawling in my room
And some pretty mama
                         better come and get this black snake soon

Ummmmh uh
                    that must have been a bed bug
                                             baby, a chinch can't bite that hard
Ummmmh uh
                    that must have been a bed bug
                                             honey, a chinch can't bite that hard
Asked my sugar for fifty cent
                         she said, Lemon, ain't a dime in the yard

Mmmmama that's all right
                         mama that's all right for you
Mmmmama that's all right
                         mama that's all right for you
Mama that's all right
                    most any old way you do

Mmmmmm mmmm
                    what's that matter now
Mmmmmm mmmm
                    honey, what's the matter now
Sugar, what's the matter:
                         don't like no black snake no how

Mmmmmm mmmm
                    wonder where is my black snake gone
Mmmmmm mmmm
                    wonder where is the black snake gone
Black snake, mama, done
                    run my darling home

BLIND LEMON JEFFERSON

Stocking Feet Blues

Somebody
        just keep on calling me
Somebody
        just keeps on calling me
She got hair
        like a mermaid on the sea

    She got up this morning come a-tipping 'cross the floor
    said mama in her
    loving stocking feet
    honey fare thee
    sweet papa fare thee well
    I done all in the world I could
    trying to get along with you

Make me down a pallet
        on your floor
Make me down
        a pallet on your floor
Make it gentle and easy
        make it down by your door

I can't stay away
        I done cried the whole night long
I can't stay away
        I've cried the whole night long
The good woman I love
        she done packed her trunk and gone

Don't mistreat me
        because I'm young and wild
Don't mistreat me
        just because I'm young and wild
Sister, you ought to remember
        that you once was a child

I don't feel welcome and I
        don't care where I go
I don't feel welcome
        I don't care where I go
The woman I love
        she drove me from her door

'Fess up brown
        where did you stay last night
'Fess up brown
        where did you stay last night
Your hair's all down
        and you know you ain't talking right

BLIND LEMON JEFFERSON

I'm a stranger here just
                    come in on the train
Mmmmmmmmmmmmmmmm
                    come in on the train
Won't some good man
               tell me some woman's name

BLIND LEMON JEFFERSON

Chock House Blues

So many wagons
                they have cut that good road down
I said so many wagons
                have cut that good road down
And the girl I love
          her mama don't want me around

Baby I can't drink whiskey
                   but I'm a fool about my home-made wine
Baby I can't drink whiskey
                   but I'm a fool about my home-made wine
Ain't no sense in leaving Dallas
                     they makes it there all the time

These here women want these men
                    to act like some *ox from dawn*
I say these women want these men
                    to act like some *ox from dawn*
Grab a pick and shovel
             and roll from sun to sun

I got a girl for Monday Tuesday Wednesday Thursday Friday too
I got a girl for Monday Tuesday Wednesday Thursday Friday too
I'm gonna sweeten up on a Saturday
                      what are the women through the week going to do

Don't look for me on Sunday
                 I want to take *baby* to Sunday School
Don't look for me on Sunday
                 I want to take *baby* to Sunday School
She's a fine looking fair brown
               but she ain't never learned Lemon's rule

                                   BLIND LEMON JEFFERSON

Broke and Hungry

I am broke and hungry
                    ragged and dirty too
I said I'm broke and hungry
                    ragged and dirty too
Mama, if I clean up can
                    I go home with you

I am motherless fatherless
                    sister- and brotherless too
I say I'm motherless fatherless
                    sister- and brotherless too
Reason I'm trying so hard to
                    make the trip with you

You miss me woman
                    count the days I'm gone
You miss me woman
                    count the days I'm gone
I'm going away to build me a
                    railroad of my own

I feel like jumping through the
                    keyhole in your door
I say I feel like jumping through the
                    keyhole in your door
If you jump this time, baby
                    you won't jump no more

I believe my good gal have
                    found my black cat bone
I say I believe my baby has
                    found my black cat bone
I can leave Sunday morning
                    Monday morning I'm slipping 'round home

I want to show you women what
                    careless love have done
I want to show you women what
                    careless love have done
Caused a man like me
                    steal 'way away from home

Well if you don't want me why
                    don't you let me know
I said if you don't want me
                    mama let me know
For I can leave at once and hunt
                    me somewhere to go

Deceitful Brownskin Blues

There's a brown 'cross town and she's
                              taller'n a sycamore tree
I got a brown 'cross town
                    taller'n a sycamore tree
That's the gal'd walk through the rain and snow
                                        for to ease that thing on me

Brownskin girl is 'ceitful
                        till she gets you all worn down
Brownskin girl is 'ceitful
                        till she gets you all worn down
She get all your pocket change
                          she gonna drive you from her town

Went home last night
                    found a note in my brownskin's door
I went home last night
                    found a note in my brownskin's door
Daddy, *State Loan has got your rule*
                          man you can't live here no more

I began to walk and
                  walked till my feet got soaking wet
I commenced to walk and
                    walked till my feet got soaking wet
Trying to find *good home* mama
                        man I ain't found none yet

Well the sun's gonna shine in
                          my back door some day
Well the sun's gon' shine
                      in my back door some day
Ahhhh it's one more drink
                      gonna drive these blues away

Lord it's heavy-hipped mama
                        and the meat shakes on the bone
I said heavy-set mama
                  and the meat shakes on the bone
Every time it shakes
                it's a sign my baby's home

BLIND LEMON JEFFERSON

Long Distance Moan

I'm flying to South Carolina
                I gotta go there this time
I'm flying to South Carolina
                I gotta go there this time
Woman in Dallas Texas
                is 'bout to make me lose my mind

Long distance, long distance
                will you please give me a credit call
Long distance, long distance
                will you give me a please cr-credit call
Want to talk to my gal in South Carolina
                who looks like a Indian squaw

Just want to ask my baby
                what in the world is she been doing
I want to ask my baby
                what in the world is she been doing
Give your loving to another joker
                and it's sure gonna be my ruin

Hey long distance
                I can't help but moan
Mmmmmmmmmmmmmmmm
                I can't help but moan
My baby's voice sound so sweet
                oh I'm gonna break this telephone

You don't know you love
                your rider till she is so far from you
You don't know you love your rider
                until she's so far from you
You can get long distance moan
                and you don't care what you do

I say no use standing and buzzing
                to get my brownie off my mind
No use standing and bawling
                get my baby off my mind
This long distance moan
                about to worry me to death this time

That Crawling Baby Blues

Well the baby crying
                    on up to his mama's knee
Well the baby crying
                    up to his mama's knee
He's crying about his sweet milk
                          and she won't feed him just that cream

Crawled up to the fireplace
                          and he stopped in the middle of the floor
Well he crawl from the fireplace
                          and stops in the middle of the floor
Said, Mama ain't that your second daddy
                          standing back there in the door

Well she grabbed my baby
                    and spanked him
                              I tried to make her leave him alone
I cried my baby and spanked him
                          I tried to make her leave him alone
I tried my best to stop her and she said the baby ain't none of mine

Some woman rocks the cradle and
                          I declare she rules her home
Woman rocks the cradle
                    and I declare she rules her home
Many man rocks some other man's baby and the fool thinks he's rocking his own

Went out late last night
                          when I learned the crawling baby blues
I said it was late last night
                          when I learned the crawling baby blues
My woman threw my clothes out doors
                              and now I got those crawling baby blues

BLIND LEMON JEFFERSON

Piney Woods Money Mama

Now I had a little mama
                     she done moved to the piney wood
I had a little mama
                     she done moved to the piney wood
She's a high stepping mama
                     and she don't mean no man no good

She got ways like the devil
                     and hair like a Indian squaw
She got ways like the devil
                     and hair like a Indian squaw
She been trying for years to get me
                     to be her son-in-law

Big mama
              never sing in her neighborhood
Ah big mama
              never sing in her neighborhood
But when she made the money
                     is when she lived in this piney wood

Blues in my kitchen
                  blues in my dining room
I've got blues in my kitchen
                  blues in my dining room
And some nice young fair brown
                     had better come here soon

Well the cook's in the kitchen
                     picking and fussing over turnip greens
I say cook's in the kitchen
                     fussing and picking over turnip greens
White folks in the parlor playing cards
                     and *they serving their cake and tea*

My baby loves my baby
                  like a cow loves to chew her cud
I say I love my baby
                  like a cow loves to chew her cud
But that fool just off and left me
                     just moved to the piney wood

BLIND LEMON JEFFERSON

Wartime Blues

What you gon-
        na do
               when they send your man to war
What you gonna do—send your man to war
What you gonna do when they send your man to war
I'm gonna drink muddy water, gonna sleep in a hollow log

I ain't got
        no body
            I'm all here by myself
Got no body, all here by myself
Got no body, all here by myself
Oh these women don't care, but the men don't need me here

Well I'm going
        to the river
            gonna walk it up and down
Going to the river, walk it up and down
Going to the river, walk it up and down
If I don't find Corinna, I'm gonna jump overboard and drown

If I could shine
        my light
            like a headlight on some train
If I could shine like a headlight on some train
If I could shine like a headlight on some train
I would shine my light, and *call a real train*

Well they tell me
        that southbound
            train had a wreck last night
Lord that southbound: train had a wreck last night
Lord that southbound: train had a wreck last night
Listen here, section foreman, they ain't treating your railroad right

Well the gal
        I love
            and the one I crave to see
Woman I love, one I crave to see
Woman I love, and the one I crave to see
Well she's living in Memphis, and the fool won't write to me

I said,
    Little woman
            what have I said and done?
Hey, mama, what I said and done?
Hey, mama, what have I said and done?
You treat me like my trouble has just begun

                                BLIND LEMON JEFFERSON

Black Horse Blues

Tell me what time do the trains come through your town
I wanna know what time the trains come through your town
I wanna laugh and talk with a long-haired teasing brown

One goes south at eight and it's one goes north at nine
One goes south at eight and one goes north at nine
I got to have a good talk with that long-haired brown of mine

Go and get my black horse and saddle up my gray mare
Go get my black horse and saddle up my gray mare
I'm going on to my good gal: she's in the world some where

I can't count these times and I'm so unsatisfied
I can't count these times and I'm so unsatisfied
Sugar, the blues ain't on me, but things ain't going on right

Easy Rider Blues

Now tell me where my easy rider gone
Tell me where my easy rider gone
I need one of these women always in the wrong

Well, easy rider, standing on the road
And it's easy rider standing on the road
I'm a poor blind man, ain't got no where to go

It's gonna be the time when a woman don't need no man
Well it's gonna be a time when a woman don't need no man
Then, baby, shut your mouth: it's gonna be *raising* sand

The train I ride don't burn no coal at all
Train I ride don't burn no coal at all
The coal house burner: everybody's *snapping* cannonballs

I went to the depot
I mean I went to the depot and set my pistol down
The blues overtake me and tears come rolling down

The woman I love, she must be out of town
Woman I love, man she's out of town
She left me this morning with a face that's *travel* bound

I got a gal 'cross town, she crochets all the time
I got a gal 'cross town, crochets all the time
Baby, if you don't quit crocheting, you gonna lose your mind

Goodbye brown, what's the matter now
Goodbye brown, what's the matter now
You turn your back to quit me: woman, and you don't know how

BLIND LEMON JEFFERSON

Awful Fix

Hey, mama
Tell me what have I
Tell me what have I
       'tain't no lie
Hey mama
Tell me what have I done
It just seem like you're trying to
Beat your loving self on down

You gonna wake up one of these mornings
Now, sweet mama, now, I be
Baby, mama, now, I be
       'tain't no lie
Tell-the-truth: you gonna wake up one of these mornings
Mama, baby, and I be gone
And you may not never
Mama, see me in your town no more

'Cause I'm a stranger in here, woman
I just blowed in your
I just blowed in your
       mamlish town
Lord, I'm a stranger to you, brownskin
Mama, I just blowed in your town
And if I ask you for a favor
Mama, please, now, don't turn me down

If you get one old woman, boy
You better get you five or
You better get you five or
       I mean six
If you get one old woman
You better get you five or six
So if that one happen to quit you
It won't leave you in a awful fix

When I had you, pretty mama
You know I tried to do the best I
       I mean could
Baby, there-was-no-doubt, I say, when I had you, little black woman
I tried to do the best I could
Now your little daddy's gone
Now who you gonna get to chop your wood?

                                     BUDDY BOY HAWKINS

Poor Boy Blues

Poor boy.   Poor boy.   Poor boy long way from home.

I was down in Louisia-a-ana-a
                            doing as I please
Now I'm in Texa-a-as
                    I got to work or leave

Poor boy.   Poor boy.   Poor boy long way from home.

If your home's in Louisiana-a-a
                                what you doing over here
Said my home ain't in Texa-a-as
                        and I sure don't care

Poor boy.   Poor boy.   Poor boy long way from home.

I don't ca-a-are
                    if the boat don't never la-and
I'd like to stay on the wate-e-e-e-er
                            as long as any man

Poor boy.   Poor boy.   Poor boy long way from home.

And my boat come a-rock-i-i-ing
                                just like a drunken ma-an
And my home's on the wate-e-e-e-er
                            and I sure don't like land

Poor boy.   Poor boy.   Poor boy long way from home.

RAMBLIN' (WILLARD) THOMAS

No Job Blues

I been walking all day
                    and all night too
I been walking all day
                    and all night too
'Cause my meal-ticket woman have quit me
                                and I can't find no work to do

I picken up the news paper
                    and I looked in the ads
Says I picken up the news paper
                    and I looken in the ads
And the policeman come along
                    and he arrested me for vag

(Now, boys, you ought to see me in my black and white suit

It won't do.)

I said, Judge,
              Judge, what may be my fine?
Lord I say Judge,
              Judge, what may be my fine?
He said, Get your pick and shovel
                    and get deep down in mine

I'm a poor vag prisoner
                    working in the ice and snow
I'm a poor vag prisoner
                    working in the ice and snow
I got to get me another meal-ticket woman
                          so I won't have to work no more

RAMBLIN' (WILLARD) THOMAS

Back Gnawing Blues

I ain't never loved
        but three womens in my life
I ain't never loved
        but three womens in my life
My mother and my sister
        and my partner's wife

My mother told me
        when I was about twelve years old
My mama told me
        when I was about twelve years old
Man, you nothing but a back biter
        may God bless your soul

(They call me back biter

        I AM a back biter

        I bite any man in the back)

I'm gonna tell all you women something
        maybe you might not like
And I'm gonna tell all you women something
        baby, you might not like
I wanna know
        if I can bite your man in the back

You might risk me, brother,
        but I will never risk you
Now you might risk me, brother,
        but I will never risk you
If you allow me a chance
        I will gnaw your backbone half in two

        RAMBLIN' (WILLARD) THOMAS

I'm Gonna Run to the City of Refuge

Well
I'm gonna run, I'm gonna run
I'm gonna run to the city of refuge
I'm gonna
Well I'm gonna run, ahhhhhhhh
Well I'm gonna run to the city of refuge
I'm gonna

       Oh Peter was preaching the gospel
       He's standing with eleven men
       I'll show you one that's in heaven
       If you would just only come in

I'm gonna run, I'm gonna run
I'm gonna run to the city of refuge
I'm gonna
Well help me to run, help me to run
Help me to run to the city of refuge
I'm gonna

       Oh Peter was preaching the gospel
       He's standing with eleven men
       I'll show you one that's in heaven
       If you would just only come in

I'm gonna run, I'm gonna run
I'm gonna run to the city of refuge
I'm gonna
Well I'm gonna run, I'm gonna run
I'm gonna run: city of refuge
I'm gonna

       And let me tell you my sinner
       If you want to join His band
       Well you got to be converted
       And give the preacher your hand

I'm gonna run, I'm gonna run
I'm gonna run to the city of refuge
I'm gonna
Yes I'm gonna run, Lord it's I'm gonna
I'm gonna run to the city of refuge
I'm gonna

       Well the Holy Ghost is a myst'ry
       God sent it in the land
       But struggling hard at the Master
       Try to stay in Jesus' hand

BLIND WILLIE JOHNSON

I'm gonna run, ahhhhhhhh
Well I'm gonna run: ah, city of refuge
I'm gonna
Well I'm gonna run, I'm gonna
Ah, I'm gonna run to the city of refuge
I'm gonna

> Well the twelfth chapter Revelation
> Come along with the thirteenth verse
> The dragons that John did preach about
> Drag us off to death in Hell

I'm gonna run, I'm gonna run
I'm gonna run to the city of refuge
I'm gonna
Well I'm gonna run, I'm gonna run
I'm gonna run: city of refuge
I'm gonna

> Well 'round that *preaching* table
> When Jesus was about to leave
> Well the God that prayed down in the earth
> Then the Holy Ghost set you free

I'm gonna run, I'm gonna run
I'm gonna run to the city of refuge
I'm gonna run
I'm gonna run, Lord it's I'm gonna run
I'm gonna run to the city of refuge
I'm gonna
Well it's I'm gonna run, I'm gonna run
I'm gonna run to the city of refuge
I'm gonna run

BLIND WILLIE JOHNSON

God Don't Never Change

Oh he's God
God don't never change
He's God
Always will be God

    God in the middle of the ocean
    God in the middle of the sea
    By the help of the great cre-ator
    Truly been a God to me

Great God
God don't never change
God
Always will be God

    God in Creation
    God when Adam fell
    God way up in Heaven
    God way down in Hell

Praise God
God don't never change
Oh
Always will be God

BLIND WILLIE JOHNSON

Spoke to the mountain
Said, How great I Am
Want you to get up this morning
Skip around like a lamb

Well he's God
God don't never change
Oh
Always will be God

God in the time of sickness
God in the doctor too
In the time of the influenzy
He truly was a God to you

Well it's God
God don't never change
Praise God
Always will be God

God in the pulpit
God way down at the door
It's God in the Amen corner
God's all over the floor

Well it's God
God don't never change
Ohhhh-ahh
Always will be God

BLIND WILLIE JOHNSON

If I Had My Way

> WELL
> If I had my way
> If I had a, a wicked one
> If I had
> Oh Lord
> > I'd tear this building down

WELL
Delilah was a woman fine and fair
Her pleasant looks, her coal black hair
Delilah gained old Samson's mind
A-first saw the woman that look so fine
Whether it was Timothy, I can't tell
A daughter of Timothy, I believe that well
A-Samson told his father to go and

> SEE—heh, Lord
> If I had my way
> Well if I had that wicked one
> If I had
> Ah Lord
> > I'd tear this building down

WELL
Samson's mother replied to him
Can't you find a woman of your kind and kin
Samson: will you be the mother of mine
Go and marry that-a Philistine
Let me tell you what old Samson
Well he broke at the lion and the lion run
Samson was the first man I'm bound to catch
He caught that lion, got upon his
And it's written that he killed a man with his
A-shoving of his hand in the lion's jaw

> Well if I had my way
> If I had, that wicked way
> If I had
> Ah Lord
> > I'd tear this building down

Well there's a mystery, declare it to me
How out of the eater there came forth meat
Well there's a mystery, declare it to me
How out of the strong-a there came forth sweet
It was not very long and he answered:
Well, THE BEES MADE HONEY IN THE LION'S EAR

Well if I had my way
Well if I had, that wicked way
If I had
Ah Lord,
        I'd tear this building down

It was only a thousand and they formed a plot
Not many days 'fore old Samson was caught
A-bind his hands while he was walking along
A-looked on the ground found a little jaw bone
He moved his arms, ropes they fell like thread
GOT THROUGH SLAYING, three thousand was dead

        Well if I had my way
        Well if I had, that wicked way
        If I had
        Ah Lord
            I'd tear this building down

WELL
Samson's strength was never found out
Tell me where your strength 'll lie if you please
A-till his wife sat upon his knees
Tell me where your strength 'll lie and happy you'll be
Samson's wife she talked so fair
Told his wife to cut off his hair:
SHAVE MY HEAD, CLEAN AS YOUR HAND
Till I become a natural man

        If I had my way
        Well if I had, that wicked way
        If I had
        Eh Lord
            I'd tear this building down

BLIND WILLIE JOHNSON

Jesus Make Up My Dying Bed

Since me and Jesus got: married
Haven't been a minute apart
With the receiver in my hand
And re-ligion in my heart

I can ring 'im up easy
Ahhhhhhhhh
Oh well
Ring 'im up easy
Go make up my

Mmmm
Weeping   that he ain't: lost
They despied the Amen
Hanging on the Cross

Hanging there in misery
Ahhhhhhhhh
Oh well
Hanging there in misery
Go make up my

Mmmmmmmmmmmmmmmm
Mmmmmm mmmmmmmmmm
Jesus gon' make up my

They despied the: Amen
Made poor Martha moan
Jesus said to his de-sciples
Come and carry my mother along

Dying will be easy
Ahhhhhhhhh
Dying will be easy
Dying will be easy
Jesus gon' make up my

I'm dead and: buried
Some body said that I was lost
When it get down to Jordan
Have to bear my *body* across

Done gone over
Ahhhhhhhhh
Oh well
Done gone over
Make up my

BLIND WILLIE JOHNSON

BLIND WILLIE JOHNSON

Jesus Is Coming Soon

Well we done told you
I got some warning
Jesus coming soon
Well I thought
I got some warning
Jesus coming soon

    In the year of 19 and 18
    God sent a mighty die-sease
    It killed many a thousand
    On land and on the seas

Well I thought
I got some warning
Jesus coming soon
Well I thought
I got some warning
Jesus coming soon

    Great disease was a-mighty
    And the people were sick every where
    It was the *vampires entering*
    It floated through the air

Well I thought
I got some warning
Jesus coming soon
Well I thought
I got some warning
Jesus coming soon

    The doctors they got troubled
    And they didn't know what to do
    They gathered themselves together
    They called it the Spanish influ

Well I thought
I got some warning
Jesus coming soon
Well I thought
I got some warning
Jesus coming soon

BLIND WILLIE JOHNSON

Soldiers died on the battlefield
Died in the camps too
Well the captain said to lieutenant
Ah, we don't know what to do

Well I thought
I got some warning
Jesus coming soon
Well I thought
I got some warning
Jesus coming soon

Well God is warning the nation
He's a-warning them every way
To turn away from the evil
And seek the Lord and pray

Well I thought
I got some warning
Jesus coming soon
Well I thought
I got some warning
Jesus coming soon

Well the noble said unto the people
You better close your public schools
And to prevent the *vampires entering*
Better close the churches too

Well I thought
I got some warning
Jesus coming soon
Well I thought
I got some warning
Jesus coming soon

Read the Book of Zacharias
Bible plainly: says
Said the people in the cities dying
'Counta their wicked ways

BLIND WILLIE JOHNSON

Motherless Children

Well well well

Ahhhhhhhhh ah

Well,
Motherless children have a hard time

Motherless children have a hard time
Mother's dead,
They don't have any where to go
Wand'ring around from door to door
                    have a hard time

Nobody on earth can take the mother's place
When   , when mother is dead, Lord
'Body on earth can take mother's place
When mother is dead,
Nobody on earth can take mother's place
When you're starting she paves the way
Nobody treat you like your mother will
When

Your wife, your husband may be good to you
                    , when mother is dead, Lord
                        may be good to you
Mother's dead
Wife and your husband may be good to you
But there's another and they'll prove untrue
Nobody treats you like mother will
When   , when mother is dead, Lord

Lord Lord Lord

Ehhhhhhhhh ehhhhh well

Ahhhhh ah

Well
Some people say that sister will do
                    , when mother is dead
                that sister will do
When, mother's dead
Some people say that sister will do
But, soon as she marry she'll turn her back on you
Nobody treat you like mother will

And
Father will do the best he can
                    , when mother is dead, Lord
Well the best he can
When mother is dead
Father will do the best he can
So many things a father can't understand
Nobody treat you like mother will

Hey,
Motherless children have a hard time
                    , when mother is dead, Lord
Motherless children have a hard time
Mother's dead
They don't have any where to go
Wand'ring around from door to door
                    have a hard time

T. B. Blues

(Now this is the T.B. Blues. The first woman had the T.B., she died.
The woman didn't have but one child in the world and that was a girl.
And every time she'd come to her bed her mother—she would look up
at her mother, and the men she was going with was maybe 25 or 30.
But anyhow, one man in the bunch was a sweet back man. And all the
rest of the men, wearing overhauls, she asked 'em Did you want anything, she wouldn't have it. She asked the sweet back man for one
dime, and he didn't have no dime. And she worried about it. All the
time he was gone.)

It's too late, too late
Too late, too late, too late
It's too late, too late
Too late, too late, too late
I'm on my way to Denver
And mama must I hesitate

T.B.'s all right to have
If your friends didn't treat you so low down
T.B.'s all right to have if your
friends didn't treat you so low down
Don't you ask 'em for no favor
They even stop a-coming around

Mmmmmmmmmmm mmmmmm
The T.B. is killing me
Mmmmmmmmmmm mmmmmm
The T.B. is killing me
My mama, I'm like a prisoner
I'm always a-working the street

When I was oooooon my feet
        Couldn't even walk down the street
        But the mens are looking at me
        From my head to my feet
        But they's dead now
And T.B. is killing me
I want my body buried
In the deep blue sea

Mmmmmmmmmmm mmmmmm
Mmmmmm mmmm mmmm

I got the tuberculosis
This consumption is killing me

(All right, get out west and talk to *the men*)

(You doing all right)

When I was oooooon my feet
    Couldn't even walk down the street
    But the mens are looking at me
    From my head to my feet
    But they's dead now
And T.B. is killing me
I want my body buried
In the deep blue sea

Roberta: Part 1.

Oh Roberta
                honey where you been so long
Oh Roberta
                honey where you been so long
Yes I been 'cross the country
                                with my long clothes on

   (He went down to see Roberta. And Roberta was running on them
freight/passenger trains. And she got tired of seeing him at the station.
And she went to running on the steamboat. He went down on the
banks of the river. When he got on the banks of the river, he looked
way up the river for Roberta.)

Oh Roberta
                sit down on my knee
Oh Roberta
                sit down on my knee
Got a lot to tell you
                        that's been worrying me

Way up the river
                far as I can see
Way up the river
                far as I can see
Well I thought I spied my
                        old time used to be

   (He thought he spied Roberta; 't was nothing but a cypress tree.)

Lord I thought I spied my
                        old time used to be
Yes I thought I spied my
                        old time used to be
And it was not nothing
                    honey, but a cypress tree

   (When he was down on the river, sitting on the banks of the river,
when Roberta come along.)

Honey I'm down on the river
                            sitting all on the ground
Way down on the river
                        sitting all on the ground
Gonna stay right here Lord
                        until Roberta come down

Oh Roberta
        tell me where you been so long
Oh Roberta
        tell me where you been so long
'Cross the country
        with my long clothes on

Roberta: Part 2.

(This man he was running after Roberta, and Roberta was running on the passenger train. And every station she would pass, this rascal would be sitting right down there looking for her. She got tired of looking at the rascal; she goes and run on the steamboat. And when the steamboat would pass along, he's sitting down on the ground. And so when the steamboat would get to the landing, the rascal would be right there looking at Roberta's face. So when Roberta come off the steamboat he looked up and he walked up and talked to her.)

Oh Roberta
        what in the world you mean
Tell me Roberta
        what in the world you mean
Honey the way you treat me
        'se'n I ever seen

(He looked at Roberta and he talked to her. Roberta wouldn't pay him no attention. He tore up to the police station and he told the chief of police. When he got up there he said to the chief of police.)

Well I'm going to the station
        gonna tell the chief police
Yes I'm going to the station
        gonna tell the chief police
Roberta done quit me
        I can't see no peace

(The police asked him How in the world you gonna know Roberta from any other brown-skin. 'Cause all of 'em is brown-skin now. The black women is brown-skin: they got so much high brown powder, you can't tell a black woman from a brown-skin. He looked at the policeman and here's what he said:)

LEADBELLY

She's a brown-skin woman
                    got black wavy hair
She's a brown-skin woman
                    got black wavy hair
And I can't describe her
                    I find her most any where

(The policeman goes on down to the landing with him. And walked
up and talked to Roberta. Here's what the police told him.)

Tell me Roberta
                    what's the matter with you
Tell me Roberta
                    what's the matter with yon
This man ain't got nobody to
                    take his troubles to

Pigmeat

Just lookee here mama
                    don't treat pigmeat the way you do
Oh
     don't treat pigmeat the way you do
If you don't believe it's pigmeat
                         ask anybody in your neighborhood

If you don't believe it's pigmeat
                    kindness you won't regret
Oh
     kindness you won't regret
I got something about this pigmeat
                    sweet mama, I ain't told you yet

I was born and raised in the country
                    mama, but I'm staying in town
                         (In New York City: what I'm talking about)
I was born and raised in the country
                    mama, but I'm staying in town
If you don't believe it's pigmeat
                    mama, from my head on down

   (She looked at the man, and I looked at the woman; she knowed this
was Leadbetter, wasn't nothing but pure pigmeat. All over Shreves-
port Louisiana and all in Texarkana. And I was running with a gal
named Sylvanna—she looked at me, and here's what she said: the last
words:)

You can take me to the mountain
                         and there will be pigmeat there
You can take me to the mountain, mama
                         will be pigmeat there
You can take the *bowl to chiny*
                    stand a test just any where

Oh
     a test just any where
Oh
     a test just any where
Take that *bowl to chiny*
               stand a test just any where

Becky Deem

Becky
Deem
She was a gambling gal
Win all the money
And she winned it fair
Becky
Deem
She was a gambling gal
She win all the money
And she winned it fair

Becky
Deem
Had the gamblers all on the ground
She win all the money
The skinners / laid / down
Becky
Deem
Had the gamblers all on the ground
She win all the money
The skinners / laid / down

She started
To hit one
With her *cigarette* case
Might-a hear the rascal hollering
Don't you murder me
She started
To hit one
With her *cigarette* case
You might-a hear the rascal hollering
Don't you murder me

Walked all
The way
From East St. Louis
She didn't have
But the one / thin / dime
She walked all
The way
From East St. Louis
And she didn't have
But the one / thin / dime

Never spent it
For whiskey
Honey, neither for wine
I spent it all on
This big ugly man of mine
Never spent it
For whiskey
Honey, and neither for wine
I spent it all on
This big ugly man of mine

Packin' Trunk Blues

(This song was made about a man and a woman. This man he married a woman, she didn't want him. But she married him anyhow. For the money that he had. And she thought that she got every dollar that he had—but she was mistaken. But she got him pretty well bent: he sat there with his head hung down. She walked by and she said, "Daddy," she said, "what's the matter with you?" He looked at her and here's what he said to her:)

I'm sitting down here wondering would a, would a matchbox hold my clothes
Sitting down here wondering would a matchbox hold my clothes
I'm sitting down here wondering would a matchbox hold my clothes

(She asked him, she said, "Papa," she said, "what's the matter with you?")

I don't want to be bothered with no suitcase on my road
Don't want to be bothered with no suitcase on my road
I don't want to be bothered with no suitcase on my road

(He said, "I'm going to see my friend, and see what he would do when his wife's packing up her trunk.")

Oh what would you do when your baby packing up her trunk?
What would you do when your baby packing up her trunk?
Oh what would you do when your baby packing up her trunk?

(He looked at him and here's what he told him:)

Get you half a gallon of whiskey and, and get on you a big drunk
Get you half a gallon of whiskey and get on you a big drunk
Get you half a gallon of whiskey and get on you a big drunk

(She said, "*Ghost,* go and play the piano a piece for me a little piece." This *ghost* jumped down and commenced playing the piano.)

All Out and Down

Honeeeeeeeeeey
      I'm all out and down
Honeeeeeeeeeey
      I'm broke, baby, and I ain't got a dime
      Every good man get in hard luck some time
           Don't he, baby?
           Don't he, baby?
           Don't he, baby?
           Don't he, baby?

(This man is a long way from home. And he got a brown skin
woman. And he know payday is coming pretty soon. And the woman
is shouting 'cause it's 'most payday. And the old mule is hungry. And
the sun is going down. And the man, he wished payday would move
off a little further so he wouldn't have to pay the woman nothin'.)

      I'm going to tell the woman like the dago told the jew
      You don't want me, honey I don't want you
           Tell me baby.
           Tell me baby.

Honeeeeeeeeeey
      What more you want me to do?
Honeeeeeeeeeey
      All the women in the levy shouting 'cause it's 'most payday
      The men on the levy hollering, "Don't you move your knee."
           Tell me baby.
           Hurry baby.
           Hurry baby.
           Hurry baby.

      All the women on the levy, honey, hollering, "Whoa, gee!"
      The men on the levy hollering, "Don't you murder me!"
           Please, baby.
           Please, baby.
           Please, baby.
           Please, baby.

Honeeeeeeeeeey
      I'm a long way from home
Honeeeeeeeeeey
      I'm down in the bottom, skinning for Johnny Ryan
      Putting my initials, honey, on a mule's behind
           With my line, babe.
           With my line, babe.
           With my line, babe.
           With my line, babe.

(I swear to God, I know that man wished that woman wouldn't

come home when payday come. He looked around and he begin to cry
the last time:)

Honeeeeeeeeeey
             I'm a long way from you
Honeeeeeeeeeey
             Yes, a brown skin woman make a preacher lay his Bible down
             A jet black woman make a rabbit hug a hound
                        Won't he, baby?

Kentucky Blues

Well, whilst we here, sonny, having fun
That's when the law jumped up, and said Nobody run
Well, you know I'm long gone
                              from Kentucky
Long gone
          I'm got away lucky
'Cause I'm gonna leave Seguin
      I'll be just like a submarine

Well, my woman poked her head out from the windows a bit
Said, Please don't let them kill Mr. Little Hat dead
I said, No use a-worrying, sweet mama, I ain't gonna be here long
Gonna let you sing this worried song
'Cause I'm gonna leave Seguin, I'll
      Be just like a submarine

I once have known a man, they called him *Austin* Jack
Stopped and put the blood hounds right on my track
'Cause the blinders could not catch my scent
You know they couldn't tell where that Little Hat went
'Cause I left Seguin
      He was just like a submarine

Well, yonder come the Santa Fee, *it's passing and* flying
You oughta see me rech up and nearly caught them blind
They said, There's another long gone
                              from Kentucky
Long gone
          and then got away lucky
'Cause he left Seguin
      He's just like a submarine

I'm gonna sing this song, ain't gonna sing no more

'Cause I'm leaving San Anton' and, I declare, ain't coming here no more

Well, I don't play the dozen and neither the ten
'Cause you keep on talking I'll ease you in
Well, you keep on talking till you make me mad
Gonna tell you 'bout the mothers that your father had
'Cause I don't play the dozen, I declare, man, and neither the ten

Fool's Blues

Some people tell me
                God takes care of old folks and fools
Some people tell me that
                God takes care of old folks and fools
But since I been born
                he must have changed his rules

I used to ask a question
                then answer that question myself
I used to ask a question
                then answer that question myself
'Bout when I was born
                wonder was there any more mercy left

Look like here of late
                I've been crying both day and night
Look like here of late
                I've been crying both day and night
Everybody talks about me
                and nobody don't treat me right

You know, until six months ago
                I hadn't prayed a prayer since God knows when
Until six months ago, people,
                I hadn't prayed a prayer since God knows when
Now I'm asking God every day
                to please forgive me for my sin

You know, this must be the Devil I'm serving; I know
                it can't be Jesus Christ
This must be the Devil I'm serving
                I know it can't be Jesus Christ
'Cause I asked him to save me
                and look like he's trying to take my life

        Now I got TB's
        I got LT's
        I got third degrees
        And both disease
My health is gone now
                and left me with the sickness blues
People, it don't seem like to me
                that God takes care of old folks and fools

"FUNNY PAPER" SMITH

No More Women Blues

Mmmmmmmmmmmmmmmmmmmm
                      mmmmmmmm mmmmmm
Mmmmmmmmmmmmmmmmmmmmmmm mmmmmm mmmmmm

Lord, she won't pick cotton
                   girl won't pull no corn
She won't pick cotton
                   girl won't pull no corn
If I don't see about, she gonna
                   hang about me so long

Now and there's one two three four
                   five six seven eight nine
And there's one two three four
                   five six seven eight nine
When I counts them blues
                   that many women is mine

Lord, if I get lucky
                   mama, in this world again
If I get lucky
                   in this world again
I ain't gonna fool with no more women
                   and a mighty few men

Mmmmmmmmmmmmmmmmmmmmm
                   mmmmmmmm mmmmmm
Mmmmmmmmmmmmm
                   mmmmmmmm mmmmmm mmmmmm

Lord, I walked all last night
                   and all last night before

TEXAS ALEXANDER

98 Degree Blues

I'm gonna get up in the morning
                  do like Buddy Brown
Gonna get up in the morning
                  do like Buddy Brown
I'm gonna eat my breakfast
                  rider, and lay back down
I say, I'm gonna eat my breakfast
                  man, and lay back down

When a man get hairy
                  know he needs a shave
When a man get hairy
                  know he needs a shave
When a woman get musty, you
                  know she needs to bathe
I say, when a woman get musty
                  oh, you know she needs a bathe

I've got something to tell you, make the
                  hair rise on your head
I've got something to tell you
                  make the hair rise on your head
Got a new way of loving a woman, make the
                  springs screech on her bed
I've got a new way of loving a woman
                  make the springs screech on her bed

If you don't believe I love you
                  look what a fool I've been
If you don't believe I love you
                  look what a fool I've been
Woman, if you don't believe I love you
                  ah, look what a shape I'm in

Says I love my baby, baby, lord
                  better'n I do myself
I says I love my baby
                  better'n I do myself
If she don't love me, she won't
                  love nobody else

TEXAS ALEXANDER

TEXAS ALEXANDER

Levee Camp Moan

Mmmmmmmmmmmmmmmmmmmmmmmm
Mmmmmmmmmmmmmmmmmmmmmmm
Mmmmmmmmmmmmmmmmmmmmmmmmm

Lord they accused me of murder
      murder murder
           I haven't harmed a man
Lord they accused me of murder
       I haven't harmed a man
Ohhhhhhhh
    they accused me of murder and I
         haven't harmed a man

Oh they accused me of forgery and I
        I can't write my name
Lord they accused me of forgery
      I can't write my name

Oh I went all around
      that whole corral
I couldn't find a mule
      with his shoulder well
Lord I couldn't find a mule
      with his shoulder well

Oh I worked old Maude
     and I worked old Belle
Lord I couldn't find a mule
     Maggie, with his shoulder well

Mmmmmmmmmmmmmmmmmmmmmmmm
Mmmmmmmmmmmmmmmmmmmmmmm
Mmmmmmmmmmmmmmmmmmmmmmmmm
        Lord that morning bell

Lord she went up the country and
       well she's on my mind
Well she went up the country
     but she's on my mind

Oh if she don't come on the big boat
       she better not land
Lord if she don't come on the big boat
       big boat
        I mean she better not land

Mmmmmmmmmmmmmmmmmmmmmmmm
Mmmmmmmmmmmmmmmmmmmmmm
Lord if she don't come on the big boat
      I mean she better not land

                TEXAS ALEXANDER

Robbing and Stealing Blues

My baby ain't good looking
                        and she don't dress fine
My baby ain't good looking
                        and she don't dress fine
But she gives me money
                  all of the time

She goes out at night
                  just like she's on wheels
She goes out at night
                  just like she's on wheels
And then I know
              she's going out to rob and steal

I lay in my bed, my
                baby brings me my meals
I lay in my bed, my
                baby brings me my meals
What good is a woman if
                she don't rob and steal

I used to live with a woman, they
                    called her Tildie Peel
I used to live with a woman, they
                    called her Tildie Peel
I soon got rid of her:
              she couldn't rob and steal

I know how you
            hungry hustlers feel
I know how you
            hungry hustlers feel
Your women don't know how to rob;
                        they're too doggone scared to steal

GENE CAMPBELL

You Never Miss the Water

Yesyounevermissyourwaterwaterwater
                              baby till your well's gone dry
Yesyounevermissyourwaterwater
                              baby till your well's gone dry
Yes you never miss your loved one
                              son, until she says good bye

Yehyehwhatyouwantwitharoosterroosterorbanty
                              who won't crow for day
Yehyehwhatyouwantwitharooster
                              son, who won't crow for day
Yeh, what you want with a woman
                              she always want to have her way

Yehdon'tyouknowyourhouselooklonesomelonesome
                              you know, when your baby gone
Yehyehdon'tyourhouselooklonesome
                              son, when your baby gone
Yeh, and you have the blues so bad
                              that you can't stay at home

Yehmylittlewomanshedoneleftmelordlord
                              please tell me what I'm gonna do
Yehyehmylittlewomanshedoneleftme
                              please tell me what I'm gonna do
Yes, she's a good little girl
                              but she just won't be true

Katie May

Yeah, you know Katie May's a good girl
>
> folks, and she don't run around at night

Yeah, you know Katie May's a good girl
>
> folks, and she don't run around at night

Yeah, you know you can bet your last dollar
>
> Katie May will treat you right

Yeah, you know I tried to give that woman
>
> everything in the world she need

That's why she don't do nothing
>
> but lay up in bed and read

You know she walks just like
>
> she got oil wells in her back yard

Yes, you never hear that woman whooping, hollering, and crying
>
> and talking 'bout these
> times being hard

You know some folks say she must be a Cadillac
>
> but I say she must be a T-model Ford

Yeah, you know some folks say she must be a Cadillac
>
> but I say she must be a T-model Ford

Yeah, you know she got the shape all right
>
> but she can't carry no heavy load

I say good bye good bye folks and
>
> these are the last words that I got to say

I say good bye good bye folks and
>
> these are the last words I got to say

Yes, if I don't see you tomorrow
>
> I hope I'll meet you early the next day

Highway Blues

I was traveling fast
one of these days
talking about
I was on my way
down

to the highway

that's when I knowed
I'm gonna meet that lady

I'm gonna take my girl
have some fun
if my money don't spend
I can shoot my gun
going

LIGHTNING HOPKINS

yes I'm going

yes I'm going
on that highway

(Now lookit here folks, here's a little story I'm gonna tell you,
but I didn't know it, right then, but I'm gonna say it, because,
I found out later that it was all right.)

(Yes, come on in there where we can get it good.)

You know there's a place
you can put your money down
take your girl
go up stairs and *clown*

I'm going

I'm gonna *clown*

I'm gonna *clown* with the people
God knows, I'm gonna break 'em

(I don't know why I didn't know there was places as that,
but I didn't.)

She spoke out loud:
Don't make me mad
looked up this morning
had everything I had
I was mad with the world

I was mad with the world

Reason why I was mad
I didn't know what she done it for

Short Haired Woman

I don't want no woman
                              if her hair ain't no longer'n mine
I don't want no woman
                              if her hair ain't no longer'n mine
Yes, you know she ain't good for nothing but trouble
She'll keep you buying rats all the time

       Yes, you know I carried my woman to the hair dresser
       And this is what the hair dresser said
       She said Sam I can't treat the woman's hair
       God know, I can treat her head

I told her no!
                              boy, if her hair ain't no longer'n mine
Yes, you know she ain't good for nothing but trouble
She'll keep you buying rats all the time

              (Wigs and rats 'll get you killed)

       Yes, you know I woke up this morning, peoples, poor Sam
       'Bout the break of day
       You know I even found a rat
       On the pillow where she used to lay

You know I don't want no woman
                                        if her hair ain't no longer'n mine
Yes, you know she ain't good for nothing but trouble
She'll keep you buying rats all the time

       You know I went to get on the good side of my woman
       Said Come and let's go and have some fun
       You know I went to make a swing out when a rat fell from her head
       Like one from a burning barn

But I just told her, I don't want no woman
                                                  if her hair ain't no longer'n mine
Yes, you know she ain't good for nothing but trouble
She'll keep you buying rats all the time

She's Mine

She's little and she's low
      she's right down on the ground
She's little and she's low
     right down on the ground
Well the way she acts
    make a rabbit hug a hound

   She's mine
   She's mine
   She's mine
   She's mine
   She's mine, but she's crippled
     and the poor child's blind

(She's still mine.)

(She's mine.)

(Yeah.)

(She's still my baby.)

Everybody in the world is laughing at me everywhere I go
'Cause I lead my wife down the road

   But she's mine
   She's mine
   She's mine, and she's little and low
     cripple, if she's blind

(Still she's mine.)

    Make no difference if she's low
    poor girl's cripple and blind

(Yeah, she's my baby.)

She's my little baby
   love her just the same

Mister Charlie

(Once in the country there was a little boy he was wandering away from his, place that he was living. He didn't have no mother, neither no father. So he decided he would try to get out on his own because he figured that the people that he was, around with, there was a little too, cruel to him. So the little kid, he wanted to see some parts of the world and he decided he would, start out on his own. So he left, his home, where, he would call a home. And he goes traveling. He travels for miles and miles, as he; he traveled a good piece, from the place, that he was located.

So he run across a rolling mill. The fact of the business: it was a saw mill. But they called it a rolling mill at that time, because they'd roll the logs down the hill, put 'em on the trolley, and roll 'em on down, and they would cut the first, off, and throw it in the junk there, and let it burn. So Mister Charlie he had, a shack, behind his mill. So he didn't have anything to be in that shack, unless 'n somebody stayed. The little boy he walked up there, and he stood, looking lonesome and 'lorn.

So Mister Charlie say, "Boy, what you doing here?"

He say, "Me me me me me me don't have no home."

So Mister Charlie say, "Well, wait a minute. I'm busy now." Mister Charlie went on, doing his work there, and things that he's supposed to do. He looked: the poor little boy was standing in the same position.

He came back there, he say, "Boy, can you work?"

"Me me can work."

He say, "Well I tell you what: by you not having no home, I got a shack back there." Said, "If you will stay in that shack and keep this fire from my cured lumber, and keep it from burning my mill burning down," he say, "I'll give you a home here, long as I got a mill."

"Th th thank you, Mister Charlie."

And so, Mister Charlie carried him back there and showed him where, that he could live, you know?

So the little boy was happy with his home.

Mister Charlie lived a few blocks from there: fact of the business. But it wasn't too far that the little boy could run to the house.

So, on Sundays they don't work. But they still got that there throw-away burning away. You know what I mean? And so the little boy he was inside of his little bunk that morning. And he looked out and he seed that the rolling mill had caught a-fire.

The little boy went to running. He run all the way. He didn't stop. 'Cause he was trying. To approve. That he meaned. To do the thing. That Mister Charlie asked him to.

So when he got there Mister Charlie was busy, doing a little old something else. What it was, the little boy don't know. And I don't either. But I know, and the little boy knows, that he was busy. So he patted Mister Charlie on the back, he said, "Mi Mi Mi Mi Mi Mi Mi Mister Charlie!"

Mister Charlie straighted up and looked at him, and said, "Boy, what you want?"

He said, "Yo yo yo yo yo."

He said, "Well wait a minute." He says, "I got something to do. You tell me later."

Mister Charlie turned around and he begins doing what he was doing. The little boy wanted to let him know that it was urgent. It was his time to go. He patted him on his back no sooner than Mister Charlie stooped over, said, "Mi Mi Mi Mi Mi Mi Mi Mi Mister Charlie!"

Mister Charlie straightened up, and said, "Boy, you trying to tell me something." Said, "Now if you can't talk it," said, "sing it." And he said:)

Ohhhhhhhhh
          Mister Charlie
                    your rolling mill is burning down
Oh Mister Charlie
          your rolling mill is burning down
He said, I ain't got no water
                Mister Charlie say, If you ain't got none,
Just let the rolling mill
          burn on down

          Mister Charlie say, Boy,
          If it ain't no water 'round
          Poke your head out the window and let that old
          Rolling mill burn on down
He said, Mister Charlie,
             do you know your rolling mill is burning down
He says, I can't help you, I can't help you,
               Mister Charlie, it ain't no water 'round

          The little boy said, Mister Charlie,
          Now don't you see
          If the mill burn down, that's
          Almost the last of me
          Mister Charlie said, Don't you worry
          Son, listen at me
          If the old mill burn down I'm gonna give you another home
                    Oh, somewhere with me
Mister Charlie
          your rolling mill is burning down
He said, Just poke your head out the window
             and let that old rolling mill burn down

          (The little boy couldn't
            help but cry—)

Ohhhhhhhhh
          Mister Charlie
            I won't have no place to stay
Mister Charlie
          I won't have no place to stay
Mister Charlie say, Son, don't you worry
           I got a home for you long
             as the day

Death Bells

Sound like I can hear this morning
them bells ringing all in my ear
Sound like I can hear this morning, baby
them bells ringing all in my ear
Yes I know I'm gonna leave on a chariot
Wonder what kind gonna carry me from here

You know every living creeper
man, was born to die
Yeah you know every living creeper
was, lord, was born to die
Yeah, but when that chariot come for you
They gonna break, run, and try to hide

Yeah, you know my mama told me
my papa told me too
She: someday, son, you know that chariot's
coming after you
I been wondering
what kinda chariot
Oh
gonna take me away from here
Yes, you know this life I'm living I been living
Oh lord, for a great many years

Captain Captain

I told my captain
            that old Maude was dead
Told my captain
            that old Maude was dead
Never mind old Maude
            put the harness on Ned

I asked my captain
            for the time of day
Well I asked my captain
            for the time of day
He looked at his watch and
            he just walked away

Got to work so hard and my
            captain pay so slow
Have to work so hard and my
            captain pay so slow
Some time I don't care whether
            I work or no

If you wake up in the morning
            I'll be seldom seen
If you wake up in the morning
            I'll be seldom seen
You can let someone else
            captain, catch my team

Went all around
            man, that whole corral
Well I went all around
            man, that whole corral
And I couldn't find a mule
            there, with his shoulder well

MANCE LIPSCOMB

Alabama Bound

Alabama bound
Alabama bound
If the boat don't sink
        and neither turn around
I'm Alabama bound

Well the preacher's in the pulpit
Just a-waving his hand
And the sisters way back
        in the a-men corners
Hollering, Go on man

What did the rooster say
To the little red hen
Want you to meet me down
        to the old barn yard
'Bout half past ten

Well the rooster crowed
Hen flew on the fence
I can see / in
        your deep blue eyes
You got to be convinced

Well the rooster crowed
And the hen replied
Said, I can see / in
        your deep blue eyes
You got to rise and fly

Well the rooster crowed
And the hen flew down
Wanna be / a
        man of mine
You got to run me down

Well I'm going up north
And going to stay
Got a long / tall
        teasing brown
Gonna pay my way

Well the preacher preached
All the sisters moaned
You want / this
        collection I got
You got to follow me home

When he got through preaching
Laid his Bible down
Said, Sisters, *I'm a missionary*
                    but for the Church
I'm Alabama bound

Don't you leave me here
Don't leave me here
But if you leave me here
                    oh darling dear
Leave a dime for beer

MANCE LIPSCOMB

Charlie Cherry

If the shack get raided
>>> ain't no body run
If the shack get raided
>>> ain't no body run
You stay right here till
>>> Charlie Cherry come

Well he cut you if you stand
>>> shoot you if you run
Well he cut you if you stand
>>> shoot you if you run
You better stay right here till
>>> Charlie Cherry come

Now he arrested my brother
>>> tied him to a tree
Well now he arrested my brother
>>> tied him to a tree
You could hear him crying,
>>> Please don't murder me

Well now Charlie Cherry
>>> meanest man I know
Well it's Charlie Cherry
>>> meanest man I know
Well now you meet him in the morning
>>> you don't know which-a-way to go

Well now where was you baby
>>> when the wind blowed cold
Well now where was you
>>> when the wind blowed cold
Well now you was in the bottom
>>> by the red hot stove

Verses 3 and 4 are from a different take than the other three.

Homeless Blues

Rocks have been my pillow, baby
                    you know bare ground have been my bed
Well now, rocks have been my pillow
                    oh Lord, bare ground have been my bed
You know I ain't got no where
                    oh Lord, to lay my poor aching head

You know I went out on the highway
                    and I tried to catch myself a ride
You know I went out on the highway
                    I tried to catch myself a ride
Well, there was no one seemed to know me
                    oh well, they kept on passing by

You know I'm ragged, I swear I'm dirty
                    baby, I got no place to go
Oh well, I'm raggedy, I swear I'm dirty
                    baby, I ain't got no place to go
Well now, I know that you don't love me
                    baby, and you don't want me no more

Oh take me out of this old bottom
                    baby, 'fore your water rise
Now take me out of this old bottom
                    baby, before your water rise
You know I ain't got no true religion, baby
                    mmmm well, I don't want to be baptized

LIL' SON JACKSON

New Orleans to Jackson

James Alley

The times ain't now
                    nothing like they used to be
Oh times ain't now
                    nothing like they used to be
And I'm telling you all the truth
                              oh take it from me

I done seen better days
                    but I'm putting up with these
I done seen better days
                    but I'm putting up with these
I could have a much better time
                              but these girls is so hard to please

'Cause I was born in the country
                              she thinks I'm easy to rule
'Cause I was born in the country
                              she thinks I'm easy to rule
She tried to hitch me to her wagon:
                                   she wanta drive me like a mule

You know I bought the groceries
                              and I paid the rent
Yeah, I buys the groceries
                         and I pays her rent
She tried to make me wash her clothes
                                   but I gòt good common sense

I said, If you don't want me
                         why don't you tell me so
You knowed if you don't want me
                              why don't you tell me so
Because it ain't like a man
                         that ain't got no where to go

I b'lieve I'm giving you sugar for sugar
                                        let you get salt for salt
I'll give you sugar for sugar
                         let you get salt for salt
And if you can't get along with me
                                   well, it's your own fault

Now you want me to love you
                         and you treat me mean
How do you want me to love you
                                   if you keep a-treating me mean
You're my daily thought
                    and my nightly dream

RABBIT BROWN

Sometime I think
        that you too sweet to die
Sometime I think
        that you too sweet to die
And another time I think
        you ought to be buried alive

The Jailhouse Blues

When I was lying in jail with my
                    back turned to the wall
When I was laying in jail with my
                    back turned to the wall
I could lay down and dream I could
                    hear my good gal squall

Lord she brought me coffee
              and she brought me tea
Lord she brought me coffee
              and she brought me tea
Fell dead at the door
          with the jailhouse key

I'm going down to the courthouse
                  see the judge and the chief police
Going down to the courthouse
                see the judge and the chief police
My good gal fell dead now and
                I sure can't see no peace

I'll tell you what I'll do and I
              sure god ain't gonna tell no lie
Tell you what I'll do and I
              sure god ain't gonna lie
I believe I'll lay down
          take mor-phine and die

SAM COLLINS

Slow Mama Slow

Take your time kind mama
                I'm gonna do it just as slow as I can
Take your time kind mama
                I'm doing it just as slow as I can
I might start shimmying
                don't let nobody in

Make your bed up higher
                and turn your lamp way low
Make your bed up higher
                turn your lamp way low
I'm gonna hug and kiss you
                ain't coming here no more

Pull down your window
                lock up on your door
Lock up on your window
                lock up on your door
I got ways like the devil
                I'm slipping on the floor

Make your bed up higher
                a-and turn your lamp around
Make your bed up higher
                turn your lamp around
Look out your back door
                see me leave this town

Whoopee Blues

Honey, you been gone all day
                    that you may make whoopee all night
Baby, you been gone all day
                    that you may make whoopee all night
I'm gonna take my razor and cut your late hours
                              you wouldn't think I been serving you right

Undertaker been here and gone
                    I give him your heighth and size
I said undertaker been here and gone
                      I give him your heighth and size
You'll be making whoopee with the devil
                    in hell tomorrow night

You done made me love you
                  now got me for your slave
Baby you done made me love you
                  now got you for your slave
From now on you'll be making whoopee,
                    baby, in your lonesome grave

Baby, next time you go out
                  carry your black suit along
Mama, next time you go out
                  carry your black suit along
Coffin gonna be your present
                  hell gonna be your brand new home

I say the devil got ninety thousand women
                      he just need one more
He's on the mountain calling for you
                  baby, broke down and surely must go

Cool cool weather we're having
                  summer's almost out
Then I got to go through Death Valley
                  there ain't a house for 25 miles around

My poor feet is so tired
                  Lord help me some way
Then I got 300 miles to go
                  traveling through the mud and clay

Mmmmmmmmmmmmmmm
Mmmmmmmmmm mmmm

The Gone Dead Train

And I'm going way down
                    lord I'm gonna try to leave here today
Tell me that's a mean old fireman
                              and that train is just that way

Gotta get on that train
                    I said I'd even *brought* my trunk
Boys if you have been running around in this world
                                    this train will wreck your mind
                                    (your life too)

Lord, I once was a hobo
                    I crossed many points
But I decided I'd *pull down* for a fast life
                              and take it as it comes
                              (I reckon these old firemen and engineer would too)

There's so many people
                    have gone down today
And these fast trains north and south have
                              settled in nice in place

Mmmmmm mmmmmmmmmmm
                              I want to ride your train
I said, Look here engineer
                    can I ride your train
He said, Look, you ought to know this train ain't mine
                                    and you asking me in vain

Said, If you go to the Western Union
                              you might get a chance
                              (I didn't know the Western Union run no trains)
If you go to the Western Union
                    you might get a chance
You might to wire to some of your people
                              and your fare will be sent right here
                              (I haven't thought of it that way before)

I want to go home
                    and that train is done gone dead
I want to go home
                    that train is done gone dead
I done lost my wife and my three little children
                              and my mother's sick in bed

Mmmmmm please
                    help me win my fare
'Cause I'm a traveling man
                    boys, I can't stay here

Out On Santa-fe—Blues

Said a woman and a dollar
      a bout the same
Said a woman and a dollar
      a bout the same
Dollar go from hand to hand and a
      woman goes from man to man

Don't let a woman know you love her
      if you do you have done wrong
Don't let a woman know you love her
      if you do you have done wrong
You come in from your work, now
      she got her clothes and gone

Then you catch you a freight train
      goin' out on the Santa-fee
Then you catch you a freight train
      goin' out on the Santa-fee
I ain't staying now
      this ain't the place for me

Your mind'll tell you to travel
      any and every where
Your mind tell you to travel
      any and every where
When you're there you won't stay long
      you can't stay no where

I can tell the day, mama
      I seen my baby's face
I can tell the day, mama
      I seen my baby's face
She *started me to* lovin' her
      then treat me this a way

You got all you wanted
      now please let me 'lone
You got all you wanted
      now please let me 'lone
It won't be long till
      back up this road I'm gone

ARTHUR PETTIES (PETTIS)

Married Man Blues

When you lose your money
                          please don't lose your mind
When you lose your money
                          please don't lose your mind
When you lose your woman
                          please don't fool with mine

Tell you married men
                          how to keep your wives at home
Tell you married men
                          how to keep your wives at home
Get you a job
            and roll for the man
                                    and try to carry your labor home
Mmmmmmmmmmm mmmmmm
                          try to carry your labor home

Tell you married women
                          how to keep your husband at home
Tell you married women
                          how to keep your husband at home
Mmmmmmmmmmm
                    mmmmmm mmmm mmmm
Take care of your husband's labor
                          and let these single boys alone

BLIND WILLIE (JOE) REYNOLDS

What make a
            single woman
                        crazy 'bout a married man
What make a single woman
                        crazy 'bout a married man
'Cause he works all the time
                        he puts money in her hand

What make a married woman
                            so crazy 'bout a single man
Mmmmmmmmmmm
                    mmmmmm mmmm mmmm
What make a married woman
                            so crazy 'bout a single man
'Cause the husband might lay down and die
                                    and leave that fellow to her hand

Let me tell you men
                    what these married women will do
Let me tell you boys
                    what these married women will do
She will get your money
                    she will catch up to you

Tell you this, men
                    ain't gonna tell you nothing else
Tell you this, men
                    ain't gonna tell you nothing else
Man's a fool if he thinks
                    he's got a whole woman by hisself

BLIND WILLIE (JOE) REYNOLDS

Nehi Blues

Some girls wear short dresses
       some of these married women wear them too
Some girls wear short dresses
       some of these married women wear them too
That's the reason we single men, lord, don't know what we want to do

Wish the proper judge would make these
         women let their dresses down
Wish the proper judge would make these
         women let their dresses down
So there'd quit being so doggone much murder in town

When they pass the law
      pulling the short dress down
When they pass the law
      pulling the short dress down
So we single men can tell a: married woman from a child

Mmmmmmmmmmmmmmm
       mmmmmmmmmm mmmmmm mmmm
Mmmmmmmmmmmmmmmm
       mmmmmmmm mmmmmm
Mmmmmmmm mmmmmm
       mmmmmm mmmm mmmm

                    BLIND WILLIE (JOE) REYNOLDS

Let me tell you boys
                    what these nehi dresses will do
Let me tell you boys
                    what these nehi dresses will do
Get you broke, naked and hungry, boy, and then come down on you

All of you women,
                    sure lord, ought to be 'shamed
All of you young women,
                        sure lord, ought to be 'shamed
Taking these old men's money when they walking on walking canes

Mmmmmmmmmmmmmmmm
                            mmmmmmmmmm mmmmmm mmmm
Mmmmmmmmmmmmmmmm
                            mmmmmmmm mmmmmmm
Mmmmmmmmm mmmmmmm
                        mmmmmm mmmm mmmm

A old man ain't nothing
                    but a young woman's slave
These old mens ain't nothing
                        but a young woman's slave
They work hard all the time trying to stay in these young men's ways

Mmmmmmmmmmmmmmmm
                            mmmmmmmmmm mmmmmm mmmm
Mmmmmmmmmmmmmmmm
                        mmmmmmmm mmmmmmm
Mmmmmmmm mmmmmmm
                    mmmmmm mmmm mmmm

Maggie Campbell Blues

Cryin', who's that yonder
                         comin' down the road
                comin'
                down the road
Mmmmm, who's that yonder
                            comin' down the road
Well it
        look like Maggie, baby,
But she walk too slow

Now, sun goin' shine
                    my back door some day
             my back
             door some day
Mmmmm, sun goin' shine in
                        my back door some day
And the
          wind gon' change, gon'
Blow my blues away

Now, see see rider
                  see what you done done
           see what
           you done done
Mmmmm, see see rider
                    see what you done done
You done
          made me love you, now you
Tryin' to put me down

Well, I'm goin' away, lord,
                        won't be back till fall
                    won't be
                    back till fall
Well, I'm goin' away, lord,
                        won't be back till fall
If I
    meet my good gal, well I
Won't be back at all

Now, who's that yonder
                        comin' down the road
                    comin'
                    down the road
Mmmmmm, who's that yonder
                            comin' down the road
Well it
        look like Maggie, baby,
But she walk too slow

Mmmmmm, goin' away
                        won't be back till fall
                    won't be
                    back till fall
Well, I'm goin' away, lord,
                        won't be back till fall
Well if I
        meet my good gal, well I
Won't be back at all

TOMMY JOHNSON

Canned Heat Blues

Cryin' canned heat
Canned heat, mama
Cryin' Sterno's,
      killin' me
Cryin' canned heat, mama
Sterno's killin' me
Say, can't you run to
        take these canned heat blues

TOMMY JOHNSON

Cryin' mama
Mama mama
You know canned heat,
            killin' me
Cryin' mama mama mama
Cryin' canned heat is killin' me
Canned heat don't kill me
                    I b'lieve I
                            never die

I woke up
Up this mornin'
With canned heat
        on my mind
Woke up this mornin'
Canned heat was on my mind
Woke up this mo—
                with canned heat on
                        on my mind

Cryin' lord
Lord I wonder
Canned heat, lord
            killin' me
Began to worry
Worryin' 'bout my soul
Take a brown skin woman
                to do the
                        easy roll

I woke up
Up this mornin'
Cryin' canned heat
            'round my bed
Run here some body
Take these canned heat blues
Run here some bo—
                and take these
                        canned heat blues

Cryin' mama
Mama mama
Cryin' canned heat
            killin' me
They took my soul, lord,
                they gonna kill me dead

Big Road Blues

Cryin' ain't goin' down this
           Big road by myself
     Now don't you
           Hear me talkin', pretty mama, lord
Ain't goin' down this
           Big road by myself
If I don't carry you, goin'
           Carry somebody else

Cryin' sun goin' shine in
           My back door some day
     Now don't you
           Hear me talkin', pretty mama, lord
Sun goin' shine in
           My back door some day
And the wind goin' change, goin'
           Blow my blues away

Baby, what makes you do
           Like you do do do
           Like you do do do
     Don't you hear me now
What makes you do me
           Do like you do do do
Now you say you goin' do me like you
           Done poor Cherry Red

TOMMY JOHNSON

Take the poor boy's money, now,
                    Sure lord won't take mine
          Now don't you
                    Hear me talkin', pretty mama
Takin' the poor boy's money
                    Sure enough won't take mine
Takin' the poor boy's money, now,
                    Sure lord won't take mine

Cryin' ain't goin' down this
                    Big road by myself
          Now don't you
                    Hear me talkin', pretty mama, lord
Ain't goin' down this
                    Big road by myself
If I don't carry you, goin'
                    Carry somebody else

Cryin' sun goin' shine, lord,
                    My back door some day
          Now don't you
                    Hear me talkin', pretty mama, lord
Sun goin' shine in
                    My back door some day
And the wind goin'
                    Blow my
                              Blues away

TOMMY JOHNSON

ISHMAN BRACEY

Leaving Town Blues

Now I tell you mama now
                      I'm sure gonna leave this town
Now I tell you mama now
                      I'm sure gonna leave this town
'Cause I been in trouble ever since I
                      sot my suitcase down

Now you don't b'lieve I'm leaving
                      just watch the train I'm on
Now you don't b'lieve I'm leaving
                      just watch the train I'm on
And you don't b'lieve I'm *looking*
                      just count the days I'm gone

Now I ain't gonna be your
                      your teasing brown no more
I mean I ain't gonna be your
                      teasing brown no more
Sugar, the way you do me, you
                      make my blood run cold

Now 'fore I stay here mama 'n'
                      be treated this-a-way
Mama 'fore I stay here now and
                      be treated this-a-way
Now I'll let some freight train
                      throw me every day

Mmm lord oh lord oh
                      oh lord oh lord oh lord
Mmm lord oh lord oh
                      oh lord oh lord oh lord
Now the woman I'm loving, she
                      treat me like a mangy dog

Now lookee yonder sugar where the
                      rising sun done gone
Mmm lookee yonder sugar where the
                      rising sun done gone
I believe I will leave here mama
                      a long way from my home

ISHMAN BRACEY

Saturday Blues

Now you
tell me mama, do you
think that's right
You with your
kid all day and run
to me at night
        With your
        kid all day and
        run to me at night
                With your kid all day and
                run to me at night

Now my
reg'lar woman totes my
pocket change
And my
sometime woman wants to
do the same
        And you
        better not let my
        reg'lar catch you here
                Don't never let my
                reg'lar catch you here

'Cause it
ain't no telling what
she might do
Now
she might cut you, she might
shoot you too
        Now
        she might cut you
        she might shoot you too
                Lord she might cut you
                she might shoot you too

Now she's the
meanest woman that I've
ever seen
And when I
asked for water give me
gasoline
        Now I
        asked her for water
        give me gasoline
                Lord when I asked for water
                give me gasoline

ISHMAN BRACEY

Now if you
want your woman to
look like the rest
You buy her
high brown powder, Palmer's
Skin Success
        You buy her
        high brown powder
        Palmer's Skin Success
                Buy her high brown powder
                Palmer's Skin Success

Now I got
four five puppies and got one
shaggy hound
It takes
all them dogs to run my
women down
        It takes
        all them dogs to
        run my women down
                Takes all them dogs to
                run my women down

Now I got
four five puppies and got one
shaggy hound
It takes
all them dogs to run my
women down
        It takes
        all them dogs to
        run my women down
                Takes all them dogs to
                run my women down

Dark Road Blues

Cryin'
    I ain't goin' down the
               dark road by myself
      Now don't you
            hear me talking' to you, pretty mama
Oh-ho, ain't goin' down the
               dark road by myself
Cryin' if I don't carry you
          carry somebody else

Cryin'
    who that yonder
          comin'
            up the road
      Now don't you
            hear me talkin' to you, pretty mama
Oh-ho, who that yonder
          baby, up the road
Cryin' it look like my faro
          but she walk too slow

Cryin'
    I won't let you do me do me
            like you
              did poor Shine
      Now don't you
            hear me talkin' to you, pretty mama
Oh-ho, I won't let you do me
          like you did poor Shine
Cryin' you taken the poor boy's money
             gonna have to kill me
                'fore you take mine

    (Yeah)

Cryin' you're gonna have to kill me
          'fore you take mine

Cryin'
    smokestack lightnin'
          shine like
            faro gold
      Now don't you
            hear me talkin' to you, pretty mama
Oh-ho, smokestack lightnin'
          shine like faro gold
Cryin' I wouldn't get in trouble
          see no body saw

Cryin'
      I spied a spider
               climbin'
                      up the wall
    Now don't you
                 hear me talkin' to you, pretty mama
Oh-ho, spied a spider
                 climbin' up the wall
Cryin' I asked the spider did he
                   want his ashes hauled

Cryin'
      I ain't gonna marry
                ain't gonna
                      settle down
    Now don't you
                 hear me talkin' to you, pretty mama
Oh-ho, ain't gonna marry
                 ain't gonna settle down
Cryin' I'm gonna stay right here till my
                      moustache dragged the ground

Cryin'
      where was you
                when the
                     'Frisco left the yard
    Now don't you
                 hear me talkin' to you, pretty mama
Where was you
              'Frisco left the yard
Cryin' I was standin' right there
                   po-lice had me barred

Ham Hound Crave

You can read my letter now
                              sure don't know my mind
You can read my letter now
                              sure don't know my mind
When you think I'm loving you
                              I'm leaving all the time

I ain't got nobody, now I'm
                              all here by myself
I ain't got nobody, I'm
                    all here by myself
I ain't got nobody, I'm
                    all here by myself

            (who you telling? tell it.)

Let me be your sometime now
                              until your always come
Let me be your sometime now
                              until your always come
And I do more for you now
                              always ever done

            I don't want no hogheads
            Don't eat no chittlins
            Don't want no spareribs
            Don't eat no backbone
            Mama, got a hambone
            I wonder can I get it boiled
'Cause these Chicago women are
                              about to let my hambone spoil

            Church's bells a-ringing
            The preacher preaching
            Secretary's writing
            The members shouting
            The dirty deacon has taken my gal and gone
And all these children are
                    prob'ly trying to sing my song

Let me be your rocker now
                              until your straight chair come
Let me be your rocker now
                              until your straight chair come
And I rock you easier
                    than your straight chair ever done

That Lonesome Train Took My Baby Away

Woke up this morning
Found something wrong
My loving baby had caught that
Train and gone
Now I want you
To starch my jumper
Iron my overhauls
I'm gonna ride that train
That they call the Cannon Ball

Mister Depot Agent, close your
Depot down
The woman I'm loving, she's fixing to
Blow this town
Now that
Mean old fireman
That cruel old engineer
Gonna take my baby
And leave me lonesome here

It ain't no telling what that
Train won't do
It'll take your baby and run right
Over you
Now that
Engineer man
Ought to be 'shamed of himself
Take women from their husbands
Babies from their mother's breast

I walked down the track when the stars re-
Fused to shine
Looked like every minute I was going to
Lose my mind
Now my
Knees was weak, my
Footsteps was all I heard
Looked like every minute
I was stepping in another world

Mister Depot Agent, close your
Depot down
The girl I'm loving, she's fixing to
Blow this town
Now that
Mean old fireman
Cruel old engineer
Gonna take my baby
And leave me lonesome here

CHARLIE McCOY

Evil Devil Woman

I'd rather be the devil
     oh rather be the devil
         be that old
            woman's man
            that woman's man

Oh she was evil
     oh she was evil
        wouldn't work
          hand in hand
          hand in hand

Oh she's all right now
     oh she's all right now
        she's all
         right with me
         all right with me

But the devil is evil
     oh the devil is evil
        evil as
         he can be
         as he can be

I tried to be
    oh tried to be
      tried to be
        nice and kind
        nice and kind

Oh she was evil
     oh she was evil
        would not
         change her mind
         change her mind

I'll cut your wood, baby
      oh I'll cut your wood, baby
         and I'll
           build your fire
           build your fire

I'll bring your water
      oh bring your water
        through that
         muddy bayou
         muddy bayou

                       (KANSAS) JOE McCOY

I'll give my money
        oh give my money
             to buy your
                shoes and clothes
                shoes and clothes

But you was evil
        oh you was evil
             throwed me
                out of doors
                out of doors

But that's all right, baby
        oh that's all right, baby
             it's coming home
                to you
                coming home to you

I tried to be
        oh tried to be
             tried to be
                a man to you
                a man to you

(KANSAS) JOE McCOY

All Around Man

Now I ain't no butcher
No butcher's son
I can do your cutting
Till the butcher man comes

       'Cause I'm a all 'round man
       Oh I'm a all 'round man
       I mean I'm a all 'round man
       And I can do most anything that come my hand

Now I ain't no plumber
No plumber's son
I can do your screwing
Till the plumber man comes

       'Cause I'm a all 'round man
       Oh I'm a all 'round man
       I mean I'm a all 'round man
       And I can do most anything that come my hand

Now I ain't no miller
No miller's son
I can do your grinding
Till the miller man comes

       'Cause I'm a all 'round man
       Oh I'm a all 'round man
       I mean I'm a all 'round man
       And I can do most anything that come my hand

(oh baby, YOU know I'm a all 'round man)

Now I ain't no milk man
No milk man's son
I can pull your titties
Till the milk man comes

       'Cause I'm a all 'round man
       Oh I'm a all 'round man
       I mean I'm a all 'round man
       And I can do most anything that come my hand

Now I ain't no spring man
No spring man's son
I can bounce your springs
Till the spring man comes

'Cause I'm a all 'round man
Oh I'm a all 'round man
I mean I'm a all 'round man
And I can do most anything that come my hand

Now I ain't no *auger* man
No *auger* man's son
I can bore your hole
Till the *auger* man comes

'Cause I'm a all 'round man
Oh I'm a all 'round man
I mean I'm a all 'round man
And I can do most anything that come my hand

BO CARTER

Old Devil

Go back, old Devil
              and look up on your shelf
Go back, old Devil
              and look up on your shelf
Go back, old Devil
                —it ain't no joke, no lie this time—
              look up on your shelf
                    and get you soap and water
                    and bathe your dirty self

I beat my baby
              man, with a rope and a line
I beat my baby oooo
                  man, with a rope and a line
I beat my baby
                —it ain't no joke, no lie this time—
              with a rope and a line
                    until she went stone blind

              (yeah)

Some low down scoundrel been
                          fishing all in my pond
Some low down scoundrel oooo
                          been fishing all in my pond
Some low down scoundrel
                —it ain't no joke, no lie this time—
              been fishing in my pond
                    catching all my game-fish
                    and grinding up the bones

What you want with a woman, man
                          and she can't rob and steal
What you want with a woman oooo
                          man, and she can't rob and steal
What you want with a woman
                —it ain't no joke, no lie this time—
              she can't rob and steal
                    you don't need no man, baby
                    don't know you in the dark when he feel

Old Timbrook Blues

Old Timbrook was a black horse
                              black as any crow
Old Timbrook was a black horse
                              black as any crow
Had a white ring 'round his fore-paw
                                   white as any snow

Yes old Timbrook he come darting
                              like a bullet from a gun
Old Timbrook he come darting
                              like a bullet from a gun
And old Molly she come creeping
                              like a *criminal to be hung*

Johnny Walker, Johnny Walker,
                              Johnny Walker my dear son
Johnny Walker, Johnny Walker,
                              Johnny Walker my dear son
Hold tight rein on Timbrook
                         so that horse could run

Oh the cuckoo was a flying bird
                              hollers when he fly
Oh the cuckoo was a flying bird
                              hollers when he fly
But he never hollers cuckoo
                         till the fourth a July

Oh the race track it was dusty
                              and the wind was high
Oh the race track it was dusty
                              and the wind was high
Well you couldn't see old Timbrook
                              as he come darting by

Oh the children they did holler
                              and the old folks squall
Oh the children they did holler
                              and the old folks squall
But old Timbrook he beat Molly
                              to the hole in the wall

I love my race horse
                    like to have my fun
Yes I love my race horse
                         like to have my fun
Old *Missus* went to the race track
                              and lost all-a her mon'

JOHN BYRD

Devil Got My Woman

I'd rather be the devil
                    to be that woman's ma-a-an
I'd rather be the devil
                    to be that woman's ma-a-an

Oh nothing but the devil
                    changed my baby's mi-i-ind
Oh nothing but the devil
                    changed my baby's mi-i-ind

I laid down last night
        laid down last night
            I laid down last night
                            tried to take my rest
My mind got to rambling
                    like the wild geese from the west
                            from the west

The woman I love
        woman that I love
            the woman I love
                            stoled her from my best friend
But he got lucky
            stoled her back again
And he got lucky
                stoled her back again

Hard Time Killin' Floor Blues

Hard times here every, where you go
Times is harder, than ever been before

Well the people are drifting, from door to door
Can't find no heaven, I don't care where they go

Oh, ho, uh, ah, ho
Oh, ho, uh, ah, ho

Let me tell you people, just before I go
These hard times will kill you, *this dry long so*

Oh, ho, uh, ah, ho
Oh, ho, uh, ah, ho

When you hear me singing, my true lonesome song
These hard times can last us so very long

Oh, ho, uh, ah, ho
Oh, ho, uh, ah, ho

If I ever get off, this killin' floor
I'll never get down, this low no more

Lord, lord, lord, lord
I'll never get down, this low no more

If you say you had money, you better be sure
'Cause these hard times will drive you, from door to door

Oh, ho, uh, ah, ho
Oh, ho, uh, ah, ho

Mm, ho, uh, ah, ho
Oh, ho, uh, ah, ho

Sing this song, and I ain't gonna sing no more
Sing this song, and I ain't gonna sing no more

Oh, ho, uh, ah, ho
Hard times will drive you, from door to door

Cypress Grove Blues

I would rather be buried
                    in some cypress grove
I would rather be buried
                    in some cypress grove
To have some woman
                    lord, that I can't control

And I'm going away now
                    I'm going away to stay
And I'm going away now
                    I'm going away to stay
That'll be all right, pretty mama
                    you gonna need my help some day

When the sun gone down
                    you know what you promised me
When the sun gone down
                    you know what you promised me
And what's the matter
                    baby, I can't see

I would rather be dead and
                    six feet in my grave
Now I would rather be dead and
                    six feet in my grave
To be *way up here, honey*
                    treated this-a-way

Well, the old people told me
                    baby, but I never did know
Now, the old people told me
                    baby, b-but I never did know
The Good Book declares you've got to
                    reap just what you sow

When your knee-bones aching
                    and your body cold
When your knee-bones aching
                    and your body cold
You just getting ready
                    honey, for the cypress grove

TOMMY McCLENNAN

Brown Skin Girl

      (yes yes
      yeah)

Mmmmmmmmmmmmmmmm
Mmmmmm mmmm mm
Now I got a brown skin girl
With her front tooth crowned with gold
      (take your time and make this one right
      'cause it's the best one you got)
I got a brown skin woman
With her front tooth crowned with gold
She got a lien on my body
And a mortgage on my soul

Now friend don't never let your good girl
Fix you like this woman got me
      (yes yes yes yes)
Friend don't never let your good girl
Fix you like this woman got me
      (how's she got you did)
Got me stone crazy 'bout her
As a doggone fool can be

Now I ain't gonna tell no body,
Baby, 'bout the way you do
      (take your time now and play it right)
Ain't gonna tell no body,
Baby, 'bout the way you do
      (how you got—to—how'd I do)
Say you always keep some
Some fat mouse following you
      (yeah: heh heh heh)

Now I done told you once now baby now
Ain't gonna tell you no more
Mmmm I told you once, baby,
Ain't gonna tell you no more
      (why?)
Next time I have to tell you
I'm sure gonna let you go

Now when you get you one of them funny women
      (take your time now)
She won't do to trust
Get you a two-by-four
And I swear you can scratch the stuff
Mmmmmmmmmmm
Baby, now that's all I want
Just a little bit of loving,
And then you can be gone

179   *TOMMY McCLENNAN*

Death Valley Blues

I went down in Death Valley
                              there's nothing but tombstones and dry bones
I went down in Death Valley
                              nothing but tombstones and dry bones
That's where poor me'll be
                              lord, when I'm dead and gone

Now if I should die,
                              I should die before my time
Baby, if I should die,
                              I should die before my time
I want you to bury my body
                              down by that 'Frisco Line

Now bury me, mama
                              low down in the sand
Oh bury me, mama
                              low down in the sand
Now bury me, mama
                              where I won't bother your next old man

Oh bye bye, baby
                              I said good bye
Oh bye bye, baby
                              I said good bye
Death Valley is my home
                              mama, when I die

Tell all the women
                              please come dressed in red
Tell all the women
                              please come dressed in red
They going down on 61 highway
                              that's where the poor boy he fell dead

Wear your patent leather slippers
                              mama, put on your mourning gown
Wear your patent leather slippers
                              put on your mourning gown
You gonna follow poor Crudup
                              down to his burying ground

                                        ARTHUR ("BIG BOY") CRUDUP

Mississippi: the Delta

Bullfrog Blues

Have you ever woke up with them
                              bullfrogs on your
                              bullfrogs on your
                                        I mean mind
Have you ever woke up, mama,
                    bullfrogs on your mind
Have you ever woke up with them
                    bullfrogs on your mind

Let it rain here, mama,
                    sun shining in your
                    sun shining in your
                              I mean door
It's gonna rain today, mama,
                    sun shine in your door
Gonna rain today
              the sun is shining in your back door

I'm gonna tell you this time, mama,
                         I ain't gonna tell you no
                         ain't gonna tell you no
                                   I mean more
I'm gonna tell you this time, mama,
                         ain't gonna tell you no more
I'm gonna tell you this time, mama,
                         ain't gonna tell you no more

I'm gonna leave you, partner,
                    and I won't be back here no more

I left you standing here, buddy,
                    in your back door
                    in your back door
                              bullfrog blues
I left you here standing, mama,
                    your back door
I left you standing here
                    in your back door crying

Got the bullfrog blues, mama,
                    can't be satis-
                    can't be satis-
                              mamlish-fied
Got the bullfrog blues, and I
                    can't be satisfied
Got the bullfrog blues, and I
                    can't be satisfied

Have you ever dreamed lucky and
                    woke up cold in

WILLIAM HARRIS

                              woke up cold in
                                        I mean hand
Have you ever dreamed lucky
                    woke up cold in hand
Have you ever dreamed lucky
                    woke up cold in hand

I'm gonna tell you, buddy, what a
                              Chinaman told a
                              Chinaman told a
                                        I mean a Jew
I'm gonna tell you what a
                    Chinaman told a Jew
You don't likee me
              well I sure god don't like you

Hey, lookee here, partner,
                        see what you done to
                        see what you done to
                                   I mean me
Lookee here, partner,
                  see what you done to me
Hey, lookee here, partner,
                    see what you done to me

Hey, the sun gonna shine in
                        my back door some
                        my back door some
                                 I say today
The sun gonna shine in
                  my back door some day
Hey, the sun gonna shine in
                    my back door some day

WILLIAM HARRIS

You Can't Keep No Brown

Now I woke up this morning, mama
                    blues all around my bed
Rose this morning, mama
              blues all around my bed
Thinking about the kind
               words that my mama had said

Now my mama's dead
            so is my daddy too
Now my mama's dead
            so is my daddy too
That's the reason I tried so hard
                 to get along with you

Now where there ain't no loving
                  ain't no getting along
Where there ain't no loving
               sure ain't no getting along
'Cause you'll have more trouble
               honey, than all the days is long

So many days
          I stoled away and cried
So many days
          I stoled away and cried
Poor boy has been mistreated
               now I can't be satisfied

Now I'm gonna write a letter
                 mail it in the air
I'm gonna write a letter
               gonna mail it in the air
Because the March wind blows
               it blows news every where

'Cause I'm going
Up the country
Won't be very long

Good gal
You can count the days I'm gone

       I oftentellmyhoney
       don'thavetofight
       thegalthatgetsyou'sgottotreatyouright
I'm crazy 'bout my Jane
               tell the world that I am
'Cause I'm going
          got to sing long distance blues

                                      BO WEAVIL JACKSON

Nowyougetwayback
youballthejack
wechangingpartnersgetyour
lovingback
I want to see my Jane
              tell the world that I do
'Cause I'm going in the world
                    to sing long distance blues

34 Blues

I ain't gonna tell no body
                        34 have done for me-e-e
I ain't gonna tell no body what
                           34 have done for me-e-e
Took my roll-a
                 I was broke as I could be

They run me from Will Dockery's
                       Willie Brown, how 'bout your jo-o-ob
They run me from Will Dockery's
                       Willie Brown, I want your jo-o-ob
           (I wonder what's the matter)
I went out and told Papa Charlie:
                  I don't want you hangin' round on my job no more

Well it's down in the country
                it almost make you cry-y-y
Well it's down in the country
                it almost make you cry-y-y
         (my God chillun)
Women and children
           flag that freight train and will ride

Come and got a little six Buick
               big six Chevrolet ca-a-ar
Come and got a little six Buick
               little six Chevrolet ca-a-ar
        (My God, what solid power)
And they don't do nothin'
            but follow behind *Holloway's farmer's plou-ou-ough*

Ah, it may bring sorrow
            Lord, and it may bring chee-e-eer
It may bring sorrow
            Lord, and it may bring chee-e-eer
Oh Lord, oh Lord
        let me see a brand new year

CHARLIE PATTON

Bird Nest Bound

Come on, mama
        Out to the edge of town
Come on, mama
        Go to the edge of town
I know where there's a bird nest
        Builded on the ground

If I was a bird, mama

If I was a bird, mama, I would
        Build my nest in the heart of town
           (Lord you gonna build it in the heart of town)
So when the times get lonesome
        I'd be bird nest bound

Ah love is at your front door
        Blues are in your room
Ah love is at your front door
        Blues are in your room
Parted at your back door, what is
        Gonna become of you

Sometime I say I need you
        Then again I don't
Sometime I say I need you
        Then again I don't
           (You know it's the truth, baby)
Sometime I think I'll quit you
        Then again I won't

Oh, I remember one morning
        Standing in my baby's door
           (Sure, boy, I was standing there)
Oh, I remember one morning
        Standing in my baby's door
           (Boy, you know what she told me)
Look-a-here papa Charlie, I
        Don't want you no more

Take me home sweet home baby
        To that Shining Star
Take me home now to
        That Shining Star
           (Lord, you know I'm just staying there)
You don't need no telling, mama
        Take you in my car

189   *CHARLIE PATTON*

High Sheriff Blues

When the trial's in Belzoni
Ain't no use in screaming and crying
Mmmmmm mmmm
When the trial's in Belzoni
Ain't no use a-screaming and crying
Mmmmmm mmmm
Mister Webb will take you
Back to Belzoni jailhouse *flying*

Let me tell you folkses
Ho-o-ow he treated me
Eeeeee eeee
Let me tell you folkses
Ho-ow he treated me
Eeeeee eeee
And he put me in a cell there
It was dark as it could be

It was late one evening
Mr. Purvis was standing 'round
Mmmmmm mmmm
It was late one evening
Mr. Purvis was standing 'round
Mmmmmm mmmm
Mr. Purvis told Mr. Webb to
Let poor Charlie down

It takes boozey booze,
Lord, to carry me through
Mmmmmm mmmm
Takes boozey booze,
Lord, to carry me through
Thirty days seem like years in a
Jailhouse where there is no booze

I got up one morning
Feeling awful—
Mmmmmm mmmm
I got up one morning
Feeling mighty bad
Mmmmmm mmmm
And it must not of been them
Belzoni jail I had
                (Blues I had, boy)

While I was in trouble
Ain't no use a-screaming
Mmmmmm mmmm
While I was in prison
Ain't no use a-screaming and crying
Mr. Purvis on his mansion
He doesn't pay no mind

Moon Going Down

Oh that moon is going down, baby,
                    Sun's about to shine
Oh that moon's going down, baby,
                    Sun's about to shine
Rosetta, Henretta told me, lord I
                    Don't want you hanging round

Oh well, where were you now, baby,
                    Clarksdale Mill burned down
Oh well, where were you now, baby,
                    Clarksdale Mill burned down
                      (Boy, you know where I was)
I was way down Sunflower, with my
                    Face all full of frown

They's a house over yonder
                    Painted all over green
They's a house over yonder
                    Painted all over green
                      (Boy, you know I know it's over there)
Some of the finest young women, lord,
                    Than, 'most ever I seen

Lord I think I heard that
                Helena whistle
                Helena whistle
                Helena whistle blow
Lord I think I heard that
                Helena whistle blow
                    (Well I hear it blowing now)
Lord I ain't gonna stop walking till I
                    Get in my rider's door

Lord the smoke stack is black and the
                    Bell it shine like
                    Bell it shine like
                    Bell it shine like gold
Oh the smoke stack is black and the
                    Bell it shine like gold
                      (Talk to me, boy: you know it looks good to me)
Lord I ain't gonna walk there or
                    Tarry round no more

Oh yeah, evil walkin' at midnight
                    When I heard the local blow
I will leave out at night when I
                    Heard the local blow
                      (Boy, I was getting lonesome—stay in there now)
I got to see my rider:
                    When she's getting on board

                      CHARLIE PATTON

High Water Everywhere: I

The back water done rose around Sumner, now,
                Drove me down the line
Back water done rose at Sumner, drove
             Poor Charlie down the line
And I tell the world the water
        Done struck through this town

Lord, the whole round country, lord
          River is overflowed
Lord, the whole round country
       Man it's overflowed
           (You know I can't stay here: I'm bound
               to go where it's high, boy)
I would go to the hilly country
       But they got me barred

Now look-a-here now, Leland
        River's rising high
Look-a-here now boys, around Leland, tell me
          River's raging high
            (Boy it's rising over there; yeah)
I'm gonna move over to Greenville
      'Fore I bid good-bye

Look-a-here, water done, now lordy, done broke
          Rose most every where
The water at Greenville and Leland
       Lord it done rose everywhere
          (Boy you can't never stay here)
I would go down to Rosedale, but they
       Tell me there's water there

Now the water, now mama
      Done struck *Charlie's* town
Well they tell me the water
      Done struck *Charlie's* town
        (Boy I'm going to Vicksburg)
Well I'm going to Vicksburg
      On the high of mine

I am going on dry water
       Where land don't never flow
Well I'm going over the hill where water
        Oh, don't never flow
          (Boy, *hit Sharkey County and everything*
              was down in Stover)
But *the whole county were leaving*
      Over in Tallahatchie sure
        (Boy I went to Tallahatchie: they got
          it over there)

                                CHARLIE PATTON

Lord the water done wrecked all of
                    That old Jackson road
Lord the water done ragëd
                Over the Jackson road
                    (Boy it got my car)
I'm going back to the hilly country
                Won't be worried no more

High Water Everywhere: 2

Back water at Blytheville
Backed up all around
Back water at Blytheville
Done took Joiner town
It was fifty families and children
Come to sink and drown

The water was rising
Up in my friend's door
The water was rising
Up in my friend's door
The man said to his women folk
Lord, we'd better go

The water was rising
Got up in my bed
Lord, the water's rolling
Got up to my bed
I thought I would take a trip, lord
Out on the big *ice sled*

Awwwwww I hear, lord lord,
Water upon my door
        (You know what I mean)
        (Look-a-here)
I hear the ice lord
Lord, we're sinking down
I couldn't get no boat there
Marion City gone down

Ohhhhhh-ah the water rising
Families sinking down
Say now, the water was rising
At places all around
        (Boy, they's all around)
It was fifty men and children
Come to sink and drown

Ohhhhhh-oh lordy
Women and grown men down
Ohhhhhh-oh
Women and children sinking down
        (Lord have mercy)
I couldn't see no body home and
Wasn't no one to be found

Revenue Man Blues

Oh, the revenue men is rising
                Boy you'd better look out
                      (Oh pshaw, that man's coming again)
Oh, the revenue men is rising
                Boy you'd better look out
                (Boy if he
                calls you
                you don't stop
                boy I'll)
If he hollers, you don't stop, you will
                Likely be knocked out

Well I don't love salt water well she
                Always wants a drink
                  (Got to have a drink)
I don't love salt water
            She always wants a drink
              (Boy if they
              see you with a bottle though)
If they see you with a bottle, they will
                Almost break your neck

Well, safe sweet home to
            Lord, that Shining Star
              (Oh pshaw)
I say safe sweet home
           To that Shining Star
             (She don't
             need no telling, daddy
             oh, pshaw)
She don't need no telling, dad will
                Take you in his car

Oh, come on mama, let us
     Go to that edge of town
       (Oh pshaw)
Come on mama, let us
     Go to that edge of town
      (Baby I know where there's a
      bird nest builded)
I know where there's a bird nest
     Builded all over the ground

Oh, I wakes up every morning now with a
       Jinx all around my bed
        (Oh pshaw)
I wakes every morning with a
     Jinx all around my bed
       (You know I
       have 'em
       jinx forever)
I have been a good provider, but I
      B'lieve I been misled

Hang It on the Wall

Justshakeityoucanbreakityoucanhangitonthewall
HollerwhenIcatchit'foreitfall
        youcanbreakityoucanhangitonthewall
HollerwhenIcatchit'foreitfall

        Sweet jelly

            MY ROLL

        Sweet mama, won't you let it fall

    I AIN'T GOT NO BODY NOW
                    Ah
                    I fooled around
                    I mean
                    When the sun go down
                    Ah
                    I had my brown

        'Bout the jelly

            MY ROLL

        Sweet mama, won't you let it fall

Justpatityoucangrabityoucanwhipityoucanpitchit
Andaway*tillI*
        flipitandgetit
                    Till I
                    Ain't had my right mind
                    I
                    Stayed *in a little old town*

        'Bout the jelly

            MY ROLL

        Sweet mama, won't you let it fall

Justshakeityoucanbreakityoucanhangitonthewall
HollerwhenIcatchit'foreitfall
    shakeit,breakit,hangitonthewa-all
HollerwhenIcatchit'foreitfall

        Sweet jelly

            MY ROLL

        Sweet mama, won't you let it fall

(Lookit here, baby, it's gettin' good to me now
and I'll help you shake it)
           Ahh
           Ahh
           I mean my brown
           Ahh
           When the sun go down

    'Bout the jelly

    MY ROLL

    Sweet mama, won't you let it fall

Justpatityoucangrabityoucanwhipityoucanpitchit
Andaway*tillI*
    flipitandgetit
        Till I
        Ain't had my right mind
        I
        Stayed *in a little old town*

    'Bout the jelly

    MY ROLL

    Sweet mama, won't you let it fall

Justshakeityoucanbreakityoucanhangitonthewall
HollerwhenIcatchit'foreitfall
    shakeityoucanbreakityoucanhangitonthewall
HollerwhenIcatchit'foreitfall

    Sweet jelly

    MY ROLL

    Sweet mama, won't you let it fall

EVERY BODY GOT A JELLY ROLL
                Like mine
                It fooled around
                I mean
                When the sun go down
                Ahh
                I had my brown

    'Bout the jelly

    MY ROLL

    Sweet mama, won't you let it fall

Justshakeityoucanbreakityoucanhangitonthewall
HollerwhenIcatchit'foreitfall
        youcanbreakityoucanhangitonthewall
HollerwhenIcatchit'foreitfall

      Sweet jelly

        MY ROLL

    Sweet mama, won't you let it fall

  EVERYBODY HAVE A JELLY ROLL
                              Like mine
                              I left the town
                              I mean
                              If the sun went down
                              Ahh
                              I had my brown

    'Bout the jelly

        MY ROLL

    Sweet mama, won't you let it fall

Justshakeityoucanbreakityoucanhangitonthewall
HollerwhenIcatchit'foreitfall
        youcanbreakityoucanhangitonthewall
HollerwhenIcatchit'foreitfall

      Sweet jelly

        MY ROLL

    Sweet mama, won't you let it fall

  EVERYBODY
      (oh pshaw, baby, you can whip it again)
                              Ahh
                              I catch it when
                              Ahh
                              Back to town again

    'Bout the jelly

        MY ROLL

    Sweet mama, won't you let it fall

Future Blues

Can't tell my future
                    I can't tell my past
Lord it seems like every minute
                              sure gon' be my last

Oh minutes seems like hours and
                              hours seems like days
Yes, it's minutes seems like hours
                              hours seems like days
And it seems like my woman oughta
                              stop her low down ways

Oh the woman I love now, she's
                              five feet from the ground
I said the woman I love, now lord, is
                              five feet from the ground
And she's tailor-made
                    and: ain't no hand-me-down

Lord, and I got a woman now, lord, and she's
                              lightning when she
                         she's lightning when she
                                        now, that's why I love the girl
I've got a woman now, and she's
                              lightning when she smiles
Five feet and four inches and she's
                              just good hugging size

Oh, I know you see that picture, now lord
                              still up on your mother's
                              up on your mother's
                                        mama's shelf
I know you see that picture now
                              up on your mother's shelf
Well you know by that I'm getting tired of
                              sleeping by myself

And it's T for Texas now, and it's
                              T for Tennessee
And it's T for Texas now, and it's
                              T for Tennessee
Lord bless that woman
                    that: put that thing on me

WILLIE BROWN

M & O Blues

I leave here I'm gonna
              catch that M and O
Now when
        I leave here I'm gonna
              catch that M and O
I'm going
      way down south where I ain't
              never been before

Once
    I had a notion
          lord and I believe I will
Once
    I had a notion
          lord and I believe I will
I'm gonna
      build me a mansion
           out on Decatur Hill

Now here's
      all of you men
           ought to be 'shamed of yourself
Hey there
      all of you men
           ought to be 'shamed of yourself
Going 'round here swearing 'fore God, you got a
              whole woman by yourself

I started to
      kill my woman till she
            lay down 'cross the bed
I started to
      kill my woman till
           lay down 'cross the bed
And she
      looked so ambitious till I
           took back everything I said

And I
      asked her how 'bout it
          lord, and she said all right
And I
      asked her how 'bout it
          lord, and she said all right
But she
      never showed up
         at the shack last night

And—

WILLIE BROWN

Tell Me Man Blues

Tell me man
             Which way to the rising sun
Tell me man
             Which way to the rising sun
It rise in the east and
             Go down in the west

I want to see you
             Go with the rising sun
I want to see you
             Go with the rising sun
So I can always tell when
             The sun is going down

When I go
             Please don't talk after me
Oh when I go
             Please don't talk after me
'Cause I'm going away where
             To my 'posed to be

Tell me man
             What you got on your mind
Tell me man
             What you got on your mind
To keep me worried
             And bothered all the time

You may want to
             See me look little and cute
You may want me
             To look little and cute
I'm going to get me
             A khaki suit

HENRY SIMS

My Black Mama

Well
black mama, what's the
matter with you today
Ain't satisfactory, don't care
what I do
Heh-eh, mama,
what's the
matter with you
Baby, it *ain't satisfactory,* baby
and I don't care
what I do

You say a brown skin woman will make a rabbit
move to town
Say a
jet black woman will make a mule kick his
stable down
Oh a brown skin woman will make a
rabbit
move to town
Well, and a real black woman
will make a
mule kick his
stable down

Yeah
it ain't no heaven now and it ain't no
burning hell
Said I
where I'm going when I die can't no
body tell
Oh it ain't no heaven no
ain't no
burning hell
Oh, where I'm going when I die
can't no
body tell

Well
my black mama's face shine
like the sun
Oh lipstick and powder sure won't
help her none
My black mama's face
shine
like the sun
Oh, lipstick and powder
well they sure won't
help her none

Well
if you see my milk cow tell her
hurry home
I ain't had no milk since that
cow been gone
If you see my milk cow
tell her
to hurry home
Yeah, I ain't had no milk
since that
cow been gone

Well, I'm
going to the race track to see my
pony run
He ain't the best in the world, but he's a running
son of a gun
I'm going to the race track
to see my
pony run
He ain't the best in the world
but he's a running
son of a gun

Oh
Lord have mercy on my
wicked soul
I wouldn't mistreat you baby, for my
weight in gold
Oh Lord have mercy
on my
wicked soul
Mmmm mmmm mmmm mmmm

Well
I solemnly swear, Lord, I raise
my right hand
That I'm gonna
        get me a woman
             you get you
another man
I solemnly swear
Lord, I raise my right hand
That I'm gonna get me a woman, baby,
you get you
another man

I got a letter this morning, how do you
reckon it read
Oh hurry hurry, gal you
love is dead

I got a letter this morning
how do you
reckon it read
Oh, hurry hurry
the gal you
love is dead

I grabbed my suitcase, I took on
up the road
I got there, she was laying on the
cooling board
I grabbed my suitcase
I took on
up the road
Oh, when I got there
she was laying on the
cooling board

Well, I
walked up close, I looked down
in her face
Good old gal, got to lay there
till judgement day
I walked up close and I
looked down
in her face
Yes, you're a good old gal
got to lay there
till judgement day

        (Ah, tell 'em now
        I feel low down this evening)

Oh
my woman's so black, she stays
apart of this town
Can't nothin' go when the poor gal
is around
My black mama
stays apart of
this town
Oh, can't nothin' go
when the poor girl
is around

Oh
some people tell me the worried
blues ain't bad
It's the worst old feeling that I
ever had
Some people tell me
the worried
blues ain't bad
But it's the worst old feeling
Lord
      I ever had

Mmmm
I fold my arms and I
walked away
That's all right, mama, your troubles will
come some day
I fold my arms
Oh, and I
walked away
Yeah
      that's all right, mama
your troubles will
come some day

The Jinx Blues

Mmmmmm hmmmmm mmmmmm
Mmmm hmmm mmmm hmmm
Mmmmmm mmmmmm mmmmmm
Mmmm hmmm hmmm mmmm

Well I got up this morning
  Jinx all around
  Jinx all around
  'Round my bed
I say I got up this morning
  With the jinx
  All 'round my bed
Know I thought about you and
  It like to kill
  Me dead

Mmmm lookee here now baby
  What you want me
  What you want me
  Me to do-ooo
Lookee here honey
  I say what do you want poor me to do
You know I done all I could
  Just trying to get along
  With you

You know the blues ain't nothing but a
  Low down shaking
  Low down shaking
  Aching chill
I say the blue-ues
  Is a low down
  Old aching chill
Well if you ain't had 'em, honey,
  I hope you ne-
  Ver will

Well the blues the blues
  Is a worried heart
  Is a worried heart
  Heart disease
Oh the blues
  Is a worried
  Old heart disease
Look like the woman you be loving, man,
  Is so doggone hard
  To please

Mmmm I rather be outdoors
        Walking up
        Walking up
        And down the road
I say I rather be outdoors
        I said, and walking
        Up and down the road
Than to be laying around here working
        Just for my board
        And clothes

Mmmm lookit here little girl
        Don't you cry
        Don't you cry
        Cry no more
I say lookit here darling honey
        Don't you cry cry no more
Well when I leave this time
        I'm gonna hang crepe on
        Your door

SON HOUSE

The Pony Blues

Mmmmmm mmmmmm mmmm mmmm
Mmmmmm mmmmmm mmmm mmmm

Why don't you
catch me a pony
and saddle
up my black mare
Oh, my pony—
saddle up
my my black mare
You know I
I'm gonna follow my baby
way out in
the world, somewhere

You know
he's a traveling horse
and he's
too black bad
He's a tra-
veling pony
and, I declare,
he's too black bad
You know
he's got a gait, now, no
traveling mare
ain't never had

You know
I take him by the reins
and I led
him around and 'round
I say I take him
by the reins and I
I led him
around and 'round
You know
he's the best in the world but
he's the best
ever
been in this time

You know
he's a traveling horse
and he don't
even know his name
He's a tra-
veling pony
and he don't
even know his name

You know
the way he can travel
is a low down
old dirty shame

Why don't you
come up here pony
now come on
please let's us go
I say
come up
get up there
please pony
now let's us go
Let's we
saddle on down on
the Gulf of
of Mexico

You know the
horse that I'm riding
he can foxtrot
he can lope and pace
I say
the pony
I'm riding
he can foxtrot and
he can lope and pace
You know
a horse: *with him in the gate*
you know
I'm bound to
win that race

Mmmmmm
he's a traveling horse
and he don't
even know his name
He's a tra-
veling pony
and he don't
even know his name
You know
the way he can travel
is a low down
old dirty shame

SON HOUSE

Preachin' the Blues

Oh, I'm gonna get me a religion
I'm gonna join the Baptist Church,

Oh, I'm gonna get me a religion
I'm gonna join the Baptist Church:

I'm gonna be a Baptist Preacher
And I sure won't have to work.

Oh, I'm gonna preach these blues and
And I want everybody to shout,

Mmmmmmmm
And I want everybody to shout:

I'm gonna do like a prisoner—
I'm gonna roll my time on out.

Oh, in my room
I bowed down to pray,

Oh—I was in my room
I bowed down to pray:

Then the blues came 'long and they
Blowed my spirit away.

Oh, I have religion
On this very day,

Oh, I have religion
On this very day:

But the womens and whiskey, well they
Would not let me pray.

Oh—I wish I had me
A heaven of my own,
                              (Great God amighty)
Yeahh
A heaven of my own:

Well, I'd give all my women
A long long happy home.

Well, I love my baby
Just like I love myself,

Well, I love my baby
Just like I love myself:

Ohhhhhh
Just like I love myself:

Well, if she don't have me
She won't have nobody else.

Well, I'm gonna fold my arms
I'm gonna kneel down in prayer,

Oh, I'm gonna fold my arms
Gonna kneel down in prayer:

When I get up I'm gonna
See if my preaching suit a man's ear

Well, I met the blues this morning
Walking just like a man,

Ohhh-oh-ohhhh
Walking just like a man:

I said, Good morning blues
Now give me your right hand.

Now there's nothing now baby
Lord, that's gonna worry my mind,

Ohhhhh
Nothing that's gonna worry my mind:

Oh, to satisfy
I got the longest *line*.

Oh, I got to stay on the job
I ain't got no time to lose,

Yeahh
I ain't got no time to lose:

I swear to God
I've got to preach these gospel blues.
                    (Great God amighty)
Oh—I'm gonna preach these blues
And choose my seat and set down,

Oh, I'm gonna preach these blues now
And choose my seat and set down:

When the spirit comes, sisters,
I want you to jump straight up and down.

Nappy Head Blues

When you hear me walking
        turn your lamp down
        turn your lamp down
           lamp down low
When you hear me walking
        turn your lamp down low
When you hear me walking
        turn your lamp down low
And turn it so your
        man'll never know

Gonna buy me a bed, it
        shine like a morning
        shine like a morning
           a morning star
I'm gonna buy me a bed, it
        shine like a morning star
Gonna buy me a bed, it
        shine like a morning star
When I get to bed, it
        rock like a Cadillac car

My head is nappy
        it's so mamlish
        it's so mamlish
           mamlish long
Your head is nappy
        your feet so mamlish long
Your head is nappy
        your feet so mamlish long
It look like a turkey
        coming through the mamlish corn

I done told you I love you
        what more can I
        what more can I
           can I do
I done told you I love you
        what more can I do
I done told you I love you
        what more can I do
And you must want me to lay
        down and die for you

Come On in My Kitchen

Hmmmmmmmmmmmmmmmmmmm
                            hmmmmmmmmmmmmmmm
Hmmmmmmmmmmmmmmmmmmmm
                            hmmmmmmmmmm
You better come on
                in my kitchen
                            well it's going to be raining outdoors

The woman I love
                    took from my best friend
Some joker got lucky
                    stoled her back again
You better come on
                in my kitchen
                            it's going to be raining outdoors

Oh oh she's gone
                    I know she won't come back
I taken her last nickel
                    out of her nation sack
You better come on
                in my kitchen
                            it's going to be raining outdoors

        (Baby can't you hear that wind howl)

        (Aww can't you hear that wind howl)

You better come on
                in my kitchen
                                it's going to be raining outdoors

When a woman gets in trouble
                            everybody throws her down
Looking for her good friends
                        none can be found
You better come on
                in my kitchen
                            baby it's going to be raining outdoors

And the time coming
                    it's going to be so
You can't make the winter babe
                        just dry long so
You better come on
                in my kitchen
                            'cause it's going to be raining outdoors

ROBERT JOHNSON

Walking Blues

I woke up this morning
                        feeling around for my shoes
Know by that I got these
                        old walking blues
Woke
        up this morning
                        feeling around
                                        oh for my shoes
But you
        know by that I
                        got these old walking blues

Lord I
        feel like blowing my
                        poor lonesome horn
Got up this morning my little Bern-
                        iece was gone
Lord
        I feel like
                blo-ow
                        my lonesome horn
Well I got up this morning
                        all I had was gone

Well
        leaving this morning if I have to
                        oh ride the blinds
I feel mistreated and I
                        don't mind dying
Leaving this morning
                        I have to ride the blinds
Babe
        I been mistreated
                        baby and I don't mind dying

ROBERT JOHNSON

Well
      some people tell me that the worried
                        blues ain't bad
Worst old feeling I most
               ever had
Some
      people tell me that these
                 oh worried
                      oh blues ain't bad
It's the worst old feeling
              I most ever had

She's got
      Elgin movements from her head down
                    to her toes
Break in on a
        dollar most any
              where she goes
Oooooooo
        from her head
            down to her toes
Lord she break in on a dollar
             oh most anywhere she goes

Terraplane Blues

I feel so lonesome,
                        you can hear me when I moan
And I feel so lonesome,
                        you can hear me when I moan
Who's been driving my Terraplane
                                for you since I've been gone

I said I flashed your lights, mama,
                                    your horn won't even blow
            (somebody's been running my battery down on this machine)
I even flashed my lights, mama,
                            this horn won't even blow
Got a short in this connection,
                        hoo-well, babe, and it's way down below

I'm going h'ist your hood, mama,
                                I'm bound to check your oil
I'm going h'ist your hood, mama,
                                I'm bound to check your oil
I got a woman that I'm loving,
                        way down in Arkansas

        Now you know the coils ain't even buzzing
        Little generator won't get the spark
        Motor's in a bad condition, you gotta have
        These batteries charged
I'm crying, Please,
                ple-hease don't do me wrong
Who's been driving my Terraplane now for
                                you-hoo since I've been gone

Mr. Highwayman,
                ple-hease don't block the road
Eeeeee heeeee
                eee-hease don't block the road
'Cause she's regist'ring a cold one hundred,
                                and I'm booked till I got to go

Hmmmmmmmmmmm hmmmmmmmmmmm
                                hmmmmm hmmm hmmm
Eeeeeeeeeeee
            you can hear me weep and moan
Who's been driving my Terraplane now for
                                you-hoo since I've been gone

I'm gonna get deep down in this connection,
                                keep on tangling with your wires
I'm gonna get deep down in this connection,
                                whoo-well keep on tangling with the wires
And when I mash down on your little starter,
                                then your spark plug would give me fire

218   ROBERT JOHNSON

Stones in My Passway

I got stones in my passway
                and my road seem dark as night
I got stones in my passway
                and my road seem dark as night
I have pains in my heart
              they have taken my appetite

I have a bird to whistle
            and I have a bird to sing
Have a bird to whistle
            and I have a bird to sing
I got a woman that I'm loving
               boy but she don't mean a thing

My innocence betrayed me
              have overtaken poor Bob at last
My innocence betrayed me
              have overtaken poor Bob at last
And that's one thing certain
              they have stones all in my pass

    Now you trying to take my life
    And all my loving too
    You laid a passway for me
    Now what are you trying to do
I'm crying please
          please let us be friends
And when you hear me howling in my passway, rider
                    please open your door and let me in

I got three legs to truck on
             boys please don't block my road
I got three legs to truck on
             boys please don't block my road
I been feeling ashame' 'bout my rider
               babe I'm booked and I got to go

Traveling Riverside Blues

If your man gets personal
                once you have your fun
If your man gets personal
                once you've had your fun
Just come on back to Friar's Point mama and
                      barrelhouse all night long

I've got womens in Vicksburg
                clean on in to Tennessee
I've got womens in Vicksburg
                clean on in to Tennessee
But my Friar's Point rider now
                hops all over me

I ain't going to state no color but her
                front teeth crowned with gold
I ain't going to state no color but her
                front teeth is crowned with gold
She got a mortgage on my body and a
                lien on my soul

Lord I'm going to *Rosedale,* gonna take my
                rider by my side
Lord I'm going to *Rosedale,* gonna take my
                rider by my side
We can still barrelhouse baby 'cause it's
                on the river side

Now you can squeeze my lemon till the
                juice run down my
      (till the juice run down my leg baby
      you know what I'm talking about)
You can squeeze my lemon till the
                juice run down my *bed*
      (that's what I'm talking about now)
But I'm going back to Friar's Point *if I be* rocking
                to my head

I Believe I'll Dust My Broom

I'm goin' get up in the morning
                          I believe I'll dust my broom
I'm goin' get up in the morning
                          I believe I'll dust my broom
'Cause then the black man you been loving,
                             girl friend, can get my room

I'm goin' to write a letter
                    telephone every town I know
I'm goin' to write a letter
                    telephone every town I know
If I can't find her in West Helena
                      she must be in East Monroe I know

I don't want no woman
                 wants every downtown man she meet
I don't want no woman
                 wants every downtown man she meet
She's a no good pony
               they shouldn't allow her on the street

I believe
       I believe I'll go back home
I believe
       I believe I'll go back home
If you mistreat me here, baby,
                 but you can't when I go home

And I'm getting up in the morning
                    I believe I'll dust my broom
I'm getting up in the morning
                  I believe I'll dust my broom
'Cause then the black man you been loving,
                   girl friend, can get my room

I'm goin' call up China
              see is my good girl over there
I'm goin' call up China
              see is my good girl over there
If I can't find her on Philippine's Island
                  she must be in Ethiopia some where

ROBERT JOHNSON

Milkcow's Calf Blues

Te-ell me milkcow
            what on earth is wrong with you
Ooooooeeee milkcow
            what on earth is wrong with you
Now you have a little new calf
            oooo-oo and your milk is turning blue

Now your calf is hungry
            I believe he needs a suck
Now your calf is hungry
            cooo-oo I believe he needs a suck
But your milk is turning blue, oooo
            I believe he's outa luck

Now I feel like milking and my
Cow won't come
I feel like churning and my
Milk won't turn
I'm crying, Please
            plea-ease don't do me wrong
If you see my milkcow baby now-ow
            plea-ease drive her home

My milkcow been rambling
            ooooee for miles around
My milkcow been rambling
            oooo for miles around
Well I better settle for some other man's milkcow
            oooo in this same man's town

ROBERT JOHNSON

Hellhound on My Trail

I've got to keep moving
        I've got to keep moving
                blues falling down like hail
                    blues falling down like hail
Ummmmmmmmmmmmmmmmmmmmmmm
                  blues falling down like hail
                    blues falling down like hail
And the days keeps on 'minding me
           there's a hellhound on my trail
                hellhound on my trail
                    hellhound on my trail

If today was Christmas Eve
        If today was Christmas Eve
                and tomorrow was Christmas Day
If today was Christmas Eve
           and tomorrow was Christmas Day
                (aw wouldn't we have a time baby)
All I would need my little sweet rider just
              to pass the time away
              uh huh
                to pass the time away

You sprinkled hot foot powder
          umm around my door
          all around my door
You sprinkled hot foot powder
          all around your daddy's door
            hmmm hmmm hmmm
It keeps me with a rambling mind, rider,
           every old place I go
             every old place I go

I can tell the wind is rising
          the leaves trembling on the trees
             trembling on the trees
I can tell the wind is rising
          leaves trembling on the trees
          umm hmm hmm hmm
All I need my little sweet woman
          and to keep my company
            hmmm hmmm hmmm hmmm
                  my company

ROBERT JOHNSON

Me and the Devil Blues

Early this morning
                    when you knocked upon my door
Early this morning oooooo
                         when you knocked upon my door
And I said, Hello Satan
                    I believe it's time to go

Me and the Devil
                    was walking side by side
Me and the Devil oooooo
                         was walking side by side
I'm going to beat my woman
                         until I get satisfied

She said you knows the way
                         that I always dog her 'round
                              (now baby you know
                              you ain't doing me right now)
She said you knows the way oooooo
                              that I be dog her 'round
It must be that old evil spirit
                    so deep down in the ground

You may bury my body
                    down by the highway side
                              (now baby I don't care where
                              you bury my body
                              when I'm dead and gone)
You may bury my body oooooo
                              down by the highway side
So my old evil spirit
                    can get a Greyhound Bus and ride

Preaching Blues

Mmmmmm mmmm
Got up this morning
The blues, walking like a man
Got up this morning
The blues walking like a man
Well the blues:
Give me your right hand

      And the blues grabbed mama's child
           And tore it all upside down
      Blues grabbed mama's child
           And tore me all upside down
      Travel on, poor Bob,
           Just can't turn you 'round

The blu-u-ues
Is a low down shaking chill
                 (yes) (I'm preaching 'em now)
Mmmm-mmmm
Is a low down shaking chill
You ain't never had 'em, I
Hope you never will

Well the blues
Is a aching old heart disease
               (Do it now.
               You gonna do it?
               Tell me all about it.)
The blues
Is a low down aching heart disease
And like consumption
Killing me by degrees

Now if it starts to raining
Gonna drive,
          gonna drive my blues
Now if it's startin' a-raining
I'm gonna drive my blues away
Going to steer it
Stay
    out
       there
          all
            day

ROBERT JOHNSON

Spike Driver Blues

Take this hammer
           and carry it
                      to my captain:
                      Tell him I'm gone;
           Tell him I'm gone;
Tell him I'm gone;
Take this hammer
           and carry it
                      to my captain:
                      Tell him I'm gone;
           Tell him I'm gone;
I'm sure he's gone.

This is the hammer
           that killed
                      John Henry:
                      But it won't kill me;
           But it won't kill me;
Well it won't kill me;
This is the hammer
           that killed
                      John Henry:
                      But it won't kill me;
           But it won't kill me;
Ain't gonna kill me.

It's a long ways
           from east
                      Colorādo:
                      And unto my home;
           And unto my home;
And unto my home;
It's a long ways
           to east
                      Colorādo:
                      And unto my home;
           And unto my home;
That's where I'm going.

John Henry
           he left
                      his hammer:
                      Laying side the road;
           Laying side the road;
Laying side the road.

MISSISSIPPI JOHN HURT

John Henry
        he left
                his hammer:
                All over in the rain;
        All over in the rain;
That's where I'm going.

John Henry's
        a steel
                driving boy:
                But he went down:
        But he went down;
But he went down;
John Henry's
        a steel
                driving boy:
                But he went down;
        But he went down;
That's where I'm going.

Candy Man Blues

Well all you ladies gather 'round
That good sweet candy man's in town
    It's the candy man
    It's the candy man

He likes a stick of candy just nine inch long
He sells as fast a hog can chew his corn
    It's the candy man
    It's the candy man

All heard what sister Johnson said
She always takes a candy stick to bed
    It's the candy man
    It's the candy man

Don't stand close to the candy man
He'll leave a big candy stick in your hand
    It's the candy man
    It's the candy man

He sold some candy to sister Bad
The very next day she took all he had
    It's the candy man
    It's the candy man

If you try his candy, good friend of mine,
You sure will want it for a long long time
    It's the candy man
    It's the candy man

His stick candy don't melt away
It just gets better, so the ladies say
    It's the candy man
    It's the candy man

MISSISSIPPI JOHN HURT

Got the Blues, Can't Be Satisfied

Got the blues, can't be satisfied
Got the blues, can't be satisfied
Keep the blues, I'll catch that train and ride

Whiskey straight will drive the blues away
Whiskey straight will drive the blues away
That be the case, I want a quart today

Bought my gal a great big diamond ring
Bought my gal a great big diamond ring
Come right back home and caught her shaking that thing

I said, Baby, what makes you act this-a-way
I said, Baby, why do you act this-a-way
Said I won't miss a thing she gives away

Took my gun and I broke the barrel down
Took my gun, broke the barrel down
Put my baby six feet under the ground

I cut that joker so long deep and wide
Cut that joker so long deep and wide
You got the blues and still ain't satisfied

Frankie

Frankie was a good girl
Everybody knows
She paid a hundred dollars
For Albert's one suit of clothes
        He's her man
         And he done her wrong

Frankie went down to the corner saloon
Didn't go to be gone long
She peeped through the keyhole of the door
And spied Albert in Alice's arms
        He's my man
         And he done me wrong

Frankie called Albert
Albert says, I don't hear
If you don't come to the woman you love
Gonna haul you outa here
         You's my man
         And you done me wrong

Frankie shot old Albert
And she shot him three or four times
Said, Stroll back out the smoke of my gun
Let me see is Albert dying
        He's my man
         And he done me wrong

Frankie and the judge walked down the stand
Walked out side by side
The judge said to Frankie,
You gonna be justified
         For killing a man
         And he done you wrong

Dark was the night
Cold was on the ground
The last word I heard Frankie say,
I done laid old Albert down
        He's my man
         And he done me wrong

I ain't gonna tell you no story
And I ain't gonna tell no lie
Well Albert passed about an hour ago
With a girl you call Alice Fry
        He's your man
         And he done you wrong

MISSISSIPPI JOHN HURT

Ain't No Tellin'

Don't you let my good girl catch you here
Don't you let my good girl catch you here
She
    might shoot you
                     may cut you and stob you too
Ain't no telling
        what she might do

I'm up the country where the cold sleet and snow
I'm
    up the country
              where the cold sleet and snow
Ain't no telling
        how much further I may go

Eat my breakfast here, my dinner in Tennessee
Eat my breakfast here, my dinner in Tennessee
Eat my break-
        fast here,
               my dinner in Tennessee
I told you I was coming,
             baby won't you look for me

        (hey, hey: *that's scooping the clam*)

The way I'm sleeping, my back and shoulders tired
The way I'm sleeping, baby, my back and shoulders tired
The way
    I'm sleeping,
           my back and shoulders tired
Gonna turn over,
        try it on the side

Don't you let my good girl catch you here

She
    might shoot you
              may cut you and stob you too
Ain't no telling
        what she might do

Dough Roller Blues

Yes I rolled and I tumbled
            and cried the whole night long
Yes I rolled and I tumbled
            and I cried the whole night long
Yes I rose this morning
           and I didn't know right from wrong

Have you ever woke up and
            and found your dough roller gone
Have you ever woke up and
            found your dough roller gone
Then you wring your hands
            and you cried "Oooo" all day long

Yes I told my woman
          just before brown left the town
Yes I told my woman
          just before brown left the town
Don't you let no body
          tear your barrel house down

Yes I fold my arms
         and I begin to walk a way
Says I fold my arms
         says I begin to walk a way
I said "That's all right sweet mama
              your troubles gon' come some day"

GARFIELD AKERS

Fare Thee Well Blues

You told me, early last fall, you never had no man at all
        Fare thee, baby, fare thee well
You told me, early last fall, you never had no man at all
Well you got more men than a 2-ton truck can haul

You told me, to my face, there's a good man in my place
        Fare thee, baby, fare thee well
You told me, to my face, there's a good man in my place
        Fare thee, baby, fare thee well

You told me, it was early spring, when the birds begin to sing
        Fare thee, baby, fare thee well
You told me, early last spring, when the birds began to sing
Well it's the last chance, kid, to be 'round here with me

I told you, early next June, when the flowers begin to bloom
        Fare thee, baby, fare thee well
I told you, early in June, when the flowers begin to bloom
You can't do no better, another good girl can take your room

Go and h'ist your window, let your curtain down
        Fare thee, baby, fare thee well
Go and h'ist your window, let your curtain down
Well you can't tell, there may be some joker around

Go and put on your night gown, baby, let's we go lie down
        Fare thee, baby, fare thee well
Go and put on your night gown, baby, let's we go lie down
Well it's the last chance, shaking in the bed with you

JOE CALICOTT

Aberdeen, Mississippi Blues

I was
      over in Aberdeen on my way to
                  New Orleans
I was
      over in
         Aberdeen on my
              way to New Orleans
Them Aberdeen women told me they will
                     buy my
                       gasoline

They's
      two little women
           that I ain't
              never seen
They has two little
        women
           that I ain't never seen
These two little women
         they's from
            New Orleans

I'm sitting
      down in Aberdeen with New Orleans
                 on my mind
I'm sitting down in
        Aberdeen with
           New Orleans on my mind
Lord, I believe these Aberdeen women gonna
               make me
                lose my mind

Aber-
    deen is my home but the mens don't
              want me around
Aberdeen is
      my home but the
          mens don't want me around
They know I will take these women and
           take them
             out of town

Listen, you
      Aberdeen women, you know I ain't
             got no dime
Oh oh listen, you
      women, you
         know I ain't got no dime
They even has the poor boy
        all
          hobbled down

                                                    BOOKER WHITE

Parchman Farm Blues

Judge gimme
            life this morning
                        down on
                                Parchman Farm
Judge gimme life this morning
                        down on Parchman Farm
I wouldn't hate it so bad, but I
                        left my
                                wife and my home

Oh
    good bye wife
                all you
                        have done gone
Oh good bye wife
                all you have done gone
But I hope some day you will
                        hear my
                                lonesome song

Oh
    listen you men
                I don't
                        mean no harm
Oh listen you men
                I don't mean no harm
If you wanna do good you better
                        stay off of
                                Parchman Farm

Well you goes to
                work in the morning
                                just the
                                        dawn of day
Well you goes to work in the morning
                                just the dawn of day
Just at the setting of the sun, that's
                        when the
                                work is done

I'm down
        on old Parchman Farm, I sure wanna
                                go back home
I'm down on old Parchman Farm, but I
                        sure wanna go back home
But I hope some day
            I will
                overcome

BOOKER WHITE

BOOKER WHITE

Sleepy Man Blues

When a man gets troubled in mind
                        he want to sleep—all the time
When a man gets troubled in mind
                        he want to sleep all the time
He knows if he can sleep all the time
                        his *trouble won't worry his mind*
                                won't,
                                        worry his mind

I'm feeling worried in mind
                        and I'm trying to keep from crying
I'm feeling worried in mind
                        and I'm trying to keep from crying
I am standing into the sunshine
                        to keep from weakin' down
                        Keep
                                from weak-
                                        in' down

I want somewhere to go
                        but I hate to go to town
I want somewhere to go
                        to satisfy my mind
I would go to town
                        but I hate to stand around
                        Hate
                                to stand
                                        a-round

I wonder what's the matter with my right mind
                                my mind keep me sleeping all the time
I wonder what's the matter with my right mind
                                my mind keep me sleeping all the time
But when I had plenty money
                        my friends would come around
                        Would
                                come
                                        a-round

If I had my right mind
                        I would write my women a few lines
If I had my right mind
                        I would write my women a few lines
I will do most anything
                        to keep from weakin' down
                        Keep
                                from weak-
                                        in' down

BOOKER WHITE

Sic 'Em Dogs On

Baby I'm going
down town
and tell the sheriff, only you
sicking your dogs on me

She went a-running
running and crying
she said, li-
   sten god I ain't gonna do it no more,
ain't gonna do it no more

You done got
my money
now you trying to
sic your dogs on me

That's all right
little girl
how you do me
you ain't gonna do it again

I'm gonna tell
the chief
you got your dogs on me, told me
you didn't want me around

Oh li-
sten chief
she done got my money, now
sicking her dogs on me

She went to running and
crying
saying, sic 'em Butch because
Fido he won't bite

If you take
me back
I won't do it no more, baby don't
sic your dogs on me

She said, li-
sten daddy
don't you drive me
don't you drive me around

BOOKER WHITE

The Panama Limited

(This old soul, you know, time she left Chicago, you know, old soul
taken down with the flus, you know, when she's taken down with the
flus, you know, the *tack* says to the chief, come 'round in the morning,
they gonna cut out, you know, when they got there, the old soul was
getting up, you know, singing and crying, you know,)

> I ain't got no-
> body to take me to this train
> Mmmmmmmmmmmmmmmmmmmmm
> Mmmmmm mmmm mm mm mm

(I know you ain't, old soul, I feel sorry for her, after a while, you know,
she *completely content* she's gonna cut out, she reckon she's got a few
little grandchildren, you know, that she's got up on the street, you
know, and while they begin to tell the *old soul lies,* she commenced
crying and singing, you know,)

> Fare
> you well if I don't see you no more
> Mmmmmmmmmmmmmmmmmmmmmmm
> Ahhhhhhhhh nahhhhhhhh nahhhh nahhhh

(That old soul, you know, went down to the Union Station, you know,
she asked the depot man what time it was, she heard eight thirty
freight blowing, but she was gonna catch that fast Panama Limited,
you know, it kind of blow a little different, you know,

And after she heard this freight, you know, she ask the man again what time it was, he told her to go and lay her head on the railroad line, and if she heard the rail popping, the train time wasn't long, old soul stooped down, and she heard the rail popping, you know, she got up and sang, you know.)

I'm a mother-
less child, I'm a long ways from my home
Mmmmmmmmmmmmmmmmmmmmmmmmm
Mmmmmmmmmmm mmmmmm mmmm mmmm

(*Don't moan* it, slowed down by hecky!

But when old soul, you know, begin to moan, you know, she heard this here train coming in there, hollering, you know, after holling, you know, she heard the bell blowing, after the bell blowing, she heard her when she cut down,

Air brakes!

When they heard it, you know, heard the train cut down, you know, the old soul got happy, you know, she commenced singing, you know,)

The train
I'm riding, it don't burn no coal
Mmmmmmmmmmmmmmmmmmmmmmmmmm
Mmmmmm mmm mmm mmmmmmmmmm
Mmmmmmmmmmmmmmmmmmmm
Mmmmmmmmmm mmmmmmmm mmmmmm
Mmmmmmmmmmmmmm mmmmmmmmmm
Mmmmmmmmmmmmmmmmmmmmm
Mmmmmmmmmm mmmm mmmmmmmmmm

Fixing to Die

I'm looking far in mind, I
        b'lieve I'm fixing to die
        b'lieve I'm fixing to die
I'm looking far in mind, I
        b'lieve I'm fixing to die
I know I was born to die
        but I hate to leave my children crying

Just as sure as we living today
        sure we's born to die
        sure we's born to die
Just as sure we live
        sure we's born to die
I know I was born to die
        but I hate to leave my children crying

Your mother treated me, children, like I
        was her baby child
        was her baby child
Your mother treated me like I
        was her baby child
That's why it's I tried so hard
        to come home to die

So many nights at the fireside
        how, my children, mother would cry
        how, my children, mother would cry
So many nights at the fireside
        how, my children, mother would cry
Because I told the mother, I
        had to say good-bye

Look over yonder
        on the burying ground
        on the burying ground
Look over yonder
        on the burying ground
Yonder stand ten thousand
        standing to see them let me down

Mother, take my children back
        before they let me down
        before they let me down
Mother, take my children back
        'fore they let me down
And don't leave them screaming and crying
        on the graveyard ground

It's Cold in China Blues

It's so cold in China
                    birds can't hardly sing
It's so cold in China, eeeeee
                        birds can't hardly sing
You didn't make me mad till you broke my diamond ring

Ehhhhhh mama
                won't be bad no more
Take me mama
                won't be bad no more
You can get my loving if you let that old black snake go

Black snake crawling
                    tumbling in my room
Black snake crawling
                    crawling in my room
Some high brown woman better come and get this here black snake soon

Ehhhhhh mama
                what have I said and done
Ehhhhhh mama
                what have I said and done
Some joker you're loving gonna sure gonna be my ruin

        Oh any time
                    mama
                        papa
                            daddy
                                I do love
                                    do love
                                I do love
                                    do love
Crying, eeeeee
                your daddy do love you
She's a high stepping mama and I don't care what you do

I was a little boy
                on my way to school
Was a little boy oooooo
                        on my way to school
Met a high brown woman and she broke my mammy's rule

Mama say I'm reckless
                        daddy say I'm young and wild
Mama say I'm reckless oooooo
                            daddy say I'm young and wild
If he's so reckless, he's my baby child

ISAIAH NETTLES

Memphis

Old Dog Blue

I'm going back where I come f'm
I'm going back where I come f'm
I'm going back to *Giles* County
My wife died and left me a bounty
We done pretty good, ganged *around*
That's the reason I'm going to *Giles* County
Had an old dog his name was Blue
You know Blue was mighty true
You know Blue was a good old dog
Blue treed a possum in a hollow log
You can know from that he's a good old dog
Blue treed a possum out on a limb
Blue looked at me and I looked at him
Grabbed that possum, put him in a sack
Do for me and Blue till I get back
Here Ring!
Here Ring, here!
Here Ring!
Here Ring, here!
   Who been here since I been gone?
   Little bitty girl with the red dress on.
   Who been here since I been gone?
   Little bitty girl with the red dress on.
Old Blue's feets was big and round

Old Blue's feets was big and round
Never 'lowed a possum to touch the ground
Me and Blue went out on a hunt
Blue treed a possum in a hollow stump
You know old Blue was a good old dog
Blue treed a possum in a hollow log
You can know from that he's a good old dog
But old Blue died and I dug his grave
I dug his grave with a silver spade
I let him down with a golden chain
And every link I called his name
Go on Blue, you good dog you
Go on Blue, you good dog you
Blue laid down and died like a man
Blue laid down and died like a man
And now he's treeing possums in the Promised Land
I'm gonna tell you just to let you know
Old Blue's gone where the good dogs go
When I hear old Blue bark
When I hear old Blue bark
Blue treed a possum in Noah's ark
Blue treed a possum in Noah's ark

'Tain't Nobody's Business

I'm gonna stay around this town
Where the gals won't allow me to walk around
    Ain't nobody's business but mine
I'm gonna stay in Memphis Tennessee
Where the gals in Memphis take a liking to me
    Now ain't nobody's business but my own

        It ain't nobody's business, honey
        How I spend my money
Nobody's business but mine
        It ain't nobody's business, kid
        Where in the world I got my money hid
It ain't nobody's business but my own

Now listen at me baby why don't you be kind
You's talkin' to me so rough all the time
    Ain't nobody's business but mine
If I had my way I'd stay with you
Think about the things you want me to do
    Baby it ain't nobody's business but my own

        It ain't nobody's business honey
        Where in the world I find my money
Nobody's business but mine
        It ain't nobody's business baby
        How I treat my Sadie
Nobody's business but mine

I'm gonna stay around in Memphis Tennessee
Where I can *have this work all on me*
    It ain't nobody's business but mine
If I had a way I'd let you alone
Wish to God I'd-a stayed at home
    It ain't nobody's business but my own

        It ain't nobody's business honey
        How in the world I spend my money
Ain't nobody's business but mine
        It ain't nobody's business honey
        Where in the world I find my money
Nobody's business but my own

        Well it ain't nobody's business kid
        Who in the world I do my business with
Said it ain't nobody's business but mine

FRANK STOKES

FRANK STOKES

You Shall

Oh well it's our Father who art in Heaven
The preacher owed me ten dollars, he paid me seven
       Thy Kingdom come
       Thy Will be done
If I hadn't took the seven, Lord, I wouldn'ta gotten none

              Had to fight him about it

              What he owed me

              My money

                  Yeah.

Well some folks say 'bout a preacher wouldn't steal
I caught about eleven in the water melon field
Just a cuttin' and a slicin', got to tearing up the vine
They's eating and talking most all the time

              They was hungry

              And they run to the . . .

              Save my vine

              Don't rob me

                  Yeah

              My melon

                  Yeah.

Oh well you see a preacher lay behind the log
A hand on the trigger, got his eye on the hog
       The hog said 'mmm
       The gun said zip
Jumped on the hog with all his grip

              He had pork chops

                  Yeah

              And backbone

              And spare ribs

                  Yeah.

    Now when the good Lord set me free

FRANK STOKES

Now when I first was over to Memphis Tennessee
I was crazy 'bout the preachers as I could be
I went out on the front porch a-walking about
I invite the preacher over to my house
He washed his face, he combed his head
And next thing he wanted to do was slip in my bed
I caught him by the head, man, kicked him out the door
Don't: allow my preacher at my house no more

I don't like 'em

They'll rob you

Steal your daughter

Take your wife from you

Yeah

Eat your chicken

Taken your money

Yeah

They'll rob you

Make change on you

Yeah.

Hey, Mona

In the morning

Yeah

Peel the spare ribs

If they're still there

Yeah.

Now when the good Lord set me free

Big Chief Blues

I'm goin' away baby
            take me seven long months to ride
I'm goin' away baby, take me seven long months to ride
January, February, March, April, May, June, July

I was three years old
            when my poor mother died
I was three years old when my poor mother died
If you mistreat me, you mistreat a mother's child

I dreamt last night
            the whole round world were mine
I dreamt last night the whole round world were mine
It wasn't nothing at all, but my good girl jumping down

She put carbolic in my coffee
                        turpentine in my tea
Carbolic in my coffee, turpentine in my tea
Strychnine in my biscuits; lord, but she didn't hurt me

Baby, when I marry
            gonna marry a Indian squaw
I mean, when I marry gonna marry a Indian squaw
Big Chief's *gonna* be my daddy-in-law

I say, when I marry gonna marry a Indian squaw
So the Big Chief can be my daddy-in-law

FURRY LEWIS

Judge Harsh Blues

Good morning, Judge
                    what may be my fine
Good morning, Judge, what may be my fine
Fifty dollars and eleven twenty-nine

They arrest me for murder
                    I ain't never harmed a man
Arrest me for murder and, lord, I ain't harmed a ma-a-an
Women hollered murder and I ain't raised my hand

I ain't got no body
                    get me out on bond
I ain't got no body to get me out on bond
I would not mind, but I ain't done nothing wrong

Please, Judge Harsh
                    make it light as you possibly can
Please, Judge Harsh, make it light as you possibly can
I ain't done no work, Judge, in I don't know when

My woman come a-running
                    with a hundred dollars in her hand
Come a-running, my woman, with a hundred dollars in her hand
Crying, Judge, please spare my man

One hundred dollars won't do
                    better run and get your three
One hundred dollars won't do, better run and get your three
I can keep your man from the pen-i-ten-tia-ry

Baby, I'm arrested
                    please don't grieve and moan
'Cause I'm arrested, baby, please don't grieve and moan
Penitentiary seems just like my home

People all hollerin'
                    'bout what in the world they will do
Judge, the people hollerin' 'bout what in the world they will do
Lots of people had justice, they'd be in the penitentiary too

Billy Lyons and Stack O'Lee

I remember one September
On one Friday night
Stackerlee and Billy Lyon
Had a great fight.
Crying, when you lose
Your money, learn to lose.

Billy Lyon shot six bits
Stack he bet he passed
Stackerlee out with his forty-five
Said, You done shot your last.
When you lose
Your money, learn to lose.

Lord a woman come a-running
Fell down on her knees
Crying, Oh Mister Stackerlee
Don't shoot my brother please.
When you lose
Your money

Now you talking about some gambler
Oughta seen Richard Lee
Shot one thousand dollars
And come out on a three.
Crying, when you lose
Your money, learn to lose.

Lord the judge told the sheriff
We want him dead or alive.
How in the world can we bring him when he
Totes a forty-five?
When you lose
Your money, learn to lose.

Lord the woman told the judge
My husband's name Jack Shelf
Wanta 'rest poor Stackerlee
Better go somewheres else.
When you lose
Your money, learn to lose.

FURRY LEWIS

Dry Land Blues

I can look through
muddy water
baby and
        spy dry land
If you don't want me honey
Let's take hand in hand

I'm going
so far
I can't hear your
        rooster crow

256   *FURRY LEWIS*

I'm going so far
can't hear your rooster crow

This is my
last time
ever knocking
          at your door
My last time
ever knocking at your door

You won't cook me
no dinner
baby you won't iron me
          no clothes
You won't do nothing
but walk the *Horn Lake Road*

Man if you love
your woman
better mess it
          in her cup
So if she have not quit you boy
won't leave you in tough luck

Now you can take my
woman
but you ain't done
          nothing smart
For I got more'n one woman
playing in my back yard

Wind storm
come
and it blowed my
          house away
I'm a good old boy
but I ain't got no where to stay

And it's trouble
here
and it's trouble
          every where
So much trouble
floating in the air

What you gonna
do
when your trouble
          get like mine
What you gonna do
when your trouble get like mine

Kassie Jones

I woke up this morning, four o'clock
Mister Kassie told his fireman get his boiler hot
Put on your water, put on your coal
Put your head out the window, see my drivers roll,
                                        See my drivers roll,
Put your head out the window, see my drivers roll.

Lord, some people said Mister Kassie couldn't run
Let me tell you what Mister Kassie done
He left Memphis, was a quarter to nine
Got to Newport News, it was dinner time,
                                     It was dinner time,
Got to Newport News, it was dinner time.

I sold my gin, I sold it straight
Po-lice run me to my woman's gate
She come to the door, she nod her head
She made me welcome to the folding bed,
                              To the folding bed,
Made me welcome to the folding bed.

Lord, people said to Kassie, You're running over time,
You'll have an occolusion with the one-o-nine.
Kassie said, Ain't in mind,
I'll run her into glory 'less I make my time.
Said to all the passengers, Better keep yourself hid,
I'm natural gonna shake it like Chaney did,
                                  Chaney did,
I'm natural gonna shake it like Chaney did.

Mister Kassie run his engine to a mile of the place
Number Four stared him in the face
The devil told Kassie, Well you must leave town
I believe to my soul I'm Alabama bound,
                              Alabama bound,

I believe to my soul I'm Alabama bound.

Mrs. Kassie said she dreamt a dream
The night she bought her sewing machine
The needle got broke and she could not sew
She loved Mister Kassie 'cause she told me so,
                                Told me so,
Loved Mister Kassie 'cause she told me so.

There was a woman name Miss Alice Frye
Said, I'm gonna ride with Mister Kassie till I die
I ain't good looking but I take my time

I'm a rambling woman with a rambling mind,
                              Got a rambling mind.

Kassie looked at his water: his water was low
Looked at his watch: his watch was slow.

                         On the road again,
Natural born eas'man, on the road again.

Lord the people tell by the thortle moan
Man at the fire Mister Kassie Jones,
                         Mister Kassie Jones.

Mister Kassie said before he died
One more road that he wants to ride
People tell Kassie, Which road is he?
Southern Pacific and the Sancta Fee,
                         Sancta Fee.

This morning I heard some one was dying
Mrs. Kassie Jones on her doorstep crying
Mama, mama, I can't keep from crying
Papa got killed on the Southern Line,
                         On the Southern Line,
Papa got killed on the Southern Line.

Mama, mama, how can it be?
Killed my father in the first degree.
Children, children, won't you hold your breath
Draw another pension from your father's death,
                         From your father's death.

                         On the road again,
I'm a natural born eas'man, on the road again.

Tuesday morning it looked like rain
Around the curve came a passenger train
Under the bar there laid Kassie Jones
Good old engineer but he's dead and gone,
                         Dead and gone.

                         On the road again,
I'm a natural born eas'man, on the road again.

I left Memphis just to spread the news
Memphis women don't wear no shoes
Had it written in the back of my shirt
Natural born eas'man, don't have to work,
                         Don't have to work,
I'm a natural born eas'man, don't have to work.

FURRY LEWIS

I Will Turn Your Money Green

When I was in Missouri, would not let me be
When I was in Missouri, would not let me be
Wouldn't rest content, till I came to Tennessee

If you follow me baby, I'll turn your money green
Follow me baby, I'll turn your money green
I show you more money, Rockefeller ever seen

If the river was whiskey, baby and I was a duck
River was whiskey, baby and I was a duck
I'd dive to the bottom, and I never would come up

Woman I hate, I see her every day
Woman I hate, I see her every day
But the woman I love, she's so far away

Talk about *sweetheart,* and I declare I'm a honest man
Talk about *sweetheart,* and I declare I'm a honest man
Give my woman money, broke her apron string

All she gimme was trouble, trouble all the time
All she gimme was trouble, trouble all the time
I been troubled so long, trouble don't worry my mind

I been down so long, till it seem like up to me
I been down so long, seem like up to me
Woman I love, heart like a rock in the sea

I would holler murder, but this *freakin'* town too small
I would holler murder, but this *freakin'* town too small
Woman quit me, throwed my trunk outdoors

Nashville Stonewall Blues

I stayed in jail and
                worked for thirty long days
I stayed in jail and
                worked for thirty long days
And that woman said she loved me I
                        could not see her face

I looked out the window
                saw the long chain man
I looked out the window
                saw the long chain man
Oh he's coming to call us,
                boys, name by name

He's gonna take me from here to
                Nashville Tennessee
He's gonna take me from here to
                Nashville Tennessee
He's gonna take me right back, boys
                    where I used to be

I got a letter from home
                reckon how it read
I got a letter from home
                reckon how it read
It read Son come home to your mama, she's
                      sick and nearly dead

I sat down and cried
                and I screamed and squalled
I sat down and cried
                and I screamed and squalled
Said, I cannot come home, mama,
                    I'm behind these walls

Every morning 'bout four
                or it might be half past
Every morning 'bout four
                or it might be half past
You oughta see me down the foundry
                    trying to do my task

Oh the judge he sentenced me
                boys, from five to ten
'Cause the judge he sentenced me
                boys, from five to ten
I get out I'm going *to* that woman, I'll
                    be right back again

ROBERT WILKINS

That's No Way to Get Along

        I'm going home
        friends, sit down
        and tell my
        ah, mama
                friends, sit down and tell my ma
I'm going home, sit down and tell my ma
I'm going home, sit down and tell my ma
      That that's no way for me to get along.

        These low down
        women, mama
        they treated your
        ah, poor son wrong

ROBERT WILKINS

          mama, treated me wrong
These low down women, mama, treated your poor son wrong
These low down women, mama, treated your poor son wrong
     And that's no way for him to get along.

     They treated me
     like my poor heart
     was made of
     a rock *of* stone
          mama, made of a rock *of* stone
Treated me like my poor heart was made of a rock *of* stone
Treated me like my poor heart was made of a rock *of* stone
     And that's no way for me to get along.

     You know that
     was enough, mama
     to make your son
     wisht he's dead and gone
          mama, wisht I's dead and gone
That 'as enough to make your son, mama, wisht he's dead and gone
That 'as enough to make your son, mama, wisht he's dead and gone
     'Cause that's no way for him to get along.

     He stood on
     the roadside
     I cried alone
     all by myself
          I cried alone by myself
I stood on the roadside and cried alone by myself
I stood on the roadside and cried alone by myself
     And that's no way for me to get along.

     I's wanting some
     train to come along
     and take me
     now, away from here
          friends, take me away from here
That train to come along and take me away from here
     And that'll be no way for me to get along.

                           ROBERT WILKINS

I'll Go With Her Blues

I'll go with her, I'll follow her, I will
      To her burying place
I'll go with her, I'll follow her, I will
      To her burying place

Hang my head and cry, friend, I will
      Mmmm as she pass away
Hang my head and cry, friend, I will
      As she pass away

Up a yonder she go, friend, please run
      Try to call her back
Up a yonder she go, friend, please run
      Try to call her back

'Cause that sure is one woman I do
      Mmmm love and like
'Cause that sure is one woman I do
      I did love and like

I b'lieve I'll go home, friend, and do this:
      Dress myself in black
I b'lieve I'll go home, friend, and do this:
      Dress myself in black

Show to the world I wants her but I can't
      Mmmm get her back
Show to the world I wants her
      I can't get her back

Every time I hear that lonesome
      Mmmm church bell ring
Every time I hear that
      Lonesome church bell ring

Makes me think about that song my
      Baby used to sing
Makes me think about that song my
      Baby used to sing

Mmmmmm mmmm, Lord have mercy on me

Stack o' Dollars

Stack o' dollars
Stack o' dollars
Long as I am tall
      Hey now mama, hear the story
Stack o' dollars just as
                 long as I am tall
If you be my woman
              you can have them all

I heard a rumbling
I heard a rumbling
Way down in the ground
      Hey now mama, hear now
Heard a rumbling
            way down in the ground
Musta been some body
             slowly jumping down

See two women
See two women
Walking hand by hand
      Hey now mama, you see
See two women, baby
            walking hand by hand
They's a *thinking* of something, Lord
             how to fool some man

Went on the mountain
Went on the mountain
Looked down in the sea
      Hey now mama, hear now
Went on the mountain and I
            looked down in the sea
Minnows had my woman
           Lord, and the blues had me

Baby done quit me
Baby done quit me
Ain't said a mumbling word
      Hey now ma-ma
Baby done quit me
           ain't said a mumbling word
It weren't nothing that she knowed of
            just something she had heard

My Black Gal Blues

Black gal,
she took a knife,
scared my brown
to death;
If I hadn't a had my pistol
think I woulda run myself;
Hadn't a had my pistol
think I woulda run myself.

When you see
me coming
hist your
window high;
When you see me leaving
hang your head and cry;
When you see me leaving
hang your head and cry.

Now if I just
had a listened
what my ma-
ma said,
I woulda been at home, Lord,
in my feather bed;
I woulda been at home, Lord,
in my feather bed.

Got a man
on your man,
kid man on
your kid; Lord
She done got so *buggy,*
don't try to keep it hid;
She done got so *buggy,*
don't try to keep it hid.

Now I got up
this morning,
blues all round
my bed;
I turned back my cover,
blues all in my bed;
Turned back my cover,
blues all in my bed.

SLEEPY JOHN ESTES

Milkcow Blues

Now,
asked sweet mama, let me
be her kid,
She says, I
might *get loved* if I could
keep it hid.
Well she
looked at me, she be-
gin to smile,
Says, I
thought I would use you for my
man awhile,
That you just don't let my
husband catch you there,
Now just, just don't let my
husband catch you there.

Now,
went upstairs to pack my
leaving trunk,
I never
saw no whiskey, the blues done made me
sloppy drunk,
Say I never saw no whiskey,
blues done made me sloppy drunk,
Now I never saw no whiskey, but the
blues done made me sloppy drunk.

Now,
some say they *dream,*
some say they was *'deemed,*
But it's a
slow consumption killing you
by degrees,
Lord it's a slow consumption
killing you by degrees
Now it's a slow consumption, and it's
killing you by degrees

Everybody Ought to Make a Change

      Now
      Change in the ocean
      Change in deep blue sea
      Take me back, baby, you'll find some
      Change in me
Everybody
      they ought to change some time
Because it's soon or late
           have to go down in that old lonesome ground

      Now
      Change my money
      Change my honey
      I change babies just to
      Keep from being funny
Everybody
      they ought to change some time
Because it's soon or late
           we have to go down in that old lonesome ground

      Now
      Change my pants
      Change my shirt
      I change, baby, to get
      Shed of the dirt
Everybody
      they ought to change some time
Because it's soon or late
           have to go down in that old lonesome ground

      Now
      Change home
      I change town
      I change babies
      All the way 'round
Everybody
      they ought to change some time
Because it's soon or late
           have to go down in that old lonesome ground

      Now
      Change walk
      I change talk
      I change babies just
      Keep from being balked
Everybody
      they ought to change some time
Because it's soon or late
           we have to go down in that old lonesome ground

                                      SLEEPY JOHN ESTES

Street Car Blues

Now
I know the people
Is all a wonder everywhere
I say I know the people
Is all a wonder everywhere
Because they heard of poor John
Started 'round the 'lectric car

Now
Catch the Central Park car
Ride it down to Summer Street
I say *I catch the Central Park car*
Ride it down to Summer Street
Lord I'm going to ease it down in Roebust, catch my
Baby out on a midnight creep

Lord
The reasoning why, baby, I
I been so long writing to you
I say the reasoning why, baby
I been so long writing to you
Because I been studying so hard
Lord how to sing these blues

Lord
I lost my papa
And my dear
          mama too
I say I lost my papa
And my dear
          mama too
Lord I'm gonna quit my bad way of living
And visit the Sunday school

Brownsville Blues

Now I can straighten your wires
        you know poor Vasser can grind your valves
Now I can straighten your wires
        you know poor Vasser can grind your valves
Man when I turn your motor loose
        and it sure will split the air

Now Vasser can line your wheels
        you know poor Vasser can tune your horn
Now he can line your wheels
        you know poor Vasser can tune your horn
Then when he set it out on the highway
        you can hear your motor hum

Now my generator is bad
        and you know my lights done stopped
Now my generator is bad
        and you know my lights done stopped
And I reckon I better take it over to Durhamville
        and I'm going to stop at Vasser Williams' shop

Now I were raised in Lau'erdale County
        you know I was schooled on Winfield Lane
Now I were raised in Lau'erdale County
        and I was schooled on Winfield Lane
Then what I made of myself
        I declare it was the cryingest shame

Now Brownsville is my home
        and you know I ain't going to throw it down
Now Brownsville is my home
        and you know I ain't going to throw it down
Because I'm 'quainted with John Law
        and they won't let me down

SLEEPY JOHN ESTES

Lawyer Clark Blues

Now
Got offices in town
Resident out on 70 Road
He got a nice little lake
Right inside the grove

        Boys you know I like Mr. Clark
        Yes he really is my friend
        He say if I just stay out of the grave
        He see that I won't go to the pen

Now
Mr. Clark is a lawyer
His younger brother is too
When the battle get hot
He tell him just what to do

        Boys you know I like Mr. Clark
        Yes you know he is my friend
        He say if I just stay out of the grave
        He see that I won't go to the pen

Now
He lawyer for the rich
He lawyer for the poor
He don't try to rob no body
Just bring along a little dough

        Boys you know I like Mr. Clark
        Yes he really is my friend
        He say if I just stay out of the grave
        He see that I won't go to the pen

        SLEEPY JOHN ESTES

Now
Once I got in trouble
You know I was gonna take a ride
He didn't let it reach the court house
He kept it on the outside

> Boys you know I like Mr. Clark
> Yes he really is my friend
> He say if I just stay out of the graveyard
> Old John I see that you won't go to the pen

Now
Mr. Clark is a good lawyer
He good as I ever seen
He's the first man that proved that
Water run up stream

> Boys you know I like Mr. Clark
> Yes he really is my friend
> He say if I just stay out of the grave
> Old John I see you won't go to the pen

273

Floating Bridge

Now I never
             will forget that floating bridge
Now I never
             will forget that floating bridge
Now I never
             will forget
                  that float-
                       ing bridge
Tell me five
         minutes time
                 under water I was hid

When I was go-
            ing down I throwed up my hands
Now when I was go-
             ing down I throwed up my hands
Now when I was go-
             ing down
                 I throwed
                     up my hands
Please,
    take me on dry land

Now they carried
             me in the house and they laid me 'cross the bank
Now they carried
             me in the house and they laid me 'cross the bank
Now they carried
             me in the house
                 and they laid me
                       'cross the bank
'Bout a gallon 'n'
         half muddy water I had drank

They dried
        me off and they laid me in the bed
Now they dried
        me off and they laid me in the bed
Now they dried
        me off
          and they laid
              in the bed
Couldn't hear nothing
           but muddy water run through my head

                                        SLEEPY JOHN ESTES

Now my mother
                often taught me, Quit playing a bum
Now my mother
                often taught me, Quit playing a bum
Now my mama
            often taught me,
                            Son, quit
                                    playing a bum
Go somewhere,
                settle down and make a crop

Now the people standing
                        on the bridge: screaming and crying
People
        on the bridge was screaming and crying
Now the—people   •
                    on the bridge
                                standing screaming
                                            and crying
Lord have mercy while we gwine

Working Man Blues

Now you done spent all my 1940 rent
                              woman, you done worked on my substitute
Now you done spent all my 1940 rent
                              woman, you done worked on my substitute
Then if you don't reach that 1941
                    oooo babe, what in the world you gonna do

Now they oughta cut off so many trucks and tractors
                              white folks, you oughta work more mules and men
Now they oughta cut off so many trucks and tractors
                              white folks, you oughta work more mules and men
                    (tell 'em about it)
Then you know that would make
                    (what?)
                    oooo boy, money get thick again

Now when a man gets *his together*
                         you know he's turning his stocks into feed
Now when a man gets *together*
                         you all know he's turning his stocks into feed
He say he gonna sell all his corn and buy gas
                         oooo boy, and it's for his little automobile

Now I been studying, I been wondering
                              what make a man turn the ground in the wintertime
Now I been studying, I been wondering
                              what make a man turn the ground in the wintertime
You know, let the snow and rain rot the grass
                         oooo boy, that make fertilizer for the ground

Now the government given us a school in Brownsville
                              boys you know I think that's very nice
Now the government given us a school in Brownsville
                              boys you know I think that's very nice
You know the children can go in the daytime
                         oooo boy, and the old folks have it at night

T-bone Steak Blues

Say you talking 'bout your red ripe tomato
                            I'm crazy 'bout my T-bone steak
Say you talking 'bout your red ripe tomato
                            I'm crazy 'bout my T-bone steak
Said I want to buy me a faro
                    to share my Cadillac 8

I got the railroad blues
                    got box cars on my mind
I got the railroad blues
                    got box cars on my mind
And the girl I'm loving
                    she sure done left this town

Say if I had wings
                    like a bull frog on a pond
Say if I had wings
                    like a bull frog on a pond
I would lie right here
                    flying in sweet mama's arms

You know one thing's forever
                            you know, baby, *two, lord,* ain't but twice
You know one thing's forever
                            you know, baby, *two, lord,* ain't but twice
But you women 'll get a good man
                            you don't know how to treat him right

Well you mistreat me, mama
                    and that's the way you do
Well you mistreat me, now mama
                            you know, and that's the way you do
But you gonna want me some of these mornings
                            and poor *James* won't have you

(JAMES) YANK RACHEL

Lake Michigan Blues

Says I went to Lake Michigan
                    stood on the banks and cried
Well I went to Lake Michigan
                    stood on the banks and cried
Says I want to see my baby over yonder
                          but it was so long and deep and wide

Says I hung my head, baby, and I
                    slowly walked away
And I hung my head, baby,
                    and I slowly walked away
I said, That's all right, Lake Michigan
                        I hope you will go dry some day

Said the moon got gloomy, Lord,
                    the clouds begin to rise
Said the moon got gloomy,
                    and the clouds begin to rise
I want to cross Lake Michigan
                    and see my gal on the other side

And I fell down on my knees, babe,
                    and prayed, What shall I do
Fell down on my knees and I
                    prayed, What shall I do
Says I hope some day my
                    baby want to cross Lake Michigan too

(JAMES) YANK RACHEL

Oh Ambulance Man

Hey daddy
hey daddy
don't let me cry in vain

you see I'm wounded
wounded and bleeding
can't you ease my pain?

Mister Amb'lance man
will you rush me to a doctor please!

                     I ask no wild a-rushing
                     your daddy can ease your pain with ease.

Can't you see I'm cut in the stomach?

                     That's the reason I can ease your pain with ease.

Hearts is aching
day is breaking
listen to me I pray

see it snowing
cold wind is blowing
so please be on your way.

Mister Amb'lance man
please don't you drive so rough!

                     I have got to do it
                     your daddy have got to strut his stuff.

Can't you see I'm wounded and bleeding?

                     That's the reason daddy have to drive so rough.

      (Oh whip it
        till it's roasted like okra now)

Mister Amb'lance man
I can't stay still to save my soul
and you ought to be careful how you
handle my jelly roll.

                     Mama you know the road is rugged baby
                     and your daddy's got to satisfy your soul.

I mean my weary

                     (I mean your
         soooooul.   soul)

             MEMPHIS JUG BAND (HATTIE HART AND WILL SHADE)

MEMPHIS JUG BAND

New Minglewood Blues

(Play it now)

I was born in the desert
                I was raised in the lion's den
I was born in the desert
                raised in the lion's den
Said my regular occupation
                taking women from their other men

(Play it boys)

(Play it now)

When you come to Memphis
                please stop by Mingle-wood
                (Play it boy)
When you come to Memphis
                please stop by Mingle-wood
They got womens in the camp don't
                mean no man no good

Going to Germany

I'm going to Germa-
                    I'll be back some old day
I'm going to Germa-
                    I'll be back some old day
I'm going to Ger-ma-
                    I'll be back some old day

Please tell me mama
                  what more can I do
Tell me mama
              what more can I do
Done all I knowed, I
                  can't get along with you

                                (Oh play it Mr. Lewis
                                play it, play it, play it)

                                (Play it Mr. Lewis
                                play it)

Get away from my window
                      stop knocking on my
                      stop knocking on my door
Go 'way from my window
                  stop knocking on my door
I got another woman
                  can't use you no more

When you's in trouble
                  I worked and paid your
                  I worked and paid your fine
When you's in trouble
                  I worked and paid your fine
Now I'm in trouble
                you don't pay me no mind

                                (Aw play it Mr. Lewis
                                play it for me now)

                                (Play it, Mr. Lewis, play it)

                                (Oh play it from down in Dixie now)

                                (Play it right on from down in Dixie)

                                                    CANNON'S JUG STOMPERS

CANNON'S JUG STOMPERS

My Babe My Babe

My babe
my babe
sure is good to me
she *tore* my troubles
broke up my misery

I can ask her
for whiskey
she give me cherry wine
don't you wish your woman would
treat you good like mine

Her hair
ain't curly
but it hang like horse's mane
don't you wish you had a woman to
treat you just the same

I can ask her
for a nickel
she give me ten and a dime
don't you wish you had a woman to
treat you just like mine

She got me
out of jail
she bought me a diamond ring
I ain't gonna do nothing, but lay
'round and shake that thing

BILL WILBER

She calls
me daddy
and she calls me sugar pie
I ain't gonna do nothing, but lay
down by her side

Now when
she's dead
six feet in the clay
won't have another woman to
treat me this-a-way

Now good bye
good bye
baby now it's fare you well
if I don't meet you in heaven, you know
I'll meet you in hell

Now I'm a-leaving
I'm a-leaving
leaving on a eagle wing
all don't see me
sho' can hear me sing

She had
an old job
making four dollars a day
I didn't have to do nothing but lay
'round and throw it away

BILL WILBER

Bad Girl Blues

Women loving each other
              man they don't think about no man
Women loving each other
              and they don't think about no man
They ain't playing no secret no more
              these women playing it a wide open hand

I buzzed a little girl the other day
I wanted a little thrill
She say, I'm so sorry Mister *Sims*
I'm putting out the same thing to Lil

I say women loving each other
              and they ain't thinking about no man
They ain't playing with no secret
              these women playing it a wide open hand

Have you ever taken her out car riding
Bought her all kind of whiskey and wine
Say you was too drunk to realize
Say, I'll see you another time

You know women loving each other
              and they don't think about no man
They ain't playing with no secret
              these women playing it a wide open hand

Have you ever left you going out jitterbugging
Smelling sweet like a rose
Come back 'bout 5 o'clock in the morning
With a *fish scent all in her clothes*

You know women is loving each other
              and they don't think about no man
They don't play it with no secret no more
              they playing it a wide open hand

Have you ever had a little woman
Give her the last dollar you had
Every time you say something to her
She'll say, My stomach hurting so bad

You know women loving each other
              and they don't think about no man
They ain't playing for no secret
              they playing it a wide open hand

MEMPHIS WILLIE B. (BORUM)

MEMPHIS WILLIE B. (BORUM)

Alabama

Frisco Whistle Blues

(Lord I hate to hear that
Frisco whistle blow)

Well I saw the Frisco when she left the yard
I saw the Frisco when she left the yard
When that train pull out, baby, it nearly broke my heart

They's two trains running, none of 'em going my way
Two trains running, none was going my way
I'm gonna leave here walking on this very day

(Oh whoop it Mister Whooper
whoop it a long time
whoop it till I get this Trinity Train)

Well there's one thing I don't like 'bout the railroad track
One thing I don't like 'bout that railroad track
They'll take your rider, never bring her back

Honey, where were you, babe, when the Frisco left the yard
Where were you, babe,—Frisco left the yard
I was on the corner, police *had me barred*

ED BELL

Hambone Blues

Jelly roll
Jelly roll
Jelly roll is so hard to find
Ain't a baker in town
      Can bake a
            sweet jelly roll like mine

I got to go to
Cincinnatti
Just to have my hambone boiled
Womens in Alabama
      Gonna
         let my hambone spoil

Well she's mine
And she's yours
And she's somebody else's too
Don't you mention 'bout rolling
      'Cause she'll
         play her trick on you

That's the way
That's the way
These barefooted soul'll do
They will get your money
      And they'll
         have a man on you

You come home
At night
She got a towel on her head
Don't you mention 'bout rolling
      'Cause she'll
         swear she nearly dead

ED BELL

Jelly roll
Jelly roll
Well you see what you went and done
You done had my grandpa
      Now you
             got his youngest son

I'm getting tired
Of walking
I believe I'll fly awhile
I'm getting tired of women
      Telling me their lies

I wonder
What made grandpaw
Hey, love your grandmaw so
She got the same jelly roll
      She had
             forty years ago

ED BELL

Tooten Out Blues

You used to be my sugar, but
You ain't sweet no
                    mamlish more
Used to be my sugar
You ain't sweet no more
You got another joker
Hanging 'round your door

I know my baby
Worrying over
                mamlish me
I know my baby
Worrying over me
'Cause every time she grin, she
Shine her light on me

                    (Play that thing Mr. Clifford)
                    (It is feeling mistreated)

Talking 'bout your rider
But you just ought to see
                        mamlish mine, you
Talking 'bout your one woman
Just ought to see mine
She's a long tall woman, and she's
Whooping out behind

She ain't so good looking
She ain't got no great long
                        mamlish hair
She ain't so good looking, she ain't
Got no great long hair
She ain't got enough gold teeth, you can
Spot her any where

Well she's standing on the corner
Be-tween 25th and
                    mamlish Main
She stood on the corner
Be-tween 25th and Main
Well now a blind man saw her
And a dumb man called her name

And the dumb man ask her, saying,
Who's your reg'lar
                    mamlish be
The dumb man ask her, saying,
Who's your reg'lar be
And the blind man say told her that you
Sure look good to me

296   *"SLUE FOOT JOE" (ED BELL?)*

From Now On

Oh you used to told me you could drive me like a cow
Oh you used to told me you could drive me like a cow
Well now you can't drive me, 'cause you don't know how

From now on, mama, I tell you just like that
From now on, mama, I tell you just like that
If you hit my dog, sure gonna kick your cat

From now on, mama, I ain't gonna have no rule
From now on, mama, I ain't gonna have no rule
I'm gonna get hard-headed, and act just like a doggone mule

From now on, mama, you gonna do what I say
From now on, mama, you must do what I say
You must understand, you can't have your way

From now on, mama, this way you got of doing
From now on, mama, this way you got of doing
Sugar you better stop that, lord it's sure gonna be your ruin

From now on, mama, starting from this very day
From now on, mama, starting from this very day
I'm gonna get some one, who can drive my blues away

I want her to drive them off, so they won't come back no more
Want her to drive them off, so they won't come back no more
From now on, mama, I said I'm gonna let you go

BAREFOOT BILL

Squabbling Blues

My baby done quit me
Talked all over
               I say town
Baby done quit me
Talked all over town
And I'm too good a man for to
Let that talk go 'round

Take the shoes I bought her
Bare foots on the
                 I say ground
Shoes I bought her, put her
Bare foots on the ground
Then the *great* Jack Frost said he
Sure gonna tear you down

Now Mister, Mister
Please to spare my
                I mean life
Mister, Mister
Please to spare my life
I got four little children
I got one little *bald*-headed wife

Now if I should die
State of Arkan-
               I say -sas
If I should die in the
State of Arkansas
I want you to send my body
Home to my mother-in-law

Said if
      she don't want it, baby
Give it to my maw
Said if my maw
          don't want it, baby
Give it to my paw

Said if my
        paw don't want it, baby
Give it to *Abbie* Lee
Said if *Abbie* don't want it, baby
Give it to my used to be

Said if
       she don't want it, baby
Cast it in the sea
Then these women in Greenville'll
Stop squabbling over me

Then I won't be worried
With these blues no
           I say more
Won't be worried
With these blues no more
Said it's train time now
Hear that ring I do adore

BAREFOOT BILL

My Crime

I got the blues for my baby
      She got the blues for
                    I say me
Blues for my baby
      She got the blues for me
But I can't see my baby
      And she can't see me

I'm gonna be condemned
      Early tomorrow
                    I say morn
Gonna be condemned
      Early tomorrow morn
But I am not guilty
      'Cause I ain't done no body wrong

My crime, my crime, I
      Really can't under-
                    I say stand
My crime, my crime, I
      Really can't understand
They got me 'scused of murder
      And I never harmed a man

Baby, please come down be-
      Fore my trial
                    I say day
Will you please come down
      On my trial day
So when I be condemned
      You can wipe my tears away

There's no need to cry
      And no need to
                        weep and mourn
They ain't no need to cry
      No need to weep and mourn
Just try to get some body
      To go on my bond

I think it's gonna be weeping
      I begin to
                I say mourn
It's gonna be weeping
      I begin to mourn
Said I'm a poor boy, yeah
      I sure ain't got no home

The jury found me guilty
      The judge say, Listen
                    I say here
The jury found me guilty
      The judge say, Listen here
It ain't no fine for you
      Get ready for the electric chair

Big Rock Jail

The
    high sheriff been here
                got my girl and gone
The high sheriff been here
                got my girl and gone
I say, left me moaning
           yes, I'm all alone

Well listen mister
         what
           have my baby done
Well listen mister
         what
           have my baby done
I just wanna know
           if she
              done any body wrong

He took her on down
           to that Big Rock Jail
He took her on down
           to that Big Rock Jail
And that brown was so evil
              nobody would go her bail

Now tell me who took her
           gun and
              hit her razor hand
You took her gun
        hit her razor hand
And you went wrong 'cause she ain't
                never harmed a man

My baby in jail and
           I can't get no sleep
I say my baby in jail and
            I can't get no sleep
I don't get nothing but the
            mean old high sheriff

Seven Sister Blues

Coal black woman
                    fry no meat for me
No coal black woman can
                    fry no meat for me
You know black is evil
                    that gal may poison me

I got a new way of spelling
                    sweet old Tennessee
New way of spelling
                    sweet old Tennessee
New way of spelling
                    sweet old Tennessee
Double T, double N,
                    double T, double S, U, Z

My girl rolled and tumbled
                    cried the whole night long
Rolled and tumbled
                    cried the whole night long
Rolled and tumbled
                    cried the whole night long
She received that message
                    that the man she loved was gone

                              (how'd she cry?)

Said my love's like water
                    it turns off and on
Love like water
                    turns off and on
Love like water
                    turns off and on
When you think I'm loving
                    I done took off and gone

When the death wagon rolled up
                    with the rumbling sound
Death wagon rolled up
                    with the rumbling sound
Death wagon rolled up
                    with the rumbling sound
Says I knowed by that
                    my gal was graveyard bound

EDWARD THOMPSON

Keep Your Windows Pinned

Keep your back door locked
                 baby, keep your windows pinned
Keep your back door locked
                 and keep your windows pinned
If your husband should knock
                 tell him you're cooking and he can't come in

You oughta buy you a bulldog
                 to watch us whilst we sleep
You oughta buy you a bulldog
                 to watch us whilst we sleep
So he can see your husband
                 if he makes a 'fore day creep

Wake up, baby
                 please don't be so still
Wake up, baby
                 please don't be so still
'Less you fixing a good way
                 to get your daddy killed

What's that, baby
                 pecking on your window pane
What's that, baby
                 pecking on your window pane
Say the stars is shining
                 I know it can't be rain

The big star's falling
                 I know it can't be long 'fore day
The big star's falling
                 I know it can't be long 'fore day
And I think it's time for me
                 to make my get a way

CLIFFORD GIBSON

CLIFFORD GIBSON

France Blues

Have you ever took a trip, baby, on the Mobile Line
       Hey lordy mama mama
       Hey lordy papa papa,
               Hollerin' 'bout the Mobile Line
That's the road to ride, baby, ease your troublin' mind

Well I got a letter, baby, this is the way it read
       Hey lordy mama mama
       Hey lordy papa papa,
               Hollerin' 'bout the way it read
Come home, come home, baby, 'cause your love is dead

Well I packed my suitcase, bundled up my clothes
       Hey lordy mama mama
       Hey lordy papa papa,
               Hollerin' 'bout bundlinup his clothes
When I got there she was layin' on the coolin' board

Well I took my baby, honey, to the buryin' ground
       Hey lordy mama mama
       Hey lordy papa papa,
               Hollerin' 'bout the buryin' ground
You oughta heard me hollerin' when they let her down

Well there's two black horses standin' on the buryin' ground
When I turned around *those big tears* run on down

When you go to heaven *gonna, babe, gonna* stop by France
       Hey lordy mama mama
       Hey lordy papa papa,
               Hollerin' 'bout stop by France
Gonna stop by there just to give these girls a chance

Baby, when I die don't bury daddy at all
   Hey lordy mama mama
   Hey lordy papa papa,
       Hollerin' 'bout bury-daddy-at-all
Well pickle daddy's bones, baby, in alkyhol

Well the boat is up the river, baby, and she won't come down
   Hey lordy mama mama
   Hey lordy papa papa,
       Hollerin' 'bout she won't come down
Well I b'lieve to my soul, baby, boat is water bound

Baby, when I die put daddy's picture in a frame
   Hey lordy mama mama
   Hey lordy papa papa,
       Hollerin' 'bout in a frame
So where daddy's goin' you can see him just the same

Hello heaven, daddy want to give you a telephone
   Hey lordy mama mama
   Hey lordy papa papa,
       Hollerin' 'bout the telephone
So you can talk with daddy anytime when he's gone

Two White Horses in a Line

There's two white horses in a line
There's two white horses in a line
There's two white horses
                in / a / line
Gonna carry me to my burying ground

My heart stopped beating and my hands got cold
My heart stopped beating and my hands got cold
My heart stopped beating
                   and my hands / got / cold
It's a long old way and I had to go

Did you ever hear the church bell tone
Did you ever hear the church bell tone
Did you ever hear
              church / bell / tone
Then you know that the poor boy's dead and gone

It's a long old lane and it ain't got no end
It's a long old lane and it ain't got no end
It's a long old lane
              ain't got / no / end
It's a bad old wind don't never change

Go dig my grave with a silver spade
Go dig my grave with a silver spade
Go dig my grave
              sil- / ver / spade
You can lower me down with a golden chain

Did you ever hear the coffin sound
Did you ever hear the coffin sound
Did you ever hear
              co- / ffin / sound
Then you know that the poor boy's in the ground

No More Good Water

There is no more good water
Because this pond is dry

I walked down to the river
Then turned around and *cried*

If the fishes in the water
Had my blues they'd die

Got a head full of *poisonous*
My baby got a rambling mind

Hey pretty mama
Tell me what have you done

JAYBIRD COLEMAN

Georgia

If It Looks Like Jelly, Shakes Like Jelly, It Must Be Gel-a-tine

Have you met Miss Mabel Green
Who makes all kind of gel-a-tine?
'Cause she sells it very high
To get any better you need not try
I've known her for a great long time
All kind of jelly is in her line
If it look like jelly, shake like jelly
      it must be gel-a-tine

If you chance to pass her way
You will hear her singing most every day
If it look like jelly, shake like jelly
      it must be gel-a-tine

You won't try it, you gonna buy it
     here's just what I mean
Maybe your jelly *kid* is good
You be satisfied to make your—
If it look like jelly, shake like jelly
      it must be gel-a-tine

Mabel's cooking is a treat
Her jelly roll cannot be beat
She always keep them fresh and clean
Clean her jelly down in between
If it look like jelly, shake like jelly
      it must be gel-a-tine

Can't get away, 'tain't no bluff
She sure knows how to strut her stuff
Now try her once and you will see
Why she's *in* her company
If it look like jelly, shake like jelly
      it must be gel-a-tine

Telling all you men she will treat you nice
To get her jelly go and pay her price
If it look like jelly, shake like jelly
      it must be gel-a-tine

There's no jelly in town sweet like mine
All of you who wants it must fall in line
Now she sold a little jelly to the man next door
He keeps laying round here for more
If it look like jelly, shake like jelly
      it must be gel-a-tine

            CHARLIE LINCOLN (HICKS)

Chain Gang Trouble

The train
run off
nine mile
from town
and killed
little Lu-
la dead.

Her head
was found
in the dri-
ving wheel;
her body
have never
been seen.

I cried,
I moaned,
I cried,
I moaned:
I asked
how long,
how long?

I asked
my captain
for the time
of day:
say he throwed
his watch
away.

If I listened
at my mother
in a far-
ther day
I never
would-a been here
today.

If I ever
get back home,
oh baby,
to stay
I never
be treated
this-a-way.

How long,
how long,
how long,
how long,
how long,
oh how
I can go on?

I rise
with the blues
and I wake
with the blues;
nothing I
can't get
but bad news.

CHARLIE LINCOLN (HICKS)

Depot Blues

Standing at the station
                        waiting for my train to come
Standing at the station
                        waiting for my train to come
Singing, Hurry up moonlight
                            let the morrow come

You can drive me to your station
                                but you cannot make me ride your train
You can drive me to your station
                                but you cannot make me ride your train
And if you treat me mean, mama, you
                                sure lost speed again

Do not call my self leaving
                            but you are driving me a way
Do not call my self leaving
                        but it's you are driving me a way
And when my blues is over
                        you gon' be sorry some sweet day

She got up last night
                    she crawled around my bed
She got uplast night
                    she crawled around my bed
                            (wonder what's the matter now)
I'm gon' love you a long time, daddy, or
                                else I will see you dead

Mmmmmm
            mmmm mmmm mmmm
Mm mm mm
            mmmm mmmm mmmm
That gal I love
            won't act right at all

I woke up this morning
                        with the blues three different ways
I woke up this morning
                        with the blues three different ways
Had two minds to leave you
                        only one to stay

CHARLIE LINCOLN (HICKS)

I left my kid gal
                    standing in the door
I left my kid gal
                    standing in the door
Hollering, Daddy, daddy
                    you ain't obliged to go

Rather drink muddy water, go
                         sleep in a hollow tree
Rather drink muddy water
                    go sleep in a hollow tree
Than to hear my kid gal
                    say she don't want me

CHARLIE LINCOLN (HICKS)

Barbecue Blues

Woke up this morning, gal
               'twixt mid night and day
I woke up this morning
               'twixt mid night and day
With my head on my pillow where my brownie used to lay

I know I ain't good looking
               teeth don't shine like pearls
I ain't good looking
            teeth don't shine like pearls
So glad good looks don't take you through this world

Gon' starch my jumper, mama
               iron my overhauls
Gon' starch my jumper
            iron my overhauls
My brown done quit me, God knows she had it all

I'm gon' tell you now, gal
               like Gypsy told the Jew
Gon' tell you now, gal
            like Gypsy told the Jew
If you don't want me, it's a cinch I don't want you

Did you ever dream lucky
               wake up cold in hand
Did you ever dream lucky
            wake up cold in hand
That's a mighty true sign your brown got some other man

My mama told me
            papa told me too
My mama told me
            papa told me too
Some brown skin woman
             gon' be·the death of you

BARBECUE BOB (HICKS)

BARBECUE BOB (HICKS)

She's Gone Blues

When you was down
      sick down on your bed
When you was down
      sick down on your bed
Nobody brought you your medicine
I still brought you bread

You is up today
    looking good again
You is up today
    looking good again
I knocked on your door
Won't even let me in

But the sun gonna shine
      once more in my back door
But the sun gonna shine
      once more in my back door
It's true I love you, sweet mama, but you
Can't mistreat me no more

I was standing at the terminal
      humped all up and cried
I was standing at the terminal
      humped all up and cried
Crying, I wonder what train
Taken that brown of mine

And I run to the telephone
                           took the receiver down
And I run to the telephone
                           took the receiver down
I say, Hello Central
Give me Doctor Brown

My baby looks for me at
                           any old hour at night
My baby looks for me at
                           any old hour at night
No matter when I goes there, she
Never turn out all her lights

Mmmmmmmmmmmmmmmmm
                           lord lord lord lord
Mmmmmmmmmmm mmmmmmm
                           lord lord lord lord
You womens in Atlanta
Treat these men like a dog

Before this time, brown
                           maybe another year
I'll be up the country
Drinking that cool canned beer

BARBECUE BOB (HICKS)

Cold Wave Blues

Winter time is coming
                 you can hear that howling wind
Winter time is coming
                 I can hear that howling wind
You better get ready
                 loving summer's done gone in

Old Jack Frost is now ready
                 to put that thing on you
Old Jack Frost is now ready to
                 put that thing on you
If you don't stop him
                 that'll be a howdy-do

Cold wave make me shiver
                 cold wave get my goat
Cold wave make me shiver
                 cold wave get my goat
I feel so disgusted:
                 ain't got no overcoat

Shoes ain't got no bottom
                 feets pattin' on the ground
Shoes ain't got no bottom
                 feets pattin' on the ground
When it start to snowing
                 be Alabama bound

Wintertime is coming
                 I ain't got a single suit
Wintertime is coming
                 I ain't got a single suit
With my pocket empty
                 tell me what I'm going to do

BARBECUE BOB (HICKS)

Mmmmmmmmmmmmmmmmmmmmmm
                                 lord lord lord lord
Mmmmmmmmmmmmmmmmmmmmmm
                                 lord lord lord lord
Mmmmmmmmmmmmmmmmmmmmmm
                                 Mmmmmmmm mmmm mmmmmm mm

    (Lord Lord, boys, this wind 'bout to cut my throat)

Wintertime is here now
                    it's right up on me
Wintertime is coming
                    slipping right up on me
Well, I mean, look, mama
                    what I'm going to do?

Cold wave, chilly cold wave
                         listen to me please
Cold wave, chilly cold wave
                         listen to me please
Cold wave, cold wave
                    don't be so hard on me

                                                        BARBECUE BOB (HICKS)

Ease It to Me Blues

Some people long to have plenty money
                              some want their wine and song
Some long to have a-plenty money
                              some want their wine and song
All I crave is my sweet mama
                    that I dreams about all night long

Once I had a dear sweet mama
                         and I didn't treat her right
Once I had a sweet mama
                    I didn't treat her right
She left this town
               with a teasing brown
                              and her name was Mandy White

     I'm leaving town today

     I'm leaving town today

     When I find that gal
     This what I'm going to say:

I've got those
               slip it to me
               ease it to me
               mama don't hold it back
Lord I've got those
               slip it to me
               ease it to me
               mama don't hold it back
Let me have,
Have your loving blues

You can have my money
                    all I want to *do is sack*
You can have my money
                    all I want to *do is sack*
I ain't got no time to lose
                    I got to hurry on back

    Now I've got those
                        slip it to me
                        ease it to me
                        please don't hold it back
    I got those
                slip it to me
                ease it to me
                mama don't hold it back
    Just let me have,
    Have your loving blues

When I find that aggravating papa
                            that tried to two-time me
When I find that aggravating papa
                            that tried to two-time me
I know I spend a great long spell
                        up in the penitentiary

I'm gonna buy me a gun,
                    airplane and a submarine
I'm gonna buy me a gun,
                    airplane and a submarine
I'm gonna kill every body
                    ever treat me mean

BARECUE BOB (HICKS)

PEG LEG HOWELL

Lowdown Rounder's Blues

Just a worried old rounder
                with a troublesome mind
Just a worried old rounder
                with a troublesome mind
'Cause of unluck from hardship
                    fate to me have been unkind

I wouldn't listen to my mother
                    wouldn't listen to my dad
I wouldn't listen to my mother
                    wouldn't listen to my dad
And by my reckless living
                I've put myself in bad

       (I wouldn't listen to nobody; I was headlong; wouldn't hear what
       nobody said; my mama talked to me all the time; but I was just a
       way'rd child; wouldn't listen to her.)

I ain't trusting no body
             I'm 'fraid of my self
I ain't trusting no body
             I'm 'fraid of my self
I've been too lowdown
             life have put me on the shelf

My friends has turned against me
                  smiling in my face
My friends has turned against me
                  smiling in my face
Since I been so disobedient
                 I must travel in disgrace

I cannot shun the devil
             he stay right by my side
I cannot shun the devil
             he stay right by my side
There is no way to cheat him
                I'm so dissatisfied

Ain't nobody wants me
             they wouldn't be in my shoes
Ain't nobody wants me
             they wouldn't be in my shoes
I feel so disgusted
             I've got them lowdown rounder blues

No No Blues

I woke up this morning my good gal was gone
I woke up this morning my good gal was gone
Stood by my bedside I hung my head I hung my head and moaned

I walked down the street I couldn't be satisfied
I walked down the street I couldn't be satisfied
I had them no no blues I couldn't keep from I couldn't keep from crying

'Tain't none of my business but it sure ain't right
'Tain't none of my business but it sure ain't right
Take another man's gal walk the streets all walk the streets all night

Take a mighty crooked woman to treat a good man wrong
Take a mighty crooked woman to treat a good man wrong
Take a mighty mean man take another man's take another man's home

I'm a stranger here I just blowed in your town
I'm a stranger here I just blowed in your town
If I ask for a favor don't turn me, don't turn me down

I'm long and tall like a cannon ball
I'm long and tall like a cannon ball
Take a long tall man make a good gal make a good gal squall

If I mistreat you I sure don't mean no harm
If I mistreat you I sure don't mean no harm
'Cause I'm a motherless child don't know right from don't know right from wrong

I ain't no gambler and I don't play no pool
I ain't no gambler and I don't play no pool
I'm a rambling roller jelly baking, jelly baking fool

She's low and squatty right down on the ground
She's low and squatty right down on the ground
She's a light weighted mama shook her kid man shook her kid man down

I'm a stranger here I come in on the train
I'm a stranger here I come in on the train
I long to hear some good gal call my good gal call my name

WILLIE BAKER

No Woman No Nickel

I'm cold in hand
        can't get nothing here
Cold in hand
        can't get nothing here
I'm hungry as a hound
        I can't travel no where

I can't help but to worry
        how my good friend done
Can't help but to worry
        how my good friend done
Spent my money by the dollar
        now won't give me nickel one

Mama told me
        times and times again
Yes, mama told me
        times and times again
Anybody laughs in my face
        just can't be my friend

Lord look down on poor me
        pity my worried cares
Lord look down on me
        pity my worried cares
Help me to rise once more
        I'm gonna change my free-hearted ways

Just give me one friend to
        keep me from feeling so sad
Just give me one friend to
        keep me from feeling so sad
Lord you know I want a friend
        like the one what Adam had

BLIND WILLIE McTELL

Savannah Mama

Mmmmmm
        lordy lordy lord
Mmmmmmmmmm
         lordy lordy lord
Say the woman I love
           treats me just, *just* like a dog

I love you, baby
        but your ways I just can't stand
I love you, mama
        but your ways I just can't stand
Say you walked away and left me
          good gal, with another man

Going back to Savannah, mama
         and sign my initial down
Going back to Savannah, baby
         and sign my initial down
Atlanta mens all hate me
        and the women don't want me 'round

Going back to Savannah, baby
         and write my initial on the wall
Going back to Savannah, mama
         and write my initial on the wall
'Cause these north Georgia women
          don't mean me no good at all

        (Play that thing low and lonesome, boy)

Mmmmmmmmmm
        baby, ain't it hard ain't it hard ain't it hard
Ohhhhhhhh
        baby, ain't it hard ain't it hard ain't it hard
Well I'd like to love you, baby
         but your good man got me barred

BLIND WILLIE McTELL

Three Women Blues

Got three womens:
                        yellow, brown, and black
I got three womens:
                        yellow, brown, and black
It'll take the Governor of Georgia
                                    to judge one of these women I like

One for in the morning
                        and one for late at night
One for in the morning
                        and one for late at night
I got one for the noon time
                        to treat your daddy right

These blues at midnight
                        they don't leave me till day
These blues at midnight
                        they don't leave me till day
I didn't have none of my three women
                                    to drive these blues away

One is a Memphis yellow
                        the other   's a Savannah brown
One is a Memphis yellow
                        the other   's a Savannah brown
One is a Statesboro dark-skin
                        she'll really turn your damper down

Now, if I had a-listened
                        to what my three women said
Now, if I had a-listened to
                        what my three women said
I'd-a been at home sleeping
                        in a doggone feather bed

BLIND WILLIE McTELL

Statesboro Blues

Wake up mama
        turn your lamp down lo-ow
Wake up mama
        turn your lamp down low
Have you got the nerve to drive Papa McTell from your door?

My mother died and left me reckless,
        My daddy died and left me wild wild wild
Mother died and left me reckless,
        Daddy died and left me wild wild wild
Lord I'm not good looking, but I'm some sweet woman's angel child.

She's a mighty mean woman
        do me this-a-way
She's a mighty mean woman
        do me this-a-way
When I leave this time, pretty mama, I'm going away to stay.

I once loved a woman
        better than I'd ever seen
I once loved a woman
        better than I'd ever seen
Treated me like I was a king and she was a doggone queen.

        Sister tell your brother
        Brother tell your aunt
        Now auntie tell your uncle
        Uncle tell my cousin
        Now cousin tell my friend
Going up the country:
        mama, don't you want to go?
May take me a fair brown—I may take one or two more.

Big Eighty left Savannah
        lord, it did not stop
You oughta saw that colored fireman when he got that boiler hot
You can
        reach over in the corner, mama, and hand me my traveling shoes
You know by that I've got them Statesboro blues.

        Papa—
        Sister got 'em
        Auntie got 'em
        Brother got 'em
        Friend got 'em
        I got 'em
I woke up this morning
        I had them Statesboro blues
I looked over in the corner: grandma and grandpa had 'em too.

        BLIND WILLIE McTELL

Searching the Desert for the Blues

You may search
the ocean,
you might go 'cross the deep blue sea;
      but mama you'll never find
      another hot shot like me.

I followed
my baby
from the station to the train,
      and the blues came down
      like dark night showers of rain.

I left her
at the station
wringing her hands and crying;
      I told her she had a home
      just as long as I got mine.

I've got
two women
and you can't tell 'em apart;
      I got one in my bosom,
      the other one in my heart.

The one
in my bosom—
she's in Tennessee;
      and the one in my heart
      don't even give a darn for me.

I used to say
a married woman
was the sweetest thing that ever been born;
      but I've changed that thing:
      you better let married women alone.

Take my
advice:
let these married women be;
      'cause their husbands 'll grab you,
      beat you ragged as a cedar tree.

When a woman
say she love you
'bout good as she do herself,
      I don't pay her no 'tention—
      tell that same line to somebody else.

                                            BLIND WILLIE McTELL

I really
don't believe
no woman in the whole round world do right:
        act like an angel in the daytime,
        mess by the ditch at night.

I'm going
pretty mama,
please don't break this rule;
        that's why I'm searching
        these deserts for the blues.

I'm going
pretty mama,
searching these deserts now;
        that's why I'm walking
        my baby home any how.

Lord
oh lord
lordy lordy lord
        oh lordy lord
        lord lord lord.

When a woman
say she love you
'bout good as she do herself,
        I don't pay her no 'tention—
        tell that same line to somebody else.

Lord lord
lord lord lord.

Female comments between verses have been omitted.

BLIND WILLIE McTELL

Talking to Myself

Eeee wah-wah-wah-wah-wah
Eeee wah-wah
Eeee wah-wah wah wah

Good Lord
Good Lord
Send me an angel down
Can't spare you no angel
                but I'll swear I'll send you a teasing brown

That new
Way of loving
Mama, it must be best
These here Georgia women
                just won't let Mr. Samuel rest

There was a crowd
Out on the corner
Wondered who
Could it be
It weren't a thing but the women
                trying to get to me

I even went down
To the depot
With my suitcase in my hand
Crying, the womens all crying
                Mr. Sammy, won't you be my man

My mama
She told me
When I was a boy playing mumble peg
Don't drink no black cow's milk
                don't you eat no black hen's egg

Black man
Give you a dollar, mama
He won't think it's nothing strange
A yellow man 'll give you a dollar
                but he'll want back 95 cents change

You may call
Me a cheater
Pretty boy, I'll real treat you
But if you'll allow me a chance
                I'll gnaw your backbone half in two

                BLIND WILLIE McTELL (BLIND SAMUEL)

I took a trip
Out on the ocean
Walked the sand of the deep blue sea
I found a crab with a shrimp
                    trying to do the shimmy-shee

I want to tell you
Something, mama
Seem mighty doggone strange
You done mess 'round, gal
                    and made me break my yo-yo string

Honey, I ain't
Gonna be
Your old work-ox no more
You done mess 'round, baby
                    and let your doggone ox get poor

My mama
She got a mojo
Believe she tried to keep it hid
Papa Samuel got something
                    to find that mojo with

        (Take it for me)

I even
Heard a rumbling
Deep down in the ground
It weren't a thing but the women
                    trying to run me down

        (Play it low and lonesome)

BLIND WILLIE McTELL (BLIND SAMUEL)

Drive Away Blues

I believe that if I had my
                sweet woman's heart in my hand
                        in my hand
I believe that if I had my
                sweet woman's heart in my hand
                        in my hand
I believe I could teach her
              how to treat a real good man

I drink so much whisky, mama
                  I can't hardly talk
                  hardly talk
                        sweet mama, hardly talk
I drink so much whisky
              I can't hardly talk
              hardly talk
Well, it's done addled on my brain
                people, I can't hardly walk

How my poor heart weeped and weary
                  baby, when you drove me away
                      drove me away
                          sweet mama, you drove me away
How my poor heart weeped and weary
                  baby, when you drove me away
It was crying for poor boy McTell
              some old rainy day

Going up on the Lookout Mountain
                and dived in Niagra Falls
                    Niagra Falls
                        sweet mama, Niagra Falls
Going up on the Lookout Mountain
                and I dived in Niagra Falls
                    Niagra Falls
Seem like to me I can hear my
              Atlanta mama call
            I hear her call

BLIND WILLIE McTELL

Don't fret and worry
         and don't grieve after me
                sweet mama
                after me
Don't grieve and worry
         and don't fret after me
                after me
Don't you scream and cry
         'Cause I'm going back to Tennessee

           (Oh boy, play the Drive Away Blues for me)

           (That's all I know)

Can't read and write
         can't even spell my name
            spell my name
                I know, spell my name
Can't read and write
         can't even spell my name
You drove me away
         and drove my heart insane

           (But I won't be back no more, mama)

                                             BLIND WILLIE McTELL

Travelin' Blues

(I was traveling through South Americas
Walked up to a lady's house
Called her "grandma"
Didn't know her name
She give me something to eat
Walked on down the road
I heard a old train getting off like this:

I heard a old bell ring kinda like this:

I went on down and I heard a old whistle blow
I heard it say:)

Look-a-yonder

Look-a-yonder

At the women

At the women

(I went on, then I began to sing to the engineer:)

Mr. Engineer
        let a man ride the blind
Mr. Engineer
        let a poor man ride the blind
Said, I wouldn't mind it, fella
             but you know this train ain't mine

(I begin to hear that old fella blowing longs and shorts
Here the way he blowed:

Then I begin to sing to him one more time:)

You's a cruel fireman
         low down engineer
You's a cruel fireman
         low down engineer
I'm trying to hobo my way
           and you leave me standing here

(Then I goes on *to follow him* and begin to sing Poor Boy to him

And he begin to smile in my face:)

BLIND WILLIE McTELL

Get up fella
           ride all around the world
Get up fella
           ride all around the world
Poor boy
       you ain't got no girl

           (Then I begin to hear him tell me about those cheese and eggs

           How he wanted 'em fixed
           Heard him say:)

Scrambled down

Scrambled do-own

Scrambled down

           (Then I begin to hear him tell me about them cheese and eggs

           I heard him say:)

Cheese

Eggs

Dinner

Dinner

           (Then I begin to hear him tell me about *Emery*:)

I love you *Emery*
I love you true
I love you *Emerald*
Tell the world I do

Em

North Carolina / Virginia

Mojo Hiding Woman

Now it's stin-
gy mama
don't be so stingy with me,
stingy mama
don't be so stingy with me;
you's a good little girl
but you so stingy with me.

Do your water
out your pitcher,
mama, let your bowl go dry,
do your water out your pitcher
let your bowl go dry?
Then I give you my loving, mama,
mama, just before you die.

My gal
got a mojo
she won't let me see,
said my baby got a mojo
she won't let me see;
one morning 'bout four o'clock
she eased that old thing on me.

Now mama,
mama,
you can't keep that mojo hid,
hey hey mama,
can't keep that mojo hid;   (why, boy?)
'cause I got something
just to find that old mojo with.

Now my mama
left me something
she called that stingeree,
my mama left me something
called that stingeree;
I done sting my baby
and she won't stay away from me.

Pistol Slapper Blues

I can tell
my dog
any where I hear him bark;
I can tell my rider
by I feel her in the dark.

You's a cold
blooded murderer
when you want me out your way;
says that's all right, mama:
you gonna need my help some day.

And I feel
like slapping
my pistol in your face:
let some brown skin woman
be here to take your place.

Hey hey
hey yeah
Mmmmmm mm hmmm
let some brown skin woman
be here to take your place.

Now you know
you didn't want me
when you lay down 'cross my bed,
drinking your moonshine whiskey, mama,
talking all out your head.

      Now gimme the money baby,
      I'll catch that train and go;
      You don't have to kill me,
      'Cause you don't want me no more;
      Hey—
      'Cause you don't want me no more;
      Now you gimme the money baby,
      And I'll catch that train and go.

Now if you see
my rider,
tell her I said bring it home;
I ain't had no loving
since my gal been gone.

There's two
kind of people
in the world that I can't stand:
that's a lying woman
and a monkey man.

Mmmmmm
mmmmmm
mmmmmmmmmmmmmmmmmmm
mmmmmmmmmmmmmm
mmmmmmmmmmmmmmm

347

Lost Lover Blues

And I went
down
by that freight depot
and that freight train come rolling by.
   Lord and I sure ain't got no loving baby now:
   And I sure ain't got no loving baby now.

And I went
Off
in that far distant land;
I weren't there long 'fore I got a telegram,   (what'd it say?)
   Saying, Man won't you please come home:
   Now man won't you please come home.

And I went
back home;
I looked on the bed,
and that best old friend I had was dead.
   Lord and I ain't got no loving baby now:
   And I ain't got no loving baby now.

And I'm sorry,
sorry,
sorry to my heart,
but that best old friend some day must part.
   Lord ain't got no loving baby now:
   And I ain't got—loving baby now.

        (play it for me now)

Now as sure
as the birds
playing in the sky above;
life ain't worth living if you ain't with the one you love.
   Lord and I ain't got no loving baby now:
   Lord I ain't got no lover now.

If I knowed
you didn't love me
and didn't want me too,
I would take mor-phine and die.
   Lord I ain't got no loving baby now:
   And I ain't got no loving baby now.

          BLIND BOY FULLER

Bye Bye Baby Blues

Which-a-way
which-a-way
do that blood red river run?
Run from my wondow
to that rising sun.

Now that dumper
says, Loader,
please send me six foot of clay,
'cause that blood red river, mama,
is rising six foot a day.

Go down
to the camp,
and tell my brother Bill,
the woman he's loving is
sure gonna get him killed.

           (yeah)

Now reason why
these here men
they sure don't draw no more,
right from that long table
back to that commissary door.

Now I love
to hear
that M & O whistle blow;
I'm in a world of trouble, God
knows, and I got to go.

           (yeah)   (yeah)

Now I got
two women,
and I don't know one apart:
there's one in my bosom,
t'other one in my heart.

You Got to Go Down

You better learn how to treat everybody
For you got to go down. You got to go down.
You better learn how to treat everybody
You got to go down. You got to go down.
    Ashes to ashes and dust to dust
    The life you're living won't do to trust
You better learn how to treat everybody
For you got to go down.

(Some of you people don't realize it; taking the world by storm;
don't even know how to treat your family; doing all kind of ways;
living all kind of lives; saying everything before your children; treat
your wife all kind of ways; treat your husband every kind of way;
God says:)

You better learn how to treat your husband
You got to go down. You got to go down.
You better learn how to treat your husband
You got to go down. You got to go down.
    Ashes to ashes and dust to dust
    The life you're living won't do to trust
You better learn how to treat your husband
You got to go down.

(*Cause* the mother to get careless; but God tells you how to raise a
child; you got to *place you* say everything before the child; and do
everything before; God says:)

You better learn how to live 'fore children
You got to go down. You got to go down.
You better learn how to live 'fore children
You got to go down. You got to go down.
    Ashes to ashes and dust to dust
    The life you're living won't do to trust
You better learn how to live 'fore children
You got to go down.

(And you're traveling through the world; and don't know how to
treat your wife; and giving everybody else the thing that you ought to
give to your wife; God says:)

You better learn how to treat your companion
You got to go down. You got to go down.
You better learn how to treat your companion
You got to go down. You got to go down.
    Ashes to ashes and dust to dust
    The life you're living won't do to trust
You better learn how to treat your companion
You got to go down.

(And you're traveling through the world; some people think; just because a man is a drunkard; and will drink liquor sometime and cut up and raise sand; if they come and carry him to your house; you got to carry him in before the Lord; when God save him *you can suggest saving your own self;* God says:)

You better learn how to treat that drunkard
You got to go down. You got to go down.
You better learn how to treat that drunkard
You got to go down. You got to go down.
    Ashes to ashes and dust to dust
    The life you're living won't do to trust
You better learn how to treat that drunkard
You got to go down. You got to go down.
You better learn how to treat that drunkard
For you got to go down. You got to go down.
You better learn how to treat that drunkard
You got to go down. You got to go down.
    Ashes to ashes and dust to dust
    The life you're living won't do to trust
You better learn how to treat that drunkard
For you got to go down.

BLIND GARY DAVIS

Blow Gabriel

Blow Gabriel!
Blow Gabriel!
Blow Gabriel!
Blow Gabriel!
Gonna walk and talk, tell it at the Judgement
Walk and talk, tell it at the Judgement, God
What you gonna do at the Judgement
What you gonna do at the Judgement
No need to run at the Judgement
No need to run at the Judgement, God
The sun'll start running at the Judgement
The sun'll start running at the Judgement, God
No use to run at the Judgement
No use to run at the Judgement
Blow: Gabriel!
Blow Gabriel!
Blow Gabriel!

Blow Gabriel
Blow Gabriel at the Judgement, God
Blow Gabriel
Blow Gabriel
Oh the Big Book is open at the Judgement
The Big Book is open at the
       Said the moon is bleeding
       Moon is bleeding
       Rocks is melting
       Trees are bowing
       Seas are boiling
       Graves are busting
       What you gonna do—
       What you gonna do—
       What you gonna do—
       Oh sinner!
Gonna walk and talk, tell it—

       Gonna meet my father
       Gonna meet my father
       Oh Lord
       Oh my Lord
       Oh my Lord
       It's gonna be a time
       Gonna meet my brother
       Gonna meet my brother
       Gonna meet my father
       Gonna meet my father

One Way Gal

There's one thing I like about that gal of mine
There's one thing I like about that gal of mine
There's one thing I like about that gal of mine
She treats me right and loves me all the time

Sometimes I'm broke and blue as I can be
Sometimes I'm broke and blue as I can be
Sometimes I'm broke and blue as I can be
But still my baby she looks after me

She walked in the rain till her feet got soaking wet
She walked in the rain till her feet got soaking wet
She walked in the rain till her feet got soaking wet
And these are the words she said to every man she met:

Mister, change a dollar and give me one lousy dime
Mister, change a dollar and give me one lousy dime
Mister, change a dollar and give me one lousy dime
So I can feed this hungry man of mine

She took me over to a cabaret
She took me over to a cabaret
She took me over to a cabaret
I ate and drank and then I went away

This gal of mine, she's one way all the time
This gal of mine, she's one way all the time
This gal of mine, she's one way all the time
She takes the blues away and satisfies my mind

WILLIAM MOORE

St. Louis

Jersey Belle Blues

My nights is so lonely
                    days is so doggone long
My bed room is so lonely
                    every doggone thing is wrong
You know I ain't had no milk and butter
                    since my Jersey Belle been gone

My milk cow has been gone
                    three long weeks today
I'm wondering what is keeping
                    my Jersey Belle away
If I ever get my Jersey Belle back
                    she'll never go away no more

I know my Jersey Belle
                    boys, by the way she low
She called me, she called me
                    so many times before
If I ever get her home again
                    I'll never let my Jersey Belle leave no more

I got a good milk cow
                    but her head is hard like a block of wood
She's a number one Jersey cow
                    but her head is like a block of wood
Boys, it's a mighty tough titty
                    but the milk is so doggone good

I know my Jersey Belle
                    by the way she chew her cud
She keeps all of the milk all the time
                    she won't be gentle like a good cow should
Boys, it's a very tough titty
                    but the milk is so doggone good

LONNIE JOHNSON

Careless Love

Love, oh love, oh careless love
Love, love, oh careless love
    You have caused me to weep
    You have caused me to moan
You have caused me to leave my happy home

Don't never drive a stranger from your door
Don't never drive a stranger from your door
    It may be your best friend knocking
    At your door
It may be your brother: you will never know

Careless love, look how you carried me down
Careless love, look how you carried me down
    You caused me to lose my mother
    And she's laying in six feet of ground
Careless love, I can't let you carry me down

Careless love, you drove me through the rain and snow
Careless love, you drove me through the rain and snow
    You have robbed me out of my silver
    And out of all of my gold
I'll be damned if you rob me outa my soul

You worried my mother until she died
You caused my father to lose his mind
    Now damn you, I'm going to shoot you
    And shoot you four or five times
And stand over you until you finish dying

LONNIE JOHNSON

Keep It Clean

I went to the river: couldn't get across,
I jumped on your papa 'cause I thought he was a horse;
                    Now I
                    rode him on over,
                    give him a Coca-Coly,
                    lemon sody,
                    saucer of ice cream;
                    takes soap and water
                    for to keep it clean.

Up she jumped, down she fell,
Her mouth flew open like a mushry shell;
                    Now
                    ride her over,
                    give her a Coca-Coly,
                    lemon sody,
                    saucer of ice cream;
                    takes soap and water
                    for to keep it clean.

Your sister was a teddy, your daddy was a bear,
Put the muzzle on your mama 'cause she had bad hair;
                    Now
                    ride her on over,
                    give her a Coca-Coly,
                    lemon sody,
                    saucer of ice cream;
                    takes soap and water
                    for to keep it clean.

If you want to hear that elephant laugh,
Take him down to the river and wash his yes yes yes;
                    Now
                    ride him over,
                    give him a Coca-Coly,
                    lemon sody,
                    saucer of ice cream;
                    takes soap and water
                    for to keep it clean.

If you want to go to heaven when you d / i / e,
You got to put on your collar and your t / i / e;
                    Now
                    ride him over,
                    give him a Coca-Coly,
                    lemon sody,
                    saucer of ice cream;
                    takes soap and water
                    for to keep it clean.

CHARLIE JORDAN

If you want to get the rabbits out the l / o / g,
You got to put on the stump like a d / o / g;
                    Now
                    ride him over,
                    give him a Coca-Coly,
                    lemon sody,
                    saucer of ice cream;
                    takes soap and water
                    for to keep it clean.

Run here doctor, run here fast,
See what's the matter with his yes yes yes;
                    Now
                    ride him over,
                    give him a Coca-Coly,
                    lemon sody,
                    saucer of ice cream;
                    takes soap and water
                    for to keep it clean.

Hunkie Tunkie

Baby, I'm going up town
Tell the
Chief of police
My
Woman done quit me, I can't
See no peace
She
Keep me worried
Bothered all the time
'Cause she keep me worried
I'm bothered all the time

Well I love you, woman
Love your
Husband too
I have to
Love your husband to get to
Be with you
'Cause
He don't allow no
Man around his house
Because he don't allow no
Man around his house

My mama told me
My
Papa too
Don't
Let no woman be the
Death of you
'Cause
She didn't allow me
To stay out all night long
Because she didn't allow me
To stay out all night long

What you gonna do when they
Tear your
Barrel house down
Gonna
Pack my suitcase, hunt some
Other town
Now
Gonna do when they
Tear your barrel house down
Gonna pack my suitcase
Hunt some other town

Well they say everybody talking 'bout your
Honkie Tonkie Blues

CHARLIE JORDAN

Everybody talking 'bout your
Honkie Tonkie Blues
Well it's every body talking 'bout your
Mothern Honkie Tonkie Blues

Well they say everybody talking 'bout your
Honkie tonkie baby
You oughta see that curly-headed monkey-head
Head is curly
Baby, and bushy too
'Cause her head is curly
Baby, and bushy too

Skin Man

Skin man's hollering
                    passing right by my door
Well the skin man's hollering
                        passing right by my door
Well he's hollering "Skin"
                    every where he goes

Some begs a nickel
                some, some begs a dime
Some begs a nickel
                some, some begs a dime
Some begs the jelly to that
                    teasing brown of mine

Well it's skins oh skins
                    skin: skin-skin-skin
Well it's skins and skins
                    skin: skin skin
I'm going away old skin, but I'm
                        coming back again

Oh skin man
            standing by your door
Lord I saw the old skin man come
                        passing by your door
And they holler "Skins"
                    every where they go

Let me tell you
            what the skin mens'll do
Oh let me tell you
            what the skin mens'll do
Well they sell your wife skins and
                    take her away from you

Titanic Blues

Early one morning
                just about 4 o'clock
It was early one morning
                  just about 4 o'clock
When the old Titanic
             'gin to reel and rock

Smith took his glasses and
                    walked out to the front
Captain Smith took his glasses, he
                        walked out to the front
And he spied the iceberg a-coming
                      oh lord, had to bump

Some was drinking
               some was playing cards
And it's some was drinking
                   some was playing cards
Some was in the corner
               praying to their God

Little children cried mama
                  mama what shall we do
Little children crying mama
                  mama what shall we do
Captain Smith said, Children
                I'll take care of you

'Tanic sinking
          in the deep blue sea
Ti-tanic sinking
           in the deep blue sea
And the band all playing
               Nearer Oh My God to Thee

Poor Man Blues

And it's never mind, never mind, baby
          I've got my doggone eyes on you
And it's never mind, never mind, baby
          got my eyes on you
And some old day, pretty baby
        do like I want you to do

When I was sick and down
        you drove me from your door
I was sick and down, baby
        drove me from your door
Now you know how I was a poor man
          sleeping out in the ice and snow

Yes, baby
    I'm gonna see you when you, baby,
            do something I swear is wrong
See you, baby,
      when you do something I swear is wrong
When you mistreat me, baby,
        I'm gonna send you clear back home

That's all right for you, baby,
        I even pawned my watch and ring
That's all right, baby,
      pawned my watch and ring
I done give you my money
       I done give you most anything

HENRY TOWNSEND

Telephone Arguin' Blues

There's so many people
                    arguing over the telegram
There's so many people
                    arguing over the telegram
This *brought a run through* my head
                            just like a *stone in sand*

Early this morning
                    trying to get a news through
Early this morning
                    trying to get a news over the line
Lord, I just want to talk to that
                            teasing faro of mine

Hello Central
                please give me five-o-nine
Hello Central
                please give me five-o-nine
I just want to talk to that
                        old time gal of mine

Hey, arguing
                arguing every where
And they arguing
                arguing every where
I can't get no message
                    over the phone, no where I go

Mmmmmm baby
                when can I speak with you?
Mmmmmm baby
                when can I speak with you?
If you don't talk to me soon
                        baby, I don't know what I'm going to do

J. D. (JELLY JAW) SHORT

I picked up the receiver
                    I could not hear a word
I picked up the receiver
                    I could not hear no word
I want to talk to my home
                    from this sad New York land

I'm asking you a question, mama
                    asking you very clear
I'm asking you a question
                    asking you very clear
And if all things true
                    man, I'm gonna leave *on the liner, here*

Mmmmmm ain't seen my baby
                    in six long months today
I ain't seen my baby
                    six long months today
Some woman *that* I used to have
                    gonna be my baby some day

J. D. (JELLY JAW) **SHORT**

Snake Doctor Blues

(I'm a snake doctor man: everybody's trying to find out my name)

(I fly by easy, but I fly low low distant land)

I'm a snake doctor man
                everybody's trying to find out my name
I'm a snake doctor man
                everybody's trying to find out my name
And when I fly by easy
                mama, I'm gonna fly low low distant land

J. D. (JELLY JAW) SHORT

I am a snake doctor
                    gang of womens every where I go
I'm a snake doctor man
                          has a gang of womens every where I go
And when I get to flying sometime
                              I can see a gang of women standing out in the door

I'm gon' fly by easy
                    man, and you know I ain't gon' fly very low
I'm gon' fly by easy
                    man, and you know I ain't gon' fly very low
What I got in these sacks on my back, man
                              you don't know: honey, no

I ain't got many crooks in my back
                              and the dyingest snake can crawl
I ain't got many crooks in my back
                              and the dyingest snake can crawl
I puts up a solid *foundation, mens*
                         and you know it don't: never fall

The evening storm might blow
                         and the midnight wind might rise
The evening storm might rise
                         and the midnight storm might blow
And when I put up the *black foundation*
                              I don't have to look for that: woman no more

I'm a snake doctor man
                    got my medicine, I say, in my bag
I'm a snake doctor man
                    got my medicine, I say, in my bag
I mean to be a real snake doctor man
                         and you know I don't mean to be no *quack*

Lord, I know many of you mens wondering
                                   what the snake doctor man got in his hand
I know many of you mens are wondering
                              what the snake doctor man got in his hand
He's got roots and herbs
                    steals a woman, man, every where he land

J. D. (JELLY JAW) SHORT

Someday Baby

Don't care when you go
How long you stay
Lord, that good kind treatment
Bring you back some day
But it's some day, baby
You won't worry
                poor Joe's mind
                        any more

Ain't but the one thing, sonny boy
Give Joe Williams the blues

I got on
My last pair of shoes
Well it's some day, baby
You ain't gonna worry
                my mind
                    any more

Yes you keep on betting
Body dodged on past
You gonna leave Chicago running
Running most too fast
Well some day, baby
You ain't gonna worry
                my mind
                    any more

Gonna ask every body
In your neighborhood
You's a no good woman
You don't mean me no good
Well it's some day, baby
You ain't gonna worry
           my mind
               any more

       (Play it right here, boy)

And you won't worry
        poor Joe's mind
           any more

Don't care when you go
How long you stay
This nice treatment, baby, gonna bring you back
Back home some day
Well it's some day, baby
You ain't gonna worry
          my mind
             any more

      (Play it a bit, Sonny Boy)

You can steal my chickens, boys,
              you sure can't make 'em lay
You can steal my chickens, but you
                 you sure can't make 'em lay
You can steal my best woman
             but you sure can't make her stay

BIG JOE WILLIAMS

Stepfather Blues

Ah, when I was a little boy, mama
                                    'bout 16 inches high
When I was a little boy, baby
                                    'bout 16 inches high
I had a mean stepfather
                        lord, he didn't want me to eat a bite

I've got a mean stepfather and I
                                know you got a one too
I've got a mean stepfather
                            and I know you have one too
And my mother dead and gone
                              nothing in the world that she will do

Well my mother she gone
                        and I hope she gone to stay
Well my mother she gone
                        ooo lord, and I hope she gone to stay
I have a mean stepfather
                      he done drove me away

When I was a little boy, lord
                          my stepfather didn't 'low me around
When I was a little boy, mama, my
                            stepfather didn't 'low me around
He's a no good weed, mama
                      and the cows gonna mow him down

Well, poor Joe leaving this morning
                          my face is full of frown
Well, I'm leaving this morning
                      face is full of frown
I got a mean stepfather and my
                      dear mother, she don't 'low me 'round

That's all right
                    may be home some day
Oooo, lord lord, mama
                         may be home some day
My mean stepfather, he
                    won't give me no: place to stay

I am a little boy
                    I'm crying all night long
Oooo, lord, I'm a little boy
                         I cried the whole night long
My stepfather, he
                swears he done done me wrong

And 'fore I'll be dogged, mama
                            I'll leave my happy home
                                        (Play it!)
'Fore I'll be dogged, now, baby
                        I'll leave my happy home
He's a no good weed
                swear he done me wrong

BIG JOE WILLIAMS

President Roosevelt

Oh yes
We got Mr. President Roosevelt
Oh yes
     ooooo
           we got Mr. President Roosevelt
Well you know he gone he gone boys
But his spirit always gonna live on

     President Roosevelt traveled by land
     He traveled by the sea
     He helped the U-nited States boys
     And he also helped Chinee

Oh yes
I *just wanted* President Roosevelt
Well you know he gone he gone sonny boy
Oooo well, but his word would never fail

     Now the rooster told the hens
     Said, When are you hens gonna lay
     Said, No, President Roosevelt's dead
     We ain't got no place to stay

Oh yes
We got Mr. President Roosevelt
Well he gone he gone boy
But his word won't never fail

Well the hen told the rooster
Say, I want you to go crow
Said, No, President Roosevelt's dead, boys
Can't work on the project no more

Oh yes
I'm talking President Roosevelt
Well he gone he gone boys, but I know his
Spirit always gonna live on

(Play it boy)

Well President Roosevelt went to Georgia
And he rid it all 'round and 'round
I *just could see that old pale-horse*
Gonna take the President down

Oh yes
We got Mr. President Roosevelt
Well he gone he gone boys
Oooo well boy the spirit always live on

President Roosevelt traveled by the land
He went across the sea
He helped the Chinee
And also helped me

Oh yes
I *accompanied* President Roosevelt
Well he gone he gone boys, but his
Spirit always gonna live on

BIG JOE WILLIAMS

378   *BIG JOE WILLIAMS*

Some Pianos

Number 29

(A little train called 29   *seems like she all was coming into* East St.
Louis   *soon as* she got to *Memphis,* there   she blowed that
whistle   she blowed the whistle this way   I caught that
train at *Memphis one night*   I was intending to get off at *Peoria,*
Illinois   I mean that train was running   she wasn't doing
nothing but running hard, something like this   just before she
got to the border   she thought she'd blow that whistle again   she
blowed that whistle something like this   she's loafing now
     I wanted to get off that train   but she's going too
fast   I hauled away and stretched one foot on the ground
my heel liked to knock my brains out   I hauled away and
stepped off right tight   and fell off   this is the noise I made
when I hit that ground   I'm rolling now   I got up and
waved my hand, told her good bye   this is the way she seems
walking on into East St. Louis   .)

Oh Oh Blues

Then this poor
           woman's blind
                     and they leads her round every day
I know it's one left here to see 'bout her:
                            please don't use her any old way
I know it's one's left here to see 'bout her:
                            don't use her any old way

Say, my baby
           she come running
                      she come hollering, holding up her hands
She hollered, Oh lord, Mister,
                   Mister, please don't let 'em hurt my man
She hollered, Oh lord, Mister,
                 please don't let 'em hurt my man

I got out on
           my knees
                I had a long talk with the God above
I cried, Oh Lord,
            Lord, send me back that woman I love
I cried, Oh Lord,
            Lord, send me back that woman I love

                  I got a gal in Alabama
                  I got one in Louisiana
                  I got one in Texarkana
                  I got one in Corsicana
                  Got one in Indiana
                  Nineteen in Tennessee
I wants another half a dozen
                  just to run around with me

Say, I'm gonna buy me two shepherds, two fox terriers
                            two bulldogs and two grey hounds
Said I will buy me two shepherds, two fox terriers
                       two bulldogs and two grey hounds
Takes that many good running dogs run these
                  good looking women down

                  Say
                  My mama's got 'em
                  My papa's got 'em
                  My auntie's got 'am
                  My uncle's got 'em too
                  Grandma she got 'em
                  Grandpa he got 'em too
I went out to the stable, I found a mule dying
                      he must have had 'em too

Mean Mistreater Mama

You're a mean mistreating mama
>and you don't mean me no good

You're a mean mistreating mama
>and you don't mean me no good

And I don't blame you, baby:
>I'd be the same way if I could

You say you're going to leave me
>well you say you going away

Now you say you're going to leave me
>and you say you going away

That's all right baby:
>maybe you'll come back home some day

Now you're a mean mistreater
>and you mistreats me all the time

Now you're a mean mistreater
>and you mistreats me all the time

I tried to love you, baby:
>I swear, but you won't pay that no mind

Can you remember, mama, in the morning, I knocked upon your door,
You had the nerve to tell me you didn't want me no more;
>Can you remember, baby,
>When I knocked upon your door,
>You had the nerve to tell me
>That you didn't want me no more?

Ain't it lonesome, sleeping all by yourself,
When the one that you love is loving someone else;
>Ain't it lonesome,
>Sleeping by yourself,
>When the one that you love,
>Baby, is loving someone else?

LEROY CARR (WITH SCRAPPER BLACKWELL)

Take a Walk Around the Corner

B'lieve I'll take me a walk 'round the
                                 corner by myself
B'lieve I'll take me a walk 'round the
                                 corner by myself
And if I can't find my baby, I don't
                                 want no body else

She went out last night and she
                                 didn't even say good-bye
She went out last night and she
                                 didn't even say good-bye
How come she left me?
                           lord I really don't know why

Now I'm going out this morning, my
                                 forty-five in my hand
Now I'm going out this morning
                                 my forty-five in my hand
Now I'm gonna kill my woman
                                 for loving a nother man

Then I'm going to the judge and I'm gonna
                                 fall down on my knees
Then I'm going to the judge and I'm gonna
                                 fall down on my knees
And ask him, Please, fair judge,
                             have mercy on me please

Judge, I done killed my woman
                                 'cause she treated me so unkind
Judge, I done killed my woman 'cause she
                                 treated me so unkind
Treated me so unkind till, I
                         swear, I lost my mind

Well it's please please please don't
                                 send me to the electric chair
Now and it's please please please don't
                                 send me to the electric chair
Just give me my time and I'll
                         try to do it any where

When I'm dead and gone and
                         six feet in the ground
When I'm dead and gone and
                         six feet in the ground
You can only say there's a
                       good man has gone down

                                             LEROY CARR (WITH SCRAPPER BLACKWELL)

Well it looks mighty cloudy and I
                          b'lieve it's going to rain
Well it looks mighty cloudy and I
                          b'lieve it's going to rain
I just love to hear my
                baby call my name

LEROY CARR

45 Pistol Blues

I'm going over to 3rd Alley
                lord, but I'm gonna carry my 45
Lord I'm going over to 3rd Alley
                lord, but I'm gonna carry my 45
Because, you know, ain't many men
                  goes there and comes back alive

They will shoot you and cut you
                lord they will knock you down
Lord they'll shoot you and cut you
                lord they will knock you down
And you can ask any body
           ain't that the baddest place in town

Mens carry 38s
      womens carry razors too
Mens carry 38s
      womens carry their razors too
And you know you better not start nothing:
             do, they'll make away with you

Says I ain't going to 3rd Alley
          unless I change my mind
Ain't going to 3rd Alley
        lord, 'less I change my mind
'Cause you know I done got shot once over there
             lord, and stobbed three or four times

Said you know I'm gonna leave
         lord, my 45 most at home
Lord
    my 45 most too big
'Cause you know when I carry that gun
          lord I can't keep it hid

Flying Crow

Flying Crow leaving Port Arthur
                    likely come to Shreveport to change a crew
Flying Crow leaving Port Arthur
                    likely come to Shreveport to change a crew
They'll take water in Texarkana
                    and for Ashdown they'll keep on through

Twenty-five minutes *in the evening*
                    for a cup of coffee and a slice of cake
Twenty-five minutes *in the evening*
                    for a cup of coffee and a slice of cake
Flying Crow is headed for Kansas City
                    and boy she just won't wait

Yonder she goes, she's gone
                    with a red and green light behind
She's gone, she's gone
                    with a red and green light behind
Well now the red means trouble
                    and the green means a rambling mind

Well I hate to hear
                    that old fireman when he tones his bell

                    (oh, ring 'em a long time)

Mmmmmmmmmm mmmmmm mmmm
                    mm mmmm mmmm
Mmmm mmmmmm
                    mmmmmm mm
Mmmmmmmmmm mmmm
                    mmmm mmmm mmmm

West Helena Blues

I got a woman in West Helena, Arkansas
Yes I got a woman in West Helena, Arkansas
She buy me them long-toed shoes, keep that Brown Mule in my jaws

She get paid off on a Saturday, just about twelve o'clock
Yeah, she get paid off on a Saturday, just about twelve o'clock
From then on, all the joints begin to roll and rock

She buys peanuts from a blind man all up and down the line
Yeah, she buys peanuts for me and her all up and down the line
We have a real ball on a Saturdays and Sundays, Monday morning she'll rise and shine

ROOSEVELT SYKES

High Price Blues

I got a gal
She's got a baker's shop
Her jelly roll is the highest
Thing she's got

> Everything's gone higher
> Way up higher
> It's giving us so much trouble
> I wonder: what shall we do?

I walked in her shop this morning
About half past four
I said, You doing all right, baby; go ahead and
Sell some more

> 'Cause everything's gone higher
> Way up higher
> It's giving us so much trouble
> I wonder: what shall we do?

I know you gonna be bothered
With beggars and bums
But don't worry baby: just don't
Give 'way a crumb

> 'Cause everything's gone higher
> Way up higher
> It's giving us so much trouble
> I wonder: what shall we do?

I'm laying here baby
Lonesome as I can be
If you have any trouble
Just contact me

> 'Cause everything's gone higher
> Way up higher
> It's giving us so much trouble
> I wonder: what shall we do?

ROOSEVELT SYKES

ROOSEVELT SYKES/LITTLE BROTHER MONTGOMERY

The First Time I Met You

The first time I met the blues, mama
　　　　　　　　they came walking through the wood
The first time I met the blues, mama
　　　　　　　　they came walking through the wood
They stopped at my house first, mama
　　　　　　　　and done me all the harm they could

Now my blues got at me
　　　　　　　　lord, and run me from tree to tree
Now my blues got at me
　　　　　　　　and run me from tree to tree
You should have heard me begging
　　　　　　　　Mr. Blues, don't murder me

Good morning, blues
　　　　　　　　what are you doing here so soon?
Good morning, blues
　　　　　　　　what are you doing here so soon?
You be's with me every morning
　　　　　　　　lord, and every night and noon

The blues came down the valley
　　　　　　　　mama, and stopped right at my door
The blues came down the valley
　　　　　　　　and stopped right at my door
They give me more hard luck and trouble
　　　　　　　　than I ever had before

LITTLE BROTHER MONTGOMERY

Y M & V Blues

I say I woke up this morning, baby
                          so dark I couldn't hardly see
Oh I woke up this morning, baby
                          so dark I couldn't hardly see
Well you couldn't see nothing
                          but that dust from that Y & V

Now hush, be still
                  thought I heard some body calling me
Oh hush, be still
                  I heard some body calling me
Well I guess I was just mistaken
                          it was that whistle on that YM & V

Bye bye baby
              I'll find you any where you go
Bye bye baby
              I'll find you any where you go
Yeah, I'll find you baby
                      'cause you rode that old YM & V

LOST JOHN HUNTER

Sweet Patuni

Ah, wake up mama: wake up and don't sleep so sound
Gimme what you promised me: before you lay down
I been getting my 'tuni:
              only thing I love
Make you weep like a willow,
                  sling snot like a turkle-dove

Now I've got a gal, and the kid: lives out on the hill
She got good doin': serve to the one she may will
She got good 'tuni
             I'm a fool about my yam yam yam
Get my yam yam yam
              I'm going back down in Alabam'

Now come-a here, baby, and sit down in my lap
Sit one side: I forgot to tell you I had the clap your hands together Charlie,
Charlie!
        where's you been so long?
I been down in Tennessee
             and I couldn't stay there very long

I got a job in the freight house trying to learn how to truck
A box fell on me this morning, like to bust one of my:
Nut-house for crazy-folks
              folks got sense don't go there
And all the friends I had
            done shook hands and left there

I got a gal, and the kid playin' deef and dumb
But the movements in her hip'll make a dead man:
Come on out my window
            don't knock on my door
And I done told you two or three times
                don't want you no more

Now run in here baby 'cause I done got kinda sick
It ain't nothin' ailin' my stomach: it's something wrong with my:
Dixie Dam was a camp in Georgia
              you can't stay there very long
All the friends I had
           done shook hands and gone

Now here's a verse I don't want a soul to miss
I been taking *charity grub:* I've got to go outside:
Shut your mouth, boy!
            poor boys can't talk at once
And I done told you two or three times
              I don't want no junk

More Good Whiskey Blues

I'm so glad
        good whiskey have made it through
Well well, I'm so glad
          good whiskey have made it through
Well now, it have saved my wife from dying
               ooo well well, and saved my sweetheart too

I'm so glad
        good whiskey has come back in time
Well now, I'm so glad
          good whiskey has come back in time
Because now I drink so much hooch
            ooo well well, I'm bound to lose my mind

I'm so glad
        good whiskey sure is here
Hmmmmm mmmm mm
          good whiskey sure is here
Well well now, if you can't drink good whiskey
              ooo well well, why not drink some doggone good beer

I'm so glad
        good whiskey has come back to me
Hmmmmm mmmm now
          good whiskey has come back to me
Well now, it brought me good things
            ooo-hoo well well, from way across the sea

You is just as welcome
        good whiskey, as the flowers is in May
Yes, just as welcome, good whiskey
          as the flowers is in May
Well, since you has come back to me
           ooo well well, I hope you have come to stay

PEETIE WHEATSTRAW

I Can Tell by the Way You Smell

Your hair all wrinkled and you
                       full of sweat, your
Under-skirt is
         wringing wet, you be
             doing something wrong
             doing something wrong
You be doing something: I can tell by the way you smell

You show your linen to
                 any man, and
That's something, mama, that I
                   just can't stand, you been
             doing something wrong
             doing something wrong
You been doing something: I can tell by the way you smell

Here you come here walking
               just like a goose
You look like somebody just
               turned you loose, you been
             doing something wrong
             doing something wrong
You been doing something: I can tell by the way you smell

Run here mama, just
           look at sis
She got her hand in her toodle-um
                   up to her wrist, she been
             doing something wrong
             doing something wrong
She been doing something: I can tell by the way she smell

Mama and papa's in the back yard trying to
                     carve up knotty
Papa ain't ready
               so help me god, he been
             doing something wrong
             doing something wrong
Been doing something: I can tell by the way they smell

He got the motion and
               she got the swing, just
Look at papa out there
               on that thing, he's
             doing something wrong
             doing something wrong
Been doing something: I can tell by the way they smell

                                                   WALTER DAVIS

The Dirty Dozens

Well I want all you women folks to fall in line
Shake your shimmy like I'm shaking mine
You shake your shimmy and you shake it fast
You can't shake your shimmy, shake your yes yes yes

    Now you's a dirty mistreater
    A robber and a cheater
    Slip you in the dozens
    Your poppy is your cousin
    Your mama do's the lawdy lawd

Yonder go your mama going out across the field
Running and a-shaking like an automobile
I hollered at your mama and I told her to wait
She slipped away from me like a Cadillac 8

    Now she's a running mistreater
    A robber and a cheater
    Poppy is her cousin
    Slip you in the dozens
    Her mama do's the lawdy lawd

I like your mama, I like your sister too
I *did* like your daddy, but your daddy wouldn't do
Met your daddy on the corner the other day
You know about that, that he was funny that way

    So now he's a funny mistreater
    A robber and a cheater
    Slip you in the dozens
    Poppy is your cousin
    Your mama do's the lawdy lawd

God made him an elephant, he made him stout
He wasn't satisfied until he made him a snout
He made his snout just as long as a rail
He wasn't satisfied until he made him a tail
He made his tail just to fan the fly
He wasn't satisfied until he made some eye
He made his eye just to look over the grass
He wasn't satisfied: he made his yes yes yes
Made his yes yes yes and didn't get it fixed
He wasn't satisfied until it made him sick
It made him sick, lord, it made him well
You know by that that the elephant caught hell

    Now he's dirty mistreater
    A robber and a cheater
    Slip you in the dozens

Your poppy is your cousin
Your mama do's the lawdy lawd

Now now boys, say, you ain't acting fair
You know 'bout that, you got real bad hair
Your face is all hid, now your back's all bare
If you ain't doing the bobo, what's your head doing there?

Now you's a dirty mistreater
A robber and a cheater
Slip you in the dozens
Now your poppy is your cousin
And your mama do's the lawdy lawd

Now your little sister, well, she asked me to kiss her
I told her to wait until she got a little bigger
She got a little bigger, says now I could kiss her
You know 'bout that, boy, that I didn't miss her

She's a dirty mistreater
A robber and a cheater
Slip you in the dozens
Now your poppy is your cousin
And your mama do's the lawdy lawd

Now the first three months there she did very well
The next three months she begin to raise a little hell
The next three months, said she got real rough
You know by that that she was strutting that stuff

Now she's a dirty mistreater
A robber and a cheater
Slip you in the dozens
Now your poppy is your cousin
And your mama do's the lawdy lawd

Now I like your mama, but she wouldn't do this
I hit her across the head with my great big fist
The clock's on the shelf going tick tick tick
Your ma's out on the street doing I don't know which

Four five six seven eight nine and ten
I like your mama but she's got too many men
Ashes to ashes, now it's sand to sand
Every time I see her she's got a brand new man

She's a dirty mistreater
A robber and a cheater
Slip you in the dozens
Now your poppy is your cousin
And your mama do's the lawdy lawd

I Don't Know

Gonna sit around for a while
Shoulda just ridden down this aisle
Deacon Jones keepin' a-prayin'
Got as much religion as *one I've had*
Wanna go to heaven, gotta stop this stuff
Going to be struttin' that thing

                        Which a way?

            I don't know
            I don't know
            I don't know
            I don't know
        I'm tellin' these lovers
        Honey, they're struttin' that thing
                        night and day

There's a lady, but her name is Lou
Shook that thing till she caught the flu
Wasn't satisfied till she jumped in bed
Then she spoke and spoke like this
Shake your shoulders, can't shake your feet
Shake nothin', mama, but your wicked knees

                        But you shouldn't-a!

                        Shouldn't-a what, darlin'?

            I don't know
            I don't know
            I don't know
            I don't know
        I'm tellin' these lovers
        Honey, they're struttin' that thing
                        night and day

                        (Play it now)

Gettin' sick and tired of the way you do
'Time, mama, I'm gonna pizen you
Sprinkle goofer dust around your bed
Wake up some mornin', find your own self dead

                        'Cause you shouldn't-a!

                        Shouldn't-a what?

            I don't know
            I don't know
            I don't know

CRIPPLE CLARENCE LOFTON

                    I don't know
          I'm tellin' these lovers
          Honey, they're struttin' that thing
                    night and day

Shake it and break it, girls, you can hang it on the wall
Pitch it out the window, catch it before it fall
Stop a while, shimmy if it's all night long
Some time the *thing's got your habit's on*

               But you shouldn't-a!

               Shouldn't-a what, darlin'?

                    I don't know
                    I don't know
                    I don't know
                    I don't know
          I'm tellin' these lovers
          Honey, they're struttin' that thing
                    night and day

                    (Let's get back)

CRIPPLE CLARENCE LOFTON

Chicago

BIG BILL BROONZY

I'm Gonna Move to the Outskirts of Town

I'm gonna move   way out on the outskirts of town
I'm gonna move   way out on the outskirts of town
I swear I don't want no body   ooo, lord, baby   always hanging 'round

          I'm gonna tell you baby
          We gonna move away from here
          I don't want no iceman: I'm gonna
          Buy me a frigidaire

When I move   way out on the outskirts of town
I swear I don't want no body   ooo, lord, baby   always hanging 'round

          I'm gonna bring my groceries
          Gonna bring them every day
          That's gonna stop that grocery boy
          I mean, and keep him away

When I move   way out on the outskirts of town
I swear I don't want no body   ooo, lord, baby   always hanging 'round

          It may look funny
          Funny as can be
          We got eight children, baby
          Don't none of 'em look like me

That's why I'm gonna move   yeh, way on the outskirts of town
I swear I don't want no body   ooo, lord, baby   always hanging 'round

Looking Up at Down

I'm just like an old rooster
     that *hollered* way out here on a hill
I'm just like an old rooster
     that *hollered* way out here on a hill
People, now I'm done scratching
      ooo lord, Big Bill is just trying to live

I'm just like *Job's* turkey
     I can't do nothing but bobble
I'm so poor, baby
    I have to lean up against the fence to gargle
  Yeah, now baby
     well I believe I'll change towns
  Yeah, I'm down so low baby
      ooo lord, yeah, I declare I'm looking up to down

The men in the mine, baby
    they all looking down on me
Yeah, and I'm down so low baby
     I'm low as I can be
  Yeah, now baby
    now I'm down as I can be
  Yeah, I'm down so low baby
     ooo lord, everybody's looking down on poor me

Everything I get ahold to baby
     it goes away like snow in June
If I get a chance now baby again
     I'm going up to the moon
  Yeah, now baby
    yeah, and I believe I'll change towns
  Yeah, poor me's down so low, baby
      ooo lord gal, Big Bill is looking up to down

BIG BILL BROONZY

Hip Shakin' Strut

(Come on in now and get in this hip shaking contest;
yeah, 'cause it's gonna be tight.)

          (Let's all of us pull off our shoes and have a stinking
          good time.

          Oh, get hot now.)

(Yes, get hotter 'n that.

Come on girls, now, and shake 'em up, shake 'em up,
raise 'em up, let 'em down.)

          (Lay 'em low.)

(Come on everybody and do something 'cause this is
too good to let it waste.

Say, big boy, what did the banty rooster say to the
elephant?)

          (Let's you and I don't step on each other.)

(Ah HA HA HA!)

          (Huh huh.)

(Oh now let's do that thing.)

          (Get right.)

(Gee, that boy can use those brushes.)

          (Oh, he's funny that way.)

(Oh yeah?

Come on everybody, let's do the yip yap yat o.)

          (What's that? Some smell?)

(No, you eat that.)

          (Huh-oh.)

(Say, big boy, what did the elephant say to the cat?)

HOKUM BOYS:GEORGIA TOM (WITH JANE LUCAS)

GEORGIA TOM

(If you don't cover that up I'm going to turn this . . .
over.)

(Oh HA HA HA!)

(Huh huh huh.)

(Gee, look at that old fat gal: she really shakes a mean
hip.)

(She shakes two of 'em.)

(You know some people say they don't give nobody
nothing, but if they had a face on'em like you, they'd
give everybody something.)

(Who you talking to?)

(Ah, you.)

(I'd like to have some chit'lins.)

(No, you don't want no chit'lins—you want a quart
of that bad gin.

Oh, shake 'em folks, shake 'em fast.)

(Can't shake your shimmy shake your yas yas yas.)

(Ah HA HA HA!)

(Oh Lord.)

(You know this is hotter 'n that.)

(Hotter 'n something else I know too.

Oh, do it now.)

(Play it, Bill.)

(Going now.)

(Oh yeah? Tight like that; get your last shake there.)

Big Woman

Got a little bitty mama, and a big mama too
Got a little bitty mama, and a big mama too
My little bitty mama don't treat me like my big mama do

Hey hey mama, don't be mean to me
Hey hey mama, don't be mean to me
'Cause, don't you know baby, you and I can't agree

(Play it)

Hey hey mama, take your big legs off-a me
Hey hey mama, take your big legs off-a me
If you had good sense you could see I'm in misery

Hey hey mama, let's go 'cross town
Hey hey mama, let's go 'cross town
How can we have any fun when your big legs is holding me down

(Play it now)

Hey hey mama, gimme my shoes and clothes
Hey hey mama, gimme my shoes and clothes
I just found out I can't satisfy your soul

(Whup it now)

There's a train at the station, and I'm ready to go
There's a train at the station, and I'm ready to go
You'll never get a chance to put your big legs on me no more

(Yeah)

I Been Treated Wrong

I don't know my real name
                I don't know when I was born
I don't know my real name
                I don't know when I was born
The trouble I been having
                seem like I was raised in a orphan home

My mother died and left me
                when I was only two years old
My mother died and left me
                when I was only two years old
And the trouble I been having
                the Good Lord only knows

I been treated like an orphan
                and been workëd like a slave
I been treated just like an orphan
                and I been workëd like a slave
And if I never get my revenge
                even this will carry me to my grave

                (Play it one time)

Now I been having trouble
                ever since I been grown
Now I been having trouble
                ever since I been grown
I'm too old for the orphan and
                too young for the old folks home

                (Play it boy, play it, play it)

                (Yes, yes)

WASHBOARD SAM

You Got to Love Her with a Feeling

> Man, if you gonna love your woman
> Love her with a thrill
> If you don't
> You know some other man will

You got to love her with a feeling
You got to love her with a feeling
Love that woman with a feeling
Or don't you love at all

> Man, you know these women
> Don't want that old half-way stuff
> So when you turn 'em loose, man
> Be sure they got enough

And just love 'em with a feeling
Love 'em with a feeling
You've got to love them with a feeling
Or don't you love at all

> The gal I love
> She's nice and fat
> She got her way of loving
> And it's good like that

Because she love me with a feeling
That woman love me with a feeling
She love me with a feeling
Or she won't love at all

> You know the women don't like this woman
> Because she speaks her mind
> But the men are crazy about her, because she
> Take her time

And really love 'em with a feeling
Man, she just love with a feeling
That woman, she love with a feeling
Or she won't have any love at all

> Well, she shakes all over
> When she walk
> She made a blind man see, and she made a
> Dumb man talk

Because she loved 'em with a feeling
She loved 'em with a feeling
She love with a feeling
Or she won't love at all

(you know what)

You know the cop took her in, she didn't
Need no bail
She shook it for the judge, and he put the
Cop in jail

You know she loved him with a feeling
You know she loved him with a feeling
She loved him with a feeling
Or she won't love at all

TAMPA RED

Go Back to the Country

Now you *clown* with your grocery man
'Cause your bill is too high
You don't want to pay taxes
You just wanta get by

You'd better go back to the country
       way back out in the wood
I'm tired of hearin' you hollerin'
       Hoo hoo hoo, city life ain't no good

You want the finest house in town
For two or three dollars a month
You seem to think it's all right for you
To go out in the park and hunt

You'd better go back to the country
       way back out in the wood
I'm tired of hearin' you hollerin'
       Hoo hoo hoo, city life ain't no good

You wants a whole lot of credit
To pay off once a year
But you owe the salary you make
For just liquor and beer

You'd better go back to the country
       way back out in the wood
'Cause the way you run your business
       hoo hoo hoo, you can't do no good

Now you decorate your window
With your big rusty feet
You want hogs in your front yard
So you can have plenty of meat

You'd better go back to the country
       way back out in the wood
Plant you forty acres of cotton
       and try to do yourself some good

Big Apple Blues

I know you got some good apples
                    right down on Mister *Rudolph's* farm
Oh, I know you got some good apples
                    right down on Mister *Rudolph's* farm
Lord, I love you so much
                    baby, I'd like to hold you in my arms

Now I want to get a truckload of your apples
                            I want to peddle your apples up north
Lord now, and I want to get a truckload of your apples
                            and I want to peddle your apples up north
Now, maybe I can keep 'em *until* the wintertime
                    and we'll make 'em be little children's Santa Claus

Now my grandmother says she want to buy a bushel of your apples
                            she want to make her some apple sauce
Oh my grandmother says she want to buy a bushel of your apples
                            she want to make her some apple sauce
Well now, I'll be delighted and taste a little
                    well I bet they would taste on out of this world

Lord, and I can see your little apple
                    hanging way up in your little apple tree
Lord, I can see your little apple
                    a-hanging way up in your little apple tree
Now you made like you love me so much
                    baby, please drop one down for me

Now you know the rain washed away my cotton
                            people, and the sun burnt up my new ground corn
Well you know the rain washed away my cotton
                            peoples, and the sun burnt up my new ground corn
Now and if somebody don't give me here something to eat pretty soon
                    I just deswear we won't be here long

SONNY BOY WILLIAMSON

Moonshine

Now and it's moon shine
     moon shine have harmed many men
Now and it's moon shine
     moon shine have harmed many men
Now that is the reason why
     you have got to believe I'll make a change

  Now moon shine will make you shoot dice
  Make you want to fight
  Now when you go home and you can't
  Treat your wife right

You been drinking moon shine
     moon shine have harmed many men
Now that is the reason why
     I believe I'll make a change

  Now moon shine will make you think that the policeman's
  A little bitty bit of a boy
  Moon shine will make you think that the street car
  Is a little children's play-toy

Then you been drinking moon shine
     moon shine have harmed many men
Now that is the reason why
     I believe I'll make a change

  Now moon shine will make you go home
  Lay down across your bed
  And your wife try to talk with you: you say
  You didn't hear a word she said

You been drinking moon shine
     moon shine have harmed many men
Now that is the reason why
     I believe I'll make a change

  Now moon shine will make you get drunk
  And walk out in the street
  Moon shine will make you cuss out most
  Any body you meet

You been drinking moon shine
     moon shine have harmed many men
Now that is the reason why
     I believe I'll make a change

SONNY BOY WILLIAMSON

417

SONNY BOY WILLIAMSON

Bad Luck Blues

Baby did you hear about the bad luck
    The bad luck that happened just about six months ago?
Now did you hear about the bad luck
    The bad luck that happened just about six months ago?
Now, and my cousin *Arthur* got shot down
    Just as he was walking out the door

Now, and he said, Please, Mister
    Said, Please don't shoot me no more
Now, and he said, Please, Mister
    Said, Please don't shoot me no more
He said, Because my breath is getting short
    And my heart is beating awful slow

And *my Arthur* said, I know I got some friends
    I want somebody to go and get my mother please
My Arthur said, I know I got some friends
    I want somebody to go and get my mother please
Then maybe she can help me with my troubles
    Peoples, I'm in so much misery

And he said, I hate to go leave my mother and father
    I hate to go leave my cousins Sonny Boy and *Sid*
And he said, I hate to go leave my mother and father
    Said, I hate to go leave my cousins Sonny Boy and *Sid*
Now, but tell 'em if they be good they'll come to see me
    People, on the Resur-rection Day

SONNY BOY WILLIAMSON

Welfare Store

Now me and my baby we talked last night
And we talked for nearly a hour
She wanted me to go down to the Welfare Store
And get a sack of that Welfare flour

      But I told her: No!
      Baby, and I sure don't wanna go
      I say I'll do anything in the world for you
      I don't want to go down to that Welfare Store

Now you need to go get you some real white man
You know, to sign your little note
They give you a pair of them keen toed shoes
And one of them old pinch-back soldier coats

      But I told her: No!
      Baby, I don't wanna go
      I say I'll do anything in the world for you
      But I don't wanna go down to that Welfare Store

President Roosevelt said them Welfare people
They gonna treat everybody right
Said, They give you a can of them beans
And a can or two of them old tripe

      But I told her: No!
      Baby, and I sure don't wanna go
      I say I'll do anything in the world for you
      But I don't wanna go down to that Welfare Store

Well now me and my baby we talked yesterday
And we talked in my back yard
She said, I'll take care of you, Sonny Boy
Just as long as these times stay hard

      And I told her: Yeah!
      Baby, and I sure won't have to go
      I say, and if you do that for me
      I won't have to go down to that Welfare Store

SONNY BOY WILLIAMSON

Mean Old Twister

Now this dark cloud is rising
                 and it's thundering all around
Now this dark cloud is rising
                 and it's thundering all around
Look like something bad is gonna happen
                       you better lower your airplane down

Now that mean old twister's coming
                   poor people running every which-a-way
Now that mean old twister's coming
                   poor people running every which-a-way
Every body's on a wonder
              what's the matter with the cruel world today

Now my mama told me
            when I was only five months old
Now my mama she told me
            when I was only five months old
If you obey your preacher
            the Good Lord is gonna bless your soul

Now the daylight is failing
            and the moon begin to rise
Now the daylight is failing
            and the moon begin to rise
I'm just down here weeping and moaning
               right by my mama's side

Now I'm going home
          I done did all in this world that I could
Now I'm going home
          I done did all in this world that I could
Says I got everybody happy
            'round here in my neighborhood

Don't Want No Hungry Woman

Lord I can't see
               how these hungry women please
Lord I can't see
               how these hungry women please
Walk the streets at night
                   like a police on his beat

She is standing on the corner till her
                       feets get soaking wet
Well it's standing on the corner
                  till her feet got soaking wet
Mister, if you ain't got a nickel
                 please gimme a cigarette

Now I'm going down in tin-can alley
                     and get drunk as I can be
Heeeeeeeeeeeeeeeeeeeeeeeeeeeeeey
               get drunk as I can be
I don't want no hungry women
             to lay their hands on me

I done phoned to the welfare
               wrote to the government too
I done phoned to the welfare
               wrote to the government too
And I asked them to help me
             get my woman a pair of shoes

Hey, the welfare didn't answer
               the government paid me no mind
Hey, the government didn't answer
             welfare paid me no mind
Hey boy, if you think we gon' help you
             swear you better change your mind

FLOYD COUNCIL

The '40's and '50's

Little Boy Blue

Little Boy Blue
Please come blow your horn
Little Boy Blue
Please come blow your horn
My baby, she gone and left me
She left me all a lone

Now the sheeps is in the meadow
And the cows is in the corn
I've got a little gal in Chicago
She loves to hear me blow my
                                    lonesome horn

Little Boy Blue
Please come blow your horn
My baby, she gone and left me
She left me all a lone

(Play it for me, boy)

I'm gonna take my whip and whip her
I'm gonna whip her down to the ground
I'm gonna take my dirk and stob her
Then you know I'm gonna turn it 'round and 'round

Little Boy Blue
Please come blow your horn
My baby, she gone and left me
She left me all a lone

I have rambled and I have rambled
Until I have broke my poor self down
I believe to my soul
That the little girl is out of town

Little Boy Blue
Please come blow your horn
My baby, she gone and left me
She left me all a lone

ROBERT LOCKWOOD

Stamp Blues

Well I woke up this mornin'
Half past four
They had a big crowd
At the charity store

'Cause they gettin' 'em stamps
Yes, they gettin' 'em stamps
Yes, they gettin' 'em stamps
That the gov'ment givin' away

Well I'm a country man
Never go to town
The women in Chicago
Tryin' to jive me 'round

'Cause they gettin' 'em stamps
Yes, they gettin' 'em stamps
Yes, they gettin' 'em stamps
That the gov'ment givin' away

(Yeh)

Well if you ever in Chicago
And the times get hard
Take a little walk
Out on South *Park*

'Cause they gettin' 'em stamps
Yes, they gettin' 'em stamps
Yes, they gettin' 'em stamps
That the gov'ment givin' away

Well the womens up here
Play me to be a fool
Think I'm the boy
Ain't never been to school

'Cause they gettin' 'em stamps
Yes, they gettin' 'em stamps
Yes, they gettin' 'em stamps
That the gov'ment givin' away

(Yeh)

TONY HOLLINS

When I got here
I had good luck
The woman I love
She keep me up

        'Cause she gettin' 'em stamps
        Yes, she gettin' 'em stamps
        Yes, she gettin' 'em stamps
        That the gov'ment givin' away

Well I woke up this mornin'
Half past two
The streets was crowded
And they couldn't get through

        'Cause they gettin' 'em stamps
        Yes, they gettin' 'em stamps
        Yes, they gettin' 'em stamps
        That the gov'ment givin' away

(Yeh
Play it a long time now boy)

427   *TONY HOLLINS*

Alley Blues

You know now mama
Take me out the alley now mama
Before the high water rise
You all know I ain't no Christian
'Cause I
Once have been baptized
   (Lord, I went to church this morning)
Yes, and they called on me to pray
Well I fell down on my knees
On my knees
Gee, I for-
Forgot just what to say

You know, and I cried, Lord, my Father, my Jesus
I didn't know what I was doing
I said that would be the Kingdom Come
I said, if you got any brownskin women in Heaven
Will you please to send Wright Holmes one
Miss *Massey,* you
      know I ain't never been in Heaven
Oh these black folks have been told
You know they tell me they got women up there
Women up there
Gee, with their mouth all lined with gold

I bet you I get my cream from a creamer
You get yourn from a Jersey cow
          (All right)
I'll bet you I'll get my meat from a pig
I bet you get your bacon from a no good sow
          (Tell the truth, darn it)
Because the woman I'm going to loving
She's a holy woman
And she
              beats that tambourine
And every time me and that old sister go to loving each other
Oooo well boy
She talks like the only one talking to me

You know I decided to get me an island in Heaven
And I'm gonna get me one of them *Jersey bulls*
          (Lord, don't you hear me now, mama
          Keep on a talking)
Yeah, I decided to get me an island in Heaven
Yes, I'm gonna get me one of them *Jersey bulls*
I'm gonna keep on *churning and churning* it
Yeah, until my churning's done got full
          (Well I believe I'll churn a little bit)
                              (Yeah)

Now some of these here days
I'm gonna have me a Heaven of my own
          (Lord, don't you hear me
          Keep on a-praying to you)
Baby, I said, Some of these here days
I'm gonna have me a Heaven of my own
Have a gang of brownskin women
Yeah, they gonna be gathering all around my throne

WRIGHT HOLMES

Six Week Old Blues

Well now you know my mama told me
            when I was only six weeks old
Well now you know my mama told me
            when I was only six weeks old
She said, Son, when you get six weeks older, well now then I'll,
                mama's gonna set your clothes out doors

Well now you know I looked at my mama well now baby then now
                                        I begin to cry
Well now you know I looked at my mama
            baby then now
                  I begin to cry
I said, And when you put your boy out mama well now
            I truly believe your poor boy die

Well now you know sometimes I weep
            then again I mourn like a mourning dove
Well I said sometimes I weeping
            then again I mourn like a mourning dove
I say that your life ain't worth living now then now
            well if you ain't with the one you love

Well now when I leave your town
            I want you to pin crepes on your door
Well now when I leave your town baby
            I want you to pin crepes on your door
I said that if I won't be dead
            well but I ain't coming back here no more

When I die
            I want you to bury my body low
When I die
            I want you to bury my body low
Just so that my evil spirit won't be
            hanging around your door no more

JOHN HENRY BARBEE

Remember Way Back

I'm sister and brotherless
I'm sister and brotherless
I'm motherless and fatherless
I'm motherless and fatherless
Too
Well, I clean up, little woman
Can I go home with you

Oh take me to the waterfront
Oh take me to the waterfront
Where the water runs co-old
Where the water runs co-old
Downstream
Well I love my little woman
She's the prettiest girl ever seen

My mother is dead now
My mother is dead now
My father is go-one
My father is go-one
Too
Well I'm sister and I'm brotherless
Motherless, fatherless, too

I 'member way back
I 'member way back
When I was the a-age
When I was the a-age
Of nine
Well I thinking 'bout my friends
All my friends all around

Oh here's my hand, babe
Oh here's my hand, babe
Won't never see me he-ere
Won't never see me he-ere
No more
Well now I love my little woman
I want the whole world to know

L. C. GREEN

Hoochie Coochie

> The gypsy woman told my mother
> Before I was born
> I got a boy child's coming
> Gonna be a son of a gun
> He gonna make pretty womens
> Jump and shout
> Then the world wanna know
> What this all about

'Cause you know I'm here
Everybody knows I'm here
Yeah, you know I'm a hoochie coochie man
Everybody knows I'm here

> I got a black cat bone
> I got a mojo too
> I got the John the Conqueroo
> I'm gonna mess with you
> I'm gonna make you girls
> Lead me by the hand
> Then the world'll know
> The hoochie coochie man

But you know I'm here
Everybody knows I'm here
Yeah, you know I'm a hoochie coochie man
Everybody knows I'm here

> On a seven hours
> On the seventh day
> On the seventh month
> The seven doctors said
> He was born for good luck
> And that you'll see
> I got seven hundred dollars
> Don't you mess with me

But you know I'm here
Everybody knows I'm here
Well you know I'm a hoochie coochie man
Everybody knows I'm here

MUDDY WATERS

Smokestack Lightnin'

Oh-ohh
Smokestack lightnin'
Shinin'
Just like gold
Oh, don't you hear me cryin':
  Wooooo-oooooo
  Wooo-oooo-oooo
  Wooooooo

Oh-ohh
Tell me baby
What's goin'
On here
Oh, don't you hear me cryin':
  Wooooo-oooooo
  Wooo-oooo-oooo
  Wooooooo

Oh-ohh
Tell me baby
Where did you
Stay last night
Oh, don't you hear me cryin':
  Wooooo-oooooo
  Wooo-oooo-oooo
  Wooooooo

Oh-ohh
Stop your train
Let a
Poor boy ride
Oh, don't you hear me cryin':
     Wooooo-oooooo
     Wooo-oooo-oooo
     Wooooooo

Oh-ohh
Fare you well
Never see
Me here no more
Oh, don't you hear me cryin':
     Wooooo-oooooo
     Wooo-oooo-oooo
     Wooooooo

Oh-ohh
Who been here, baby, since
I—I been gone
Little bitty boy
Derby on
     Wooooo-oooooo
     Wooo-oooo-oooo
     Wooooooo

JOHN LEE HOOKER

Black Snake

There's a mean black snake been
                              suckin' my rider's tongue
There's a mean black snake been
                              suckin' my rider's tongue
And if I catch him there mmmm
                              he won't come back no more

And he crawl up to my window
                              and he crawl up in my bed
He crawl up to my window
                              and he crawl up in my baby's bed
He's a mean mean black snake
                              that's been suckin' my rider's tongue

                Get me some toad-frogs' hips
                Mix it up together
                Gonna whoop it up good
                And I betcha my bottom dollar
                He won't suck my rider's tongue no more

Mean mean mean black snake
                              been crawlin' round my back door
Mmmmmmmmmmmmmmmm mmmmmmmmmm mmmmmmmm mmmmmmmm
Been crawlin' round my back door

He worry me all through the day
                              he worry me all night long
He worry me all through the day
                              he worry me all day long
I betcha my bottom dollar
                    I'm gonna kill
                              kill that old black snake
He won't
        suck my rider's tongue
He won't suck my baby's tongue no more
That mean mean black snake
He won't bother
              me no more
Mmmmmmmmmmmmmmmmmmmmm

JOHN LEE HOOKER

Somewhere to End

Hottest Brand Goin'

Well I say I work in the Conoco station
On Sixteen sixty-eight Plank Road
I work for Mr.
                    Domaine, I say now
Conoco
        oil station
                    happy motor
                                super service
You know they got the
                    hottest brand going

You want super service
Come to the Conoco station on Plank Road
You want super service station
Come down on Sixteen sixty-eight Plank Road
I say come to Mr. Ed Domaine
                                service station
He got the best gas gonna be on the road

            You want your car to be served
            Want it served just right
            Put some of that royal gasoline in there
            Roll all night or day

Sixteen sixty-eight Plank Road
That's where Robert Brown'll wait

            You might need a tune-up job
            Your brakes might be out of fix
            I reckon you might need tires
            Everything's all right

Come to Sixteen sixty-eight
Sixteen sixty-eight Plank Road
I say down
        by that Conoco station I know

                    (People, you know what I'm talking about
                    I'm talking about the hottest brand going
                    Get that royal feeling
                    Buy that royal gasoline)

Come down on sixty-eight, Sixteen sixty-eight
                                Sixteen sixty-eight Plank Road

            Say you want super service
            Bring it in to Mr. Ed Domaine

            (I'm talking about my boss now

That's my boss, where I work at, see
Sixteen sixty-eight Plank Road
You want super service
Come right there
Buy that royal gasoline
Get that royal feeling
Royal riding
And I'll tell you
That's the hottest brand that's going
Just a minute, I'll buy me one, Mr. Robert Brown
And he knows me
And that's my boss)

Come down on Sixteen sixty-eight Plank Road
Buy the hottest brand going
Now you want your car super serviced
Get your super right there

(Talking 'bout the Conoco station)

Alabama Bus

Stop that Alabama bus   I don't wanna ride
Stop that Alabama bus   I don't wanna ride
Stop that Alabama bus   I don't wanna ride
Lord an Alabama boy   'cause I don't wanna ride

Stop that Alabama bus   I don't wanna ride
Stop that Alabama bus   I don't wanna ride
Stop that Alabama bus   I don't wanna ride
Lord an Alabama boy   'cause I don't wanna ride

Lord, there come a bus don't have no load
You know, they tell me that a human being stepped on board
You know, they tell me that the man stepped on the bus
You know, they tell me that the driver began to fuss
He said, Lookit here, man, you from the Negro race
And don't you know you sitting in the wrong place?
The driver told the man, I know you paid your dime
But if you don't move you gonna pay a fine
The man told the driver, My feets are hurting
The driver told the man to move behind the curtain

Stop that Alabama bus   I don't wanna ride
Stop that Alabama bus   I don't wanna ride
Stop that Alabama bus   I don't wanna ride
Lord an Alabama boy   'cause I don't wanna ride

I wanna tell you 'bout the Reverend Martin Luther King
You know, they tell me that the people began to sing
You know, the man God sent out in the world
You know, they tell me that the man had a mighty nerve
You know, the poor man didn't have a bus to rent
You know, they tell me, Great God, he had *a mighty spent*
And he reminded me of Moses in Israel land
He said, A man ain't nothing but a man
He said, Lookit here, Alabama, don't you see
He says, A all of my people gonna follow me
You know, they tell me Reverend King was very hurt
He says, A all of my people gonna walk to work
They said, Lookit here, boy, you hadn't took a thought
So, don't you know you broke the anti-boycott law
They tell me Reverend King said, Treat us right
You know, in the Second World War my father lost his sight
You know, they tell me Abraham signed the pledge one night
He said that all of these men should have their equal rights
You know, they had the trial and Clayton Powell was there
You know, they tell me Clayton Powell asked the world for prayer
You know, they sent down there to go his bail
You know they PUT REVEREND KING IN A ALABAMA JAIL

Stop that Alabama bus   I don't wanna ride

BROTHER WILL HAIRSTON

Stop that Alabama bus	I don't wanna ride
Stop that Alabama bus	I don't wanna ride
Lord an Alabama boy	'cause I don't wanna ride

Stop that Alabama bus	I don't wanna ride
Stop that Alabama bus	I don't wanna ride
Stop that Alabama bus	I don't wanna ride
Lord an Alabama boy	'cause I don't wanna ride

You know, they tell me Reverend King was *a violence 'bide*
A when all the buses passed, and no body will ride
You know, they tell me that the Negroes was ready to go
They had a walked along the streets until their feets was sore
You know, they tell me Reverend King had spreaded the word
'Bout an Alabama bus ride, so I heard
You know, they spent a lot of money since King go on
You know, in nineteen and twenty-nine that man was born
You know, the five hundred dollars aren't very heavy
You know, the poor man was born the fifteenth of January

Stop that Alabama bus	I don't wanna ride
Stop that Alabama bus	I don't wanna ride
Stop that Alabama bus	I don't wanna ride
Lord an Alabama boy	but I don't wanna ride

I Got So Old

I got up this morning
And I put on my shoes
I strung my shoes
Then I washed my face
I walked to the mirror
For to comb my head
I made a move
Didn't know what to do
I stepped a way forward
Start to break and run
Oh baby
Oh baby
Baby, this ain't me
I got so old
       I don't even know myself

I'm going to town
Have a picture made
I'm gonna bring me home
Put 'em side by side
I'm gonna take a good look
See if it same as me
Oh no
Oh no
Baby, this ain't me
I got so old
I don't even know myself

Mama say when I was a baby
Prettiest thing she had
That's what remains
Of the things of the past
Baby
Oh baby
Baby, this ain't me
I got so old
       I don't even know myself

I's standing on the porch
Looking down the street
I look like something
Hadn't *saw in the week*
Baby, this ain't me
Oh baby, this ain't me
I got so old
       I don't even know myself

Title usually interpreted as "I Got So Ugly."

ROBERT PETE WILLIAMS

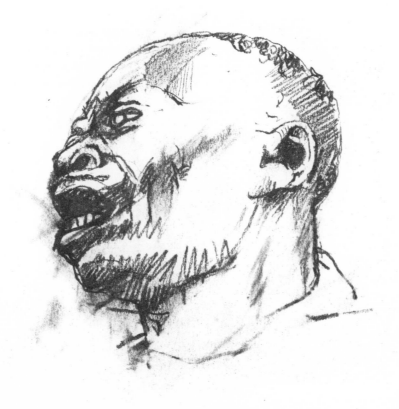

ROBERT PETE WILLIAMS

. . . .
We've grown used to him; like everything else you're used to
he doesn't stand for anything
and I talk to you about him because I can't find
anything that you're not used to;
I pay my respects.

GEORGE SEFERIS

A Survey of Sorts: Various Voices

Song . . . is a ladder whereby man comes to a heightened consciousness. It has many rungs and must descend into dark depths before it can rise to luminous heights. It unites what is above with what is below and it evokes forms yet unseen. Great is the song composed of words and melodies, greater is the song in which melody suffices, but greatest is the song that needs neither words nor music. (Ruth Finer Mintz)

The song Kuan Chü is full of joy, but it is not dirty; | It is full of grief, but it is not mean. (Confucius)

Through the hush of air a voice sang to them, low, not rain, not leaves in murmur, like no voice of strings or reeds or whatdoyoucallthem dulcimers, touching their still ears with words, still hearts of their each his remembered lines. Good, good to hear: sorrow from them each seemed to from both depart when first they heard . . . first merciful lovesoft oftloved word. (James Joyce)

To love music | more than anything, that | is unhappiness. (Paul Klee)

I have heard from a man of learning that the composer of Odes began by mentioning the deserted dwelling-places and the relics and traces of habitation. Then he wept and complained and addressed the desolate encampment, and begged his companion to make a halt, in order that he might have occasion to speak of those who had once lived there and afterwards departed; for the dwellers in tents were different from townsmen or villagers in respect of coming and going, because they moved from one water spring to another, seeking pasture and searching out the places where rain had fallen. Then to this he linked the erotic prelude (nasib), and bewailed the violence of his love and the anguish of separation from his mistress and the extremity of his passion and desire, so as to win the hearts of his hearers and divert their eyes towards him and invite their ears to listen to him, since the song of love touches men's souls and takes hold of their hearts, God having put it in the constitution of His creatures to love dalliance and the society of women, in such wise that we find very few but are attached thereto by some tie or have some share therein, whether lawful or unpermitted. Now, when the poet had assured himself of an attentive hearing, he followed up his advantage and set forth this claim: thus he went on to complain of fatigue and want of sleep and travelling by night and of the noonday heat. . . . (Ibn Qutaiba)

In the final analysis, the aim . . . is to delight the people present. (Yoshimoto Nijō)

Tell us, poet, what it is you do?—I praise. | But the deathly and the monstrous, | how do you bear them, how do you accept them?—I praise. | But the nameless, anonymous, | how then, poet, do you summon them?—I praise. | What is your right, in all disguises, | in every mask, to be true?—I praise. | And how come the still and violent, | like star and storm, know you?—Because I praise. (Rainer Maria Rilke)

Why do you say to me: poet? | I'm not a poet. | I'm only a very small child, crying. | You see: I've nothing but tears to offer the Silence. | Why do you say to me: poet? || . . . Even my sorrows are everyone's poor common sorrows | . . . Today I am thinking of dying. || . . . And I die, a little bit, every day. | You see? just as all things do. . . . (Sergio Corazzini)

. . . the duende *is a power and not a behavior, it is a struggle and not a concept. I have heard an old guitarist master say: 'The* duende *is not in the throat; the* duende *surges up from the souls of the feet.' Which means that it is not a matter of ability, but of real live form; of blood; of ancient culture; of creative action.*

. . . the dark and quivering duende *that I am talking about is a descendant of the merry daemon of Socrates . . . ; a descendant also of Descartes' melancholy Daemon. . . .*

To help us seek the duende *there is neither map nor discipline. All one knows is that it burns the blood like powdered glass, that it exhausts, that it rejects all the sweet geometry one has learned, that it breaks with*

*all styles, that it compels Goya . . . to paint with his knees and with
his fists horrible bitumen blacks. . . . (Federico Garcia Lorca)*

*To say more than human things with human voice, | That cannot be;
to say human things with more | Than human voice, that, also, cannot
be; | To speak humanly from the height or from the depth | Of human
things, that is acutest speech. (Wallace Stevens)*

*Poetry is a composition of words set to music. Most other definitions
of it are indefensible, or metaphysical. The proportion or quality of the
music may, and does, vary; but poetry withers and 'dries out' when it
leaves music . . . too far behind it. (Ezra Pound)*

*The movement of poetry is limited only by the nature of syllables and
of articulate sound, and by the laws of music, or melodic rhythms. (Ezra
Pound)*

*Poetry finds its own form; form should never be superimposed; the
structure should rise out of the words and the expression of them. (Dylan
Thomas)*

*Forms have ten thousand varieties | Things are not of one measure.
(Lu Chi)*

*Forms are chosen by poets because the most important part of what they
have to say seems to go better with that form than any other . . ., and
then, in its turn, the form develops and shapes the poet's imagination. . . .
(W. H. Auden)*

*If I hammer, if I recall in, and keep calling in, the breath . . . it is for
cause, it is to insist upon a part that breath plays in verse which has
not (due, I think, to the smothering of the power of the line by too set
a concept of the foot) has not been sufficiently observed. . . . (Charles
Olson)*

*. . . the line seems to be born of itself, born of necessity . . . and finds
that it is . . . at once the uniting element of memory, act, and perception,
a fixed novelty and yet an organized, repeatable function; an energy
and a generator of energy. (Paul Valéry)*

*What about measure, I learnt: | Look in your own ear and read.
(Louis Zukofsky)*

. . . grete vertue in a mannys eres. (Diogenes)

SOMEWHERE TO BEGIN

Doc Reed

Wanne mine eyhen misten, | And mine heren sissen, | And my nose coldet, | And my tunge foldet, | And my rude slaket, | And mine lippes blaken, | And my muth grennet, | And my spotel rennet, | And mine her riset, | And mine herte griset, | And mine honden bivien, | And mine fet stivien—| Al to late! | Wanne the bere is ate gate. (13 century English lyric)

Doc Reese

So what said the others and the sun went down. . . . (Wallace Stevens)

Blind Blake

Hayim of Volozhin, his disciple, once asked the Gaon the meaning of the word ḥesed (kindness) in a certain passage of the Zohar, which seemed out of place and unrelated to the preceding or following words. Without consulting the text, the Gaon informed him that several lines were missing. The copyist had found the passage unintelligible, and had written on the margin ḥasar ("missing"). The printer mistook the last letter, the resh, for the dalet, and the word became ḥesed. (Meyer Waxman)

. . . that boy would take me out with him at night and get me so turned around that I'd be lost if I left his side. He could see more with his blind eyes than. . . . (Gus Cannon)

SOME WOMEN

Lottie Kimbrough

Gentle lady, do not sing | Sad songs about the end of love. . . . (James Joyce)

Louise Johnson

Read, all you women   so that you may understand . . . obey your menfolk   so that you may not be touched by the sorrows. . . . (Mwana Kupona)

Bertha Lee

He watch'd th' Ideas rising in her Mind, | Suddenly he view'd, in spite of all her Art, | An Earthly Lover lurking at her Heart. (Alexander Pope)

GEECHIE WILEY

> *Eagle! eagle over your mountains, an eagle is flying over your mountains! | Slow the light—it seems as if for a moment—it is merely floating, | Floating, sailing in a sea of blue, alert to the song of delight in the heart | Of the heavens—of the sky, circling mutely in searing light. (Saul Tchernichovsky)*

ELVIE THOMAS

> *O, like the smoke of a chimney | and like the smoke of a train, | so, faithful mother, | is the love of a man. (Itzik Manger)*

LILLIAN MILLER

> *Long drunk: then bother how hinder? | Unsober time: having what thoughts? (Po P'u)*

NELLIE FLORENCE

> *Gentle men, love | Lovely women! | Love lifts your spirits | And shows you off to good advantage. | Look at me, | Young men! | Take your pleasure in me. (13 century German Easter Play)*

> *. . . in the heat, the mirage flowers and blazing fruits spread themselves in silence. (Edith Sitwell)*

JENNY POPE

> *So good-bye to the house with its wallpaper red | Good-bye to the sheets on the warm double bed. . . . (W. H. Auden)*

IVA SMITH

> *He knows he hath a home, but scarce knows where: | He says it is so far | That he hath quite forgot how to get there. (Henry Vaughan)*

LIL JOHNSON

> *Some women of kynde be ever wepyng | And under that they can both prick and stynge. (Marcus Porcius Cato)*

BESSIE JACKSON (LUCILLE BOGAN)

> *You see, a woman could get a job at that time, but a man couldn't hardly get it. Want a little money, had to get it from her. That's was in the time of the depression. And it give a man the blues: he's been the boss all the time and now the depression come and she's washing at the white folk's yard. And she's cooking there and she can get a little money, but*

she's feeding him so he can't cut up too much. So if he wants a little money . . . and she won't give him anything, naturally he says, "I'm broke and I ain't got a dime." And she says, "Well, you ought to have something . . . I gave you two bits last week!" And most any man get in hard luck some time. (Willie Thomas)

Some folks say black is evil, but I will tell the world they're wrong / 'Cause I'm a seal-skin brown I and been evil every since I been born.

MA RAINEY

And rising on one elbow Cynthia cried: / "Back to my bed? From some rebuff, no doubt! / What other woman's door has shut you out? / Where have you spent long hours that should be mine, / Till stars are sinking, and your powers decline?" (Sextus Propertius)

BESSIE SMITH

I got to make it, I got to find the end. . . .

(That was her song, for she was the maker. Then we, /As we beheld her striding there alone, / Knew that there never was a world for her / Except the one she sang and, singing, made. (Wallace Stevens))

BESSIE TUCKER

He's where? / With whom, held hands? / Small tower, silver screen: slow songs, wine / Already forgotten curse / No longer remembered low whispers. (Kuan Han-ch'ing)

SARA MARTIN

The world is too fucking with us. (Ezra Pound)

VICTORIA SPIVEY

There, there! O terror! What is this new sight? / A hunting net, Death's weapon of attack! / And she who hunts is she who shared his bed. / Howl, Furies, howl, you bloody ravening pack. . . . (Aeschylus)

MEMPHIS MINNIE

Through countless wanderings, / Hastenings, lingerings, / From far I come, / And pass from place to place . . . / To seek my home. (Edwin Muir)

I'd not dreamed, burdensome bane, / My face not fine and handsome, /

Till I lifted, lucid thing, | The glass: and see, it's ugly! (Dafydd ap Gwilym)

ALICE MOORE

Who knows three? I know three. Three are the fathers.... (Haggadah)

JIMMY AND MA YANCEY

Poet, be seated at the piano. | ... If they throw stones upon the roof | While you practice arpeggios, | It is because they carry down the stairs | A body in rags. | Be seated at the piano. (Wallace Stevens)

... you don't notice him; you feel him. ... (Art Hodes)

CHIPPIE HILL

If you can't sell it, sit on it.

TEXAS

HENRY THOMAS

The old man, loving leisure: notions odd | Fishing: T'ung River ... | ... Holding a hook, fragrant bait | Looking at Fu-ch'un Mountain, returning. (Hsü Tsai-ssu)

Simon Peter said, 'I go a-fishing;' and they said, 'We also will go with thee.' (John xxi. 3.)

BLIND LEMON JEFFERSON

Well I hate to tell you it ain't nobody there | If a man stay here he'll stay 'most any where.

Light snow's | In garden spread-fallen | Cold night | Arm pillow unpillowed | Sleeping alone? (Ōtomo Yakamochi)

I now must lie unpartnered on my bed, | And study, while my lamentations jar | On my own ears, how long the night-times are. (Sextus Propertius)

Of course my mother didn't let me go to them country suppers often. They was rough. Men was hustling women and selling bootleg, and Lemon was singing for them all night. They didn't even do any proper kind of dancing—just stompin'. (Alec Jefferson)

Everybody knew him . . . a chunky fellow in a big black hat.
(Sammy Price)

Oh he was a great big fat dark man with a big stomach. He'd lay
that guitar across his stomach, man, it was a shame . . . . (Lightning
Hopkins)

. . . He was a blind man and I used to lead him around . . . we'd
sit down and talk to one another. . . . (Leadbelly)

. . . Catch me by the hand, oh baby, / Blind Lemon was a blind
man . . . / . . . Catch me by the hand, oh baby, / And lead me
through the land. . . . (Leadbelly)

. . . he wouldn't allow you to lead him 'cause he'd say you called
him blind. No, don't call *him* blind. . . . (Lightning Hopkins)

> *(The crier soon came, leading that man of song / whom the muse*
> *cherished; by her gift he knew / the good of life, and evil— / for she*
> *who lent him sweetness made him blind. (Homer))*

Wasn't It Sad about Lemon?: The weather was below zero on the
day he passed away. . . . (Walter Taylor & John Byrd)

Well it's one kind favor I ask of you: / See that my grave is kept
clean. . . .

BUDDY BOY HAWKINS

> *Zeus and Hera bickered constantly. Vexed by his infidelities, she often*
> *humiliated him by her scheming ways. Though he would confide his*
> *secrets to her, and sometimes accept her advice, he never fully trusted*
> *Hera, and she knew that if offended beyond a certain point he would flog*
> *or even hurl a thunderbolt at her. (Robert Graves)*

RAMBLING (WILLARD) THOMAS

> *. . . I determined on keeping the sea, in spite of the weather. . . .*
> *(William Carlos Williams)*

BLIND WILLIE JOHNSON

> *. . . we haue be flytted wth ffeare of the sycknes. . . . Rownd a bowte*
> *vs yt hathe bene all moste in every howsse abowt vs & wholle howsholdes*
> *deyed & yt my frend the baylle doth scape but he smealles monstrusly*
> *for feare & dares staye no wheare for ther hathe deyed this laste weacke*
> *in generall 1603 of the wch nomber ther hathe died of them of the plage*
> *113 [5]-0-5. . . . (Philip Henslowe)*

[His father] married another lady. After Willie's mama died, why he married another lady. She kept company with another man. And she throwed lye in Willie's face to put his eyes out. . . . He was the age of seven years old.

He was singing on the streets, and he was singing, '*If I Had-a My Way I Would Tear the Building Down!* And I went walking behind him: 'If I had-a my way, oh lordy lordy, / If I had-a my way, / Oh, I'd tear that building down.' And I went on to, you know, talking with him. And then I said, 'Say, are you married or single?' He said, 'I'm single.' So I says, 'Come go to my house: I have a piano;' and I says, 'and we will get together and sing.' And he says, 'Have you ever singed anywhere?' I says, 'Well,' I say, 'I sing over the radio,' I said, 'out of church.' And so he said, 'All right,' and he went on over. Well, we went on over to the house, and we set down, and taking a few drinks, you know, and played. Then he played his guitar, and I got up to the piano, and I went to playing, 'If I Had-a My Way.' He said, 'Go on gal, tear it up!' Ha ha ha ha ha. Ahhhhhhhhh. Well, we went on back, and so he says, 'Well, let's get on the streets.' I said, 'All right.' So I said, 'Well look,' I said, 'don't you want something to eat?' He said, 'What have you cooked?' I said, 'Well, I have some crabs.' I said, 'We're making the old time Nigger's Gumbo.' I said, 'Don't you want some?' And he says, 'Well, yes.' He says, 'I'll take some.' And so he went and, and accepted a bowl. Of gumbo. And I broke it up, you know, the claws, you know, so that he could enjoy it. And then we set down and eat. . . . He told me, he says, 'Say, let's marry.' I said, 'Ok.' That's what I wanted. And then he says, 'Well, when can you get ready?' I said, 'I'll get ready tomorrow.' That was the twenty-second of June.

He died from pneumonia. We had a—we burnt out there in the North End . . . and when we burnt out, why, we didn't know many people, and so I just, you know, drug him back in there, and we laid on the wet bed covers—with a lot of newspaper. It didn't bother me, but it bothered him. Yes. You see, he'd turn over. And I just lay up on the paper. And I thought that if you put a lot of paper on, you know, that it would, you know, keep us from getting sick. We didn't get wet, but just the dampness. You know, and then he singing, you know, and his veins opened, and everything. And it just made him—uh, you know, sick. . . . [The hospital] wouldn't accept him. He'd-a been living today if they'd accepted him. 'Cause he's blind. Blind folks has a hard time—you can't get in the hospital. . . . (Angeline Johnson)

Wouldn't mind dying if dying was all.

LEADBELLY

> . . . *she was passing joious ffor she had hym lever ferre than nyghe.*
> (*Raoul Lefevre*)

A SURVEY OF SORTS: VARIOUS VOICES

. . . T. B. Blues . . . I'll never know what made me make that record. . . . But at that time I had been looking at people who had the T.B. in part of the country, and at that time if you had the T.B. nobody would have no part with you: they put you away in hospital and you was just doomed then—you gonna die. So I figured it was a nice thing to write about. (Victoria Spivey)

Little Hat Jones

Having abdicated with comparative ease | And dismissed the greater part of your friends, | Escaping by submarine | . . . You have got here . . . | How shall we celebrate your arrival? (W. H. Auden)

"Funny Paper" Smith

Hey, who are you, you? | Who has come to disturb | the dark repose of wise men? | Who has come to sow believing seeds? | Suddenly everybody saw | gleaming on his head | Moses' foolish, credulous | starlike horns. (Jacob Glatstein)

Preacher told me God will 'give a black man 'most anything he do; / I ain't black but I'm dark complected: look like he ought to forgive me too.

Texas Alexander

. . . he who seeking Asses found a Kingdom. . . . (John Milton)

He couldn't play no music. Never played an instrument in his life. But he'd tote a guitar. He'd buy a guitar. But he'd tote it in case that he'd run upon you, or me, or somebody could play, and he'd sing. And he kept a guitar 'cause if he asked you could you play a guitar, and you said "Yeah," well he had one, see, and then you all'd tear off. And that's when I met Texas Alexander, many year ago. . . .

I accompanied him for quite a bit there in Crockett, Texas, and Grapeland, Palestine Oakwood, and Buffalo, and Centerville . . . and back in them places. I never followed Texas no further 'n Houston for a long ways, see. 'Cause he was a man who would get up and go.

First Cadillac that I'd ever known to be—you know, one of them expensive bad cars—he went somewhere and he come . . . in a Cadillac, and it was the longest old ugly car, old long Cadillac, one of them there first made, but it was new—that's—he got over there—and everybody admired him, you know, because colored people didn't have no—they didn't even have T-model Fords then, you know: he come in a Cadillac. Texas was doing all right for hisself.

And he got singing them bad songs, you know, I guess he thought that it was all right, and you know in times you couldn't sing a bad song—you know, not on the box and jukes and things. So he sung a bad song, and they sent him down, see . . . yeah, they put him in the can for a while. But he sung on outa there. He got out. He wasn't in there too long, I don't think he was in there too long. 'Cause he come back. But he never been singing that kind of song again. Now, you know, they're singing everything —and they're not condemning 'em. (Lightning Hopkins)

When you gets to yoyoing you jumps it up and down, / But when you 'earn how to yoyo you turn it round and round.

GENE CAMPBELL

> . . . the burglary, while being performed, is always the last, not that you think you are not going to perform another after that one—you don't think—but because such a gathering of self cannot take place (not in life, for to push it further would be to pass out of life); and this oneness of an act which develops (as the rose puts forth its corolla) into conscious gestures, such of their efficacy, of their fragility and yet of the violence which they give to the act, here too confers upon it the value of a religious rite. Often I even dedicate it to someone. The first time, it was Stilitano who had the benefit of such homage. . . . To his beauty, to his tranquil immodesty, I dedicated my first thefts. (Jean Genet)

L. C. WILLIAMS

> Put out your light and sleep! The ever wakeful / Splashing of the old fountain is the only sound. / But whoever's been a guest under my roof, / Has soon become used to this sound. // Though it may sometime happen, when you're already in mid- / Dream, that a restlessness will go around the house, / The gravel by the fountain will crackle under heavy steps, / The light splashing sometime will stop, // And you'll awake,—but don't be startled! / The stars all still stand above the earth, / And it's only a wanderer stepping up to the marble basin, / Who scoops from the fountain with cupped hands. . . . (Hans Carossa)

LIGHTNING HOPKINS

Here in Houston I can be broke and hungry and walk out and someone will buy me a dinner. It ain't always like that in a strange place where you don't know no one.

> Philaenis always weeps with one eye. / Know why? / She only has one eye. (Marcus Valerius Martialis)

> Who says that fictions only and false hair / become a verse? (George Herbert)

Places I was playing—they were *small* places. Oh, four or five stores, and nearly each of them didn't have much more than that ... and they call Buffalo—that sounds a big place: small. Brenham, Texas: small place. Crocket: it was small. But to listen to all them names you'd think they was great big places. They're small.

MANCE LIPSCOMB

> *Who hath sent out the wild ass free? or who hath loosed the bands of the wild ass? (Job 39.5)*

... you're a man but you still a boy 'cause you had to do what the man told you—or else you couldn't stay on his place or either he'd whoop you. ...

I been playing the guitar now 'bout forty-n'ne years, and then I started out by myself, just heard it and learned it. Ear music.

> *(Thus passyth he the tyme both nyght and day, | Sumtyme with sadnes, sumtyme with play. . . . (John Skelton))*

LIL' SON JACKSON

... I think that the blues is more or less a feeling that you get from something that you think is wrong, or something that somebody did wrong to you, or something that somebody did wrong to some of your own people or something like that . . . and the onliest way you have to tell it would be through a song, and that would be the blues . . . but the blues is really aimed at an object of some kind or an indirect person. It's not aimed at the whole public; the blues cannot be aimed at the whole public.

> *David called out to him: "Kouz-Badin, how are you going to escape from me this time?. . . . David caught Ohan of Aghbak alive and tore him in two from limb to limb. Kouz-Badin tried to get away on his six-footed horse but David caught him also. He knocked out his remaining teeth. . . . He cut off his ears. He cut up his lips. He tore out an eyeball. . . . (Gurbo, of the Plain of Moush)*

Whether a man sing the blues or ballads or what have you, there is no way in the world that he can get round and not make a sin out of it in some way. In other words, there's so many ways he can make it a sin, and there's too many different ways the average entertainer *will*. He can't go wrong and keep himself clean with singing ballads or blues or boogie woogie, because it's on the wrong side. It's a two-sided road and you on the wrong side all the time.

NEW ORLEANS TO JACKSON

RABBIT BROWN

A good time won't come again. ("Li Ling")

Rabbit Brown, coloured, sang to his guitar in the streets of New Orleans, and he rowed you out into Lake Ponchartrain for a fee and he sang to you as he rowed. (*Bookman*, July 1928)

(From a small Boat, that row'd along, | The listning Winds receiv'd this Song. (Andrew Marvell))

Again I am in love and not in love, am mad and not mad. (Anacreon)

SAM COLLINS

. . . Hear you amid the drowsy even | One who is singing by your gate. | His song is softer than the dew | And he is come to visit you. (James Joyce)

My mama signify that my black snake was dead.

KING SOLOMON HILL

I have a journey up-country   as far as the town of Iringa . . . | I would not have composed this song   if it were not that you are my friends   and the reasons [for my going] are nothing special   the circumstances are the usual ones   and so I packed my things. . . . (Ustadh Ahmad Basheikh b. Husein of Mombasa)

Joe Williams . . . recorded in Grafton, Wisconsin for Paramount under the pseudonym of *King Solomon Hill,* derived from the name of a town in Mississippi. He used a falsetto voice to disguise himself. (Robert G. Koester)

. . . Gayle Wardlow . . . discovered "Hill" to have been a one-time resident of . . . Sibley (La.) named Joe Holmes. (Horace Butterworth)

. . . there have been suggestions that Hill was Collins using a pseudonym to avoid trouble with the American Recording Corporation . . . it could be that Hill was from Texas, and the similarities between his style and Collins' were only coincidental. (Samuel Charters)

(We purposed to begin with his Life, Parentage, and Education: But as to these, even his contemporaries do exceedingly differ. One saith, he was educated at home; another, that he was bred at St. Omer's by

Jesuits; a third, not at St. Omer's, but at Oxford; a fourth, that he had no University education at all. Those who allow him to be bred at home, differ as much concerning his Tutor: One saith, he was kept by his father on purpose; a second, that he was an itinerant priest; a third, that he was a parson; one called him a secular clergyman of the Church of Rome; another, a monk. As little do they agree about his Father, whom one supposeth, like the Father of Hesiod, a tradesman or merchant; another, a husbandman; another a hatter, &c. . . . Finding, therefore, such contrariety of opinions, and (whetever be ours of this sort of generation) not being fond to enter into controversy, we shall defer writing the life of our Poet, 'till authors can determine among themselves what Parents or Education he had, or whether he had any Education or Parents at all. (M. Scriblerus))

(There is no solution because there is no problem. (Marcel Duchamp))

ARTHUR PETTIES (PETTIS)

*That day was doom's first birthday and that first day was the cause of |
Evils: Dido recked nothing for appearance or reputation: | The love she brooded on now was a secret love no longer. . . . (Publius Vergilius Maro)*

BLIND WILLIE (JOE) REYNOLDS

When I loved the wife, weak now, | Then, of the bald-head burgess, | The hunchback, show of servants, | A top man's wife, Robin Nordd's, | Ellen, eager for riches. . . . (Dafydd ap Gwilym)

Three smiles that are worse than grief: the smile of snow melting, the smile of your wife to you after sleeping with another man, the smile of a leaping dog. (Irish triad)

If you can't do my rollin', mama, you can't spend my change.

TOMMY JOHNSON

When a man goes on his road he goes with a friend. . . . (Swahili song)

ISHMAN BRACEY

I sawe . . . a lady . . . the whiche as men saide blanked and popped or peynted herself. I sawe also hym that gaf to her every yere suche thynges wherewith she popped her. . . . (Geffroy de la Tour Landry)

Please take me, rider, take me to your hand / Let me in your darkest corner, woman, hide me from your man.

Willie Lofton

In the corner's spider: | cool it! | I ain't gonna sweep. (Kobayashi Issa)

Rube Lacy

Still I did not take her from her father's hand | Into a house fragrant with Assyrian odors | But she gave me her furtive gifts in the marvelous night, | Stolen from her husband's bed. | Therefore it is enough if she gives me alone | The day she marks with a white pebble. (Gaius Valerius Catullus)

Charlie McCoy

My lefe is faren in a lond— | Alas! why is she so? | And I am so sore bound | I may nat com her to. | She hath my hert in hold, | Where-ever she ride or go, | With trew love a thousandfold. (15 century English song)

(Kansas) Joe McCoy

Her only fault, and that is faults enough, | Is, that she is intolerable curst. . . . (William Shakespeare)

Bo Carter

. . . man is not Engineer, Mechanic, Local Constable, Mayor, or Lawyer, etc., he is simply someone who fulfills, among his other functions, the function of mechanic, etc., a function that does not contain the whole of him and cannot totally absorb him. (Eugene Ionesco)

Well, we called us the Mississippi Sheiks, all of us Chatmans,
'cause my name's Bo Chatman, only they call me Bo Carter.

Well, we just go from place to place and we commence to getting older and older and we was scattering out and commence to getting weaker and weaker until now we cut down to four brothers. Bo Carter, he went by the name of Carter because he went to recording by himself, so instead of putting out Chatman he put out Carter. Just changed his name as is. . . . So now I farmed, I have night-watched, and fired at a big plant up there in Memphis. Oh, lots of different kinds of work. I'm a carpenter: I can do 'most any sort of carpenter work you can bring up. (Sam Chatman)

One time a boy got at me. He run at me with his horse. Then he
had his mules set at me and he drove them with his brother one
morning right across my cotton-patch, and my lock was taken.
My wife and kids was up and I was lying in the bed. So I said,
"Gene, why didn't you speak to me, 'stead of coming and getting

at me this morning?"

He said, "Well, I just want to see who is the *man* this morning. You talk to me like I was a kid, not a man, so I just want to see who *is* the man."

. . . So I say, "Well, hear me mister, you better forget about it." Say to my wife, "Hand me that shot-gun." He say, "I wanna see who *is* the man!"

Wife handed me that pop-gun and I pointed it out there to where he was. Wife says, "He's gone!" I say, "Who is the man . . .?" He hollered back, "You!"

So then me and him made it up and now when I see him he say, "Who is the best man now?, 'cause you can't see—you blind." But I say, "No, I can't see no more, but I got my knife in my pocket and I can reach it in my pocket. I got my hand on my knife and I'll open it with my teeth and cut your throat."

"Would you do that?" I say, "Sure I'll do it. . . ." So me and him we have no more fuss. That's settled. 'Cause I'll do it all right.

JOHN BYRD

> *Just when Vronsky was thinking that it was time to pass Mahotin, Frou-Frou herself, already understanding what was in his mind, without any urging, considerably increased her speed and began to draw nearer Mahotin on the inside. . . . Vronsky passed Mahotin but was aware that Mahotin was close upon him, and he kept hearing at his back the regular rhythm of Gladiator's hooves and the still quite fresh breathing of his nostrils. (Leo N. Tolstoy)*

SKIP JAMES

. . . I'd skip around at the parties people used to have in their houses so they give me the name of Skippy.

I could compose a song in three minutes.

It was just in me I guess, and I was just grafting after it. . . .

After I got that much from those [other guitar players], then I just used my own self: Skip. I don't pattern after anyone or either copycat. I may hear something, but if it's nice enough for me to get an idea about, I think I like a phrase or something, I may get it and put it in where it will be befitting in some of my pieces. But other than that, I don't. It's just Skip's music . . . I don't sing other people's songs, I don't sing other people's voices. I can't.

Back in Dallas, the people was on soup lines. You know, lines just getting soup, wasn't having anything, just what the government was giving us.

. . . just got so case-hardened and discouraged . . . I just gave up,
quit playing altogether.

> *Pine and cypress flank a broad path | Below are the long dead men |*
> *Dark, dark, passing eternal night | Hidden asleep below the Yellow*
> *Spring | A thousand years forever unwaking (Second century Chinese*
> *poem)*

TOMMY MCCLENNAN

The hell with them. I'll sing my song. . . .

ARTHUR (BIG BOY) CRUDUP

> *Where, when tired of wandering | Will the last resting-place be | . . .*
> *Will I, somewhere in a desert, | Be buried by a strange hand?. . . .*
> *(Heinrich Heine)*

MISSISSIPPI: THE DELTA

WILLIAM HARRIS

> *He was learning the song with which the frogs praise God. It takes a*
> *very long time to learn that song. (Martin Buber)*

> *. . . kikukku kukukku kukkuku gugugu | gugugugu gugunk' | gugugugu*
> *gugunk' | gululut gululut iiiiiiiiiiiiiiii | gululut gululut iiiiiiiiiiiiiiii. . . .*
> *(Kusano Shimpei)*

Oh come on daddy, this ain't no joke, | if you got a good cigarette
better gimme a smoke. . . .

BO WEAVIL JACKSON

> *. . . without love, men cannot endure to be together. (Thomas Carlysle)*

CHARLIE PATTON

> *Then the gods of the abyss rose up; Nergal pulled out the dams of the*
> *nether waters, Ninurta the war-lord threw down the dykes, . . . A stupor*
> *of despair went up to heaven when the god of the storm turned daylight*
> *into darkness, when he smashed the land like a cup. . . . Even the gods*
> *were terrified at the flood, they fled to the highest heaven, the firmament*
> *of Anu; they crouched against the walls, cowering. . . . (Epic of*
> *Gilgamesh)*

> *LEAR: Blow winds, and crack your cheeks; rage, blow | You cataracts,*
> *and hurricanoes spout, | Till you have drenched our steeples, drowned*
> *the cocks. . . .*

FOOL: O nuncle, Court holy-water in a dry house, is better than this rain-water out o' door. . . . (William Shakespear)

Charlie Patton, he's dead. (a man)

Charlie Patton was living here when I came here back in 1917. He traveled all around but always came back. . . . Then, a few years later he left for good. Mr. Jed fired him. (Johnny Wilder)

Charlie was a great blues singer: he taught them all. . . . He was born on a farm outside Edwards in 1887. . . . Charlie's first wife was named Gertrude. He met Minnie Franklin in Merigold in 1921. . . . Then he followed her on down to Vicksburg. . . . Charlie played all over. (Viola Cannon)

He used to play the guitar and he'd make the guitar say, "Lord have mercy, Lord have mercy, Lord have mercy, pray, brother, pray, save poor me." Now that's what Charlie Patton'd make the guitar say. (J. D. Short)

. . . Willie and I got near to the house and we heard such a grunting and rattling coming up through the stalks, and I said, "Wait a minute, Willie, hold it. I hear something coming through the cotton field. Don't you hear it?" He said, "Yeah, it's something" . . . . Finally, who should pop out to the roadside but Charlie! He looked and saw us and said, "I'll kill 'em all. I'll kill 'em all." Me and Willie started laughing and told him, "How you gon' kill 'em all? We heard you running." (Son House)

Mr. Calloway sent for us to come up on the train and we were there about three weeks making records. We didn't work all the time, because it took the morning before Charlie had his voice ready. (Bertha Lee Patton)

. . . This man wanted Charlie to get Willie and I to come down to Jackson to make some church songs. . . . After that, we went on back to Charlie's, and we stayed about three more weeks. We went all around through the country playing, all three of us together. So Willie and I went on back to Lake Cormorant, where we were living then, and about two weeks after we got back, we got a telegram from Bertha; that was the girl said to be his wife. The telegram said that Charlie was dead. . . . (Son House)

(I always wanted to be like old Charlie Patton. . . . I wants to come to be a great man like Charlie Patton, but I didn't want to get killed like he did. . . . I've always realized I knew I had to die, but I didn't want one of them old sandfoot womens to come up and cut my throat, or do something to me that was unnecessary. . . . (Booker White))

Charlie was playing for a white dance—you have to work so much harder at a white dance in the South: they don't want to stop dancing. When he come home he was so hoarse he couldn't talk and he couldn't get his breath. He had to get up out of bed at night and open the windows so he could get some air. He lived three weeks after that but he was too weak to do anything. He was laying across my lap when he died. (Bertha Lee Patton)

(. . . how gladly would I meet | Mortalitie my sentence, and be Earth | Insensible, how glad would lay me down | As in my Mother's lap? there I should rest | and sleep secure. . . . (John Milton))

True, birds rebuild | Old nests and there is blue in the woods. (Wallace Stevens)

WILLIE BROWN

The girl who promised | To meet me | On Mount Tsukuba— | Was it because she listened to someone else?— | Did not meet and sleep with me. (Hitachi Fudoki)

"Coming soon" | just said, yet | long moon's | dawn's moon: | waiting till it's gone (the Priest, Sosei)

He was shorter than they were, but thicker. . . . Willie was a better guitar player than Charlie was, Son House too. At least he thought so, and they thought so too. (Bertha Lee Patton)

The gleam of the lightning over the mountain-folds gave unto us the flash of thy teeth; and it was the best of gifts. (Ibn al Fārid)

HENRY SIMS

. . . I seen Patton and Sims playing together around here. Charlie died some time ago. Son Sims didn't want to play anymore after that. He took it real bad. . . . (a woman)

SON HOUSE

. . . They called it Riverton, and right down the road a little past Riverton—about two miles—is where I was born. I got up around seven or eight years old, my mother took me to Louisiana, and that's mostly where I grew up to call myself a man . . . and when I got up to be some size, I started working. One while, I was gathering moss down in Algiers. . . .

After my mother died, I left and came back up in Mississippi where the rest of my people was. So I was just to and fro then. I wouldn't stay anywhere too long after I got to be called myself a man, you know. . . . I was just ramblified, you know. Especially after I started playing music. That was the one thing gave it to me.

. . . I bought an old piece of guitar from a fella named Frank Hopkins. I gave him a dollar and a half for it. It was nearly all to pieces, but I didn't know the difference.

. . . I kept on playing and got better and better, you know. I'd set up and concentrate on the songs, and then went to concentrating on me rhyming words, rhyming my own words. "I can make my own songs," I said. And that's the way I started.

. . . "Preachin' Blues," "Black Mama," "Mississippi County Farm," and "Clarksdale Moan." Willie Brown and I played that last one together. I think that's about all. Close as I can get to it. It's been so long. . . . I got paid forty dollars for making those records . . . forty dollars! . . . It'd take me near about a year to make forty dollars in the cotton patch. . . .

This is one on me. Just as well admit it. This is the truth. 'Course some of it is a little addition, but the biggest of it is the truth. I used to be a preacher. I was brought up in church and started preaching before I started this junk. . . . And I began to wonder, now how can I stand up in the pulpit and preach to them, tell them how to live, and quick as I dismiss the congregation and I see ain't nobody looking and I'm doing the same thing. . . . I says, well, I got to do something, 'cause I can't hold God in one hand and the Devil in the other one. . . . I got to turn one of 'em loose. So I got out of the pulpit. So I said, the next time I make a record, I'm gon' to name it "Preachin' Blues." I'm preaching on this side and the blues on that side. . . .

(He took the scroll of the Torah in his hand and danced with it. Then he laid the scroll aside and danced without it. (Martin Buber))

(He that remains plays on an instrument | | a good agreement between himself and night | A chord between the mass of men and himself, | Far, far beyond the putative canzones | Of love and summer. (Wallace Stevens))

After he [Willie Brown] died, I just decided I wouldn't fool with playing any more. I don't even know what I did with the guitar.

BOBBY GRANT

. . . one MUST buy beds. . . . (Ezra Pound)

ROBERT JOHNSON

If I had possession over Judgement Day | Lord, the woman I'm loving wouldn't have no right to pray.

Then of course there was Robert, Robert Johnson. He used to work the jukes. . . . I never did talk to him much. He was the kind of guy you wanted to listen to. . . . Robert was a nice looking man—sort of brownskin, sort of medium height, and got good hair. But he didn't seem to stay in one place too long—you know, kind of restless. Think I heard he went to Helena. (Muddy Waters)

I met Robert Johnson in Helena. I met him in *West* Helena and West Memphis and also in Mississippi—all over. . . . He could play those barrelhouse things and he was pretty much moving all the time. (Sunnyland Slim)

He was my stepfather, Robert Johnson. . . . I didn't see too much of him because he wasn't around so much. . . . (Robert Junior Lockwood)

You couldn't run with Robert for long. . . . (Walter Horton)

We were staying someplace—I don't remember where it was—and he got up in the middle of the night and left. Just like that! (Johnny Shines)

(Call me traveler!: first winter rain. (Matsuo Bashō))

. . . I was living on, I believe it was 2320 Carr Street during that time and I was playing at Earnest Walker's House Party on Jefferson. Robert Johnson had come over to find me, and he was a stranger in the town so he told me, "Look, I've heard about you." He was just traveling through and he says, "Where you working at tonight?," so I told him and he says, "Can I come over?," and I said, "Yeah," so he come over to Walker's. . . .

Well, we sat in the back yard and that fellow, he went one some guitar and I thought, well, this guy's got it. I mean he was amazing. I was a little bit older than him, but I didn't think anybody had any seniority over me on the guitar, but this guy made me look little. During the time I was fixing to leave town, really, and he played for Earnest Walker for about three weeks and I come back and he stayed with me another week over there, for a very small scale of course. He held the job until I came back and the truth is it was Robert's job when I came back. Robert continued until he was ready to leave; then the boss put me back to work. Robert was very decent about it; I mean we worked together, but as far as the job was concerned it belonged to Robert. . . . I don't really know where he was going when he left. He said he was going to Chicago. . . . (Henry Townsend)

. . . I gave him a little instruction. Said, "Now, Robert. You

going around playing for these Saturday night balls. You have
to be careful 'cause you mighty crazy about the girls. When you
playing for these balls and these girls get full of that corn whiskey
and snuff mixed together, and you be playing a good piece and
they like it and come up and call you, 'Daddy, play it again,
Daddy'—well, don't let it run you crazy. You liable to get
killed." He must not have paid it much attention. . . . So he left
and went out there from Greenwood, Mississippi. Somewhere
out in there. . . . (Son House)

> *(The mind between this light or that and space, | (This man in a room
> with an image of the world, | That woman waiting for the man she
> loves), | Grows large against space. . . . (Wallace Stevens))*

I'm lonesome and there's a lady here. She wants fifty cents and I
lacks a nickel. . . .

. . . The next word we heard was from his mother who told us
that he was dead. We never did get the straight of it. We heard
first that he got stabbed to death. Next, a woman poisoned him,
and then we heard something else. I can't remember what it was
now, but it was three different things. Never did get the straight
of it. Close as I can get to it, he was about twenty-three or -four.
(Son House)

> *(Soon will I leave you | Gone, a stranger in a strange land. (Joseph
> von Eichendorff))*

MISSISSIPPI JOHN HURT

New York's a good town, but it's not for mine, | Going back to
Avalon, there where I see my mama all the time.

> *Slepe fyrst on thy ryght syde. . . . And after thi fyrst slepe turne on thy
> lifte syde that thy ryght side may be rested . . . and when thou hast layen
> theron a good while and slept, turn ayen on thi ryght side and then slepe
> all nyght forth. (William Caxton)*

GARFIELD AKERS

> *Still yearning, and disquieted | Still sleepless tossing on his bed. . . .
> (Ibn Ḥazm)*

JOE CALICOTT

> *When you come next time, | Go to the back: | The window at the front
> | Is noisy! (Japanese song)*

I wasn't paying the time no attention—was traveling so fast. . . .

> *She was an old woman of a family with a long genealogy. Leza Shikakunamo—"The Besetting One"—had stretched out his hand against her family. He slew her mother and her father while she was yet a child; and in the course of the years all connected with her perished. . . . She became withered with age, and it seemed to her that she herself was at last to be taken. . . . Then came into her heart a desperate resolution to find Leza and ask the meaning of it all. . . .*
>
> *So she began to travel, going through country after country, nation after nation. . . . As she passed through the different countries the people asked her, "What have you come for old woman?"*
>
> *And her answer would be, "I am seeking Leza."*
>
> *"Seeking Leza! For what?"*
>
> *"My brothers, you ask me! Where in the nations is there one who suffers as I have suffered?"*
>
> *And they would ask again, "How have you suffered?"*
>
> *"In this way. I am alone. As you see me, a solitary old woman: that is how I am!"*
>
> *And they answered again, "Yes, we see. That is how you are! Bereaved of friends and kindred? In what do you differ from others? Leza Shika-kunamo sits on the back of every one of us, and we cannot shake him off."*
>
> *. . . she died. . . . (Baila tale)*

I just reach up and pull them out of the sky—call them sky songs.

> *Moor grass, how vast vast . . . | Carried me out to the distant wasteland . . . | The dark room, once closed, | A thousand years, no dawn again . . . | The men who've just carried me | Each has returned to his own home | Relations, perhaps, still grieve | Others: already sing | Dead, gone— what's to be said? . . . (T'ao Ch'ien)*

I like to talk and have a nice time—like a fish—take him out of
the water and lay him on the bank in the hot sun and he'll soon
dry up and die—that's the way I am—if you don't put me someplace where I can have fun I won't live long. . . .

> *(Since | Living men | In the end die too | While in the world | Let's have fun. (Ōtomo no Tabito))*

Like I said, though, things used to get rough in them days. Not
that they don't these days, but back then they wouldn't think no

more about killing a Negro than they would about killing a chicken. I became more acquainted with lynchings than I was with hanging up my socks. . . .

I had a first cousin to get lynched. His name was Robert Lee Hatchett. He was just about 18 years old. A bunch of white boys was drinking one Saturday night and Robert Lee was coming home and they killed him and laid his body on the railroad tracks for the train to run over. But the engineer stopped. The white boys went home and went to bed and nothing was ever done to them. And that was one of the things that started me to being mean. . . .

I never wrote songs about nothing like that, though. I didn't do it then and I won't do it now. It just get on my nerves. I can think of other things to sing about. It's so much of that kind of thing happening every day and I just don't want to make no songs out of it. . . .

I had to burn a guy a little and they gave me a little time down there on Parchman's Farm—they treat you like you treat yourself—. . . and I seen better days there than I did at home—when I got out I felt like shooting somebody else. . . .

(In his service in the Low Countries, he [Ben Jonson] had, in the face of both the camps, killed ane enemy, and taken optima spolia *from him; and since his coming to England, being appealed to the fields, he had killed his adversary, who had hurt him in the arm, and whose sword was ten inches longer than his; for the which he was imprisoned and almost at the gallows. . . . In the time of his close imprisonment, under Queen Elizabeth, his judges could get nothing of him to all their demands but* Ay *and* No. *(Drummond of Hawthornden))*

I was in Parchman, a collector come through looking for songs. I sang him three songs, but I didn't sing him no more 'cause I knew there wasn't no money in it.

(No man but a blockhead ever wrote except for money. (Samuel Johnson))

I think I did do nice. I gave him a little something to go with. He come with nothing, but he left with a little something. . . .

I could lay down and die today. What am I gon' worry about? All I want to do is make it in. On the earth, I have really gained a victory of a poor man having what he's supposed to have and I have no kick coming. When I die, I don't want to die with a frown on my face, 'cause I don't want nobody to think that I left something that I was supposed to get and I didn't get it and I left with a frown. . . .

They'd ask me to play and I played the best I knew how.

ISAIAH NETTLES

Ah, you Chinaman! (Louis Aragon)

MEMPHIS

JIM JACKSON

> *The blue dogs rue, | as he does, as he would howl, confronting | the wind which rocks what was her, while prayers | striate the snow, words blow | as questions cross fast, fast | as flames, as flames form, melt | along any darkness || Birth is an instance as is a host, namely, death. . . . (Charles Olson)*

Me and Jim Jackson played on the shows together, all down the Mississippi and through Arkansas, Alabama, all over. We were with the Red Rose Minstrels it was called, but it was a medicine show. It was just a show where the man sold all kinds of medicine and soap and stuff. One medicine good for a thousand things— and wasn't good for *nothin'*. . . .

He was a big fat fella, weighed about 235 pounds. Tall stately fella too, and he danced, sang, played guitar, cracked jokes. . . . He died back in 1937. (Speckled Red)

FRANK STOKES

> *Now some folks say that a preacher won't steal | But he will do more stealing than I get regular meals. (Kansas Joe McCoy)*

> *Many executives queried were, in fact, outraged that the press should poke so far into what they regard as purely personal business. "I certainly* would *mind discussing it," snapped Robert W. Minor, New York Central vice president, who reported that in November he sold 1,540 shares of Central stock, reducing his holdings to 460. Minor promptly slammed down the telephone. (Forbes, March 1, 1968)*

FURRY LEWIS

Well, one thing, when you write the blues and what you be thinking about, you be blue and you ain't got hardly nothing to think about. You just already blue, and you just go on and write. . . .

The time when you get a blues, what you call the blues, you just haven't come out like you s'posed to and it don't be right. You have to go all over it again until you rhyme it. It got to be rhymed up if you call yourself being with the blues. If it ain't rhymed up

A SURVEY OF SORTS: VARIOUS VOICES

it don't sound good to me or nobody else.

Oh, the first recording session was when I was around—going around then, you know, getting people could play, and we was going to Chicago, to, you know, to make records. And so I went on there, and I met Mr. Jack Kapp, he's a fine fella. Mr. Jack Kapp is a fine fella. And so I made two or three records there with Mr. Jack Kapp. . . .

I done two sides. I done two sides at a time. . . .

The first record I was made was "Good Looking Girl Blues". . . .

I went many times on Beale Street and hear them play it. . . . I felt fine, but there was a whole lot of 'em there didn't know who I was, you see, and I put about a dollar and some in there myself, to hear my own self, and everybody say, "That fella sure can play, I like to see him," and I'm right there. . . .

I used to play with a pocket knife, but I noticed sometime the pocket knife slip between my fingers, and I just thought of the bottle-neck myself, you see that can't slip off: can't go no further up or down either, just there . . . Royal Crown, R.C. . . . I takes a steel saw, you see, it's one of them steel saws, and saw it off even, smooth, you know, where it can't cut you. That can't even cut you nowhere.

> You don't hear any kind of music like that these days and times.
> Of course it's quiet here now, not like it used to be. (a woman)

> *If casino managers don't like to lose, they should sell vegetables. (Dr. Richard Jarecki)*

ROBERT WILKINS

We'd play on the streets in town Saturday evening . . . and the law would have to come along and get them back so you could walk the streets. . . . And there'd be some nights through the week, when I felt like it, I go over there and play, and the people in town—they'd get up out of their beds when they heard me.

In winter I'd go in houses. You know, they was going from house to house to house—if I could go. Yeah, they just wanted me to play because I was the best that was—anyhow, there at that time. I over-ran all the old musicians that I learned under.

> *. . . as the Bryde did rome | Abrode accompanyde with a trayne of Nymphes to bring her home, | A serpent lurking in the grasse did sting her in the ancle: | Whereof shee dyde incontinent, so swift the bane did rancle. | Whom when the Thracian Poet had bewayled sufficiently | On earth, the Ghostes departed hence he minding for to trie, | Downe at the gate of Taenarus did go to Limbo lake. | And thence by gastly folk*

and soules late buried he did take | His journey to Persephonee and to the king of Ghosts | That like a Lordly tyran reignes in those unpleasant coasts. | And playing on his tuned harp he thus began to sound. . . . (Ovidius Naso)

Fair girl in the chest of oak, | I'm bent on wrath, you left me. | Lovely form, Gwynedd's candle, | Though you are closed in the grave, | Arise, come up, my dearest, | Open the dark door of earth, | Refuse the long bed of sand, | and come to face me, maiden. (Llywelyn Goch ap Meurig Hen)

In blues it's what you call a felt-inward feeling—of your own self. It's not a spiritual feeling that you have; it's some kind of sorrowful feeling that you have of your own self. It's something that happened to you and cause you to become sorry or something, maybe grievous about it. Then you would compose the song to that feeling that you have. And then you would sing it and after you begin to sing it, then you become accustomed to it through psychology that 'most anybody could have that same feeling as you did. It's universal, but it don't bring joy in the spirit.

SLEEPY JOHN ESTES

The drama's done. Why then here does any one step forth?—Because one did survive. . . . On the second day, a sail drew near, nearer, and picked me up at last. It was the devious-cruising Rachel, that in her retracing search after her missing children, only found another orphan. (Herman Melville)

. . . Oh, and in that same river | You won't swim a second time. (Johann Wolfgang von Goethe)

YANK (JAMES) RACHEL

Tomatoes are at their succulent best when they are vine-ripened to a brilliant red. . . . (F. M. Farmer)

WILL SHADE

We had plenty of fish-fries, Saturday night fish-fries, and I made plenty then. I did pretty good. See, at that time you could get fish for a nickel; get a nickel's worth of fish you get a garbage-can full. Two pieces of corn-bread and all that fish. Used to be a place on Market and Main, you go up there and buy all that fish for a nickel. Nickel's worth of fish and you get seven or ten pieces of fish. Then you get two pieces of corn-bread, you could have another piece of fish. In them days you could get anything you want for a nickel. Ain't like it is now, you got to pay a thousand

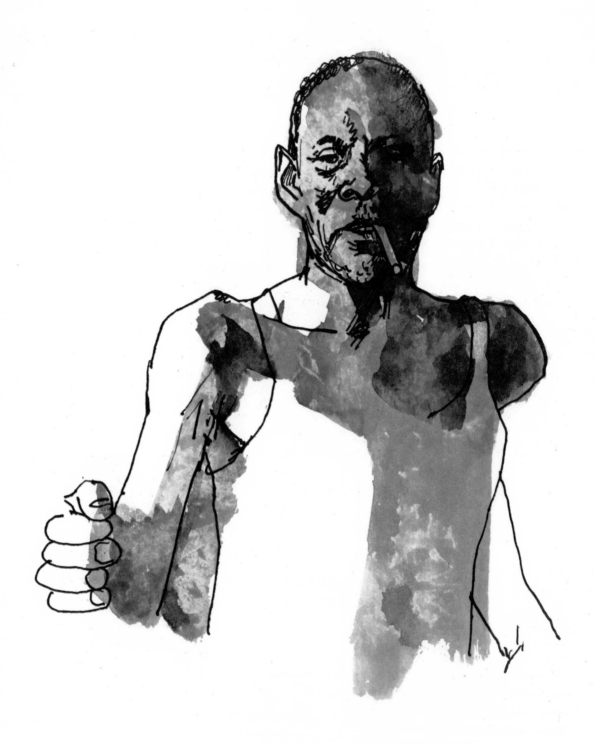

WILL SHADE

dollars for a piece of fish. Get neck-bones at that time for a penny a pound, half a penny a pound. Not like it is now, you got to pay nineteen cents for 'em. So that's why they had plenty of picnics and plenty of fish-fries and we'd go play for 'em.

Used to be wide open houses in them days. You could used to walk down the street in days of 1900 and like that, and you could find a man with throat cut from ear to ear. Also you could find people lying dead with not their throat cut, money took and everything in their pockets took out of their pockets, and thrown outside the house. Sometimes you find them with no clothes on and such as that. Sometimes you find them throwed out of windows and so forth, here on Beale Street. Sportin' class o' women running up and down the street all night long . . . get knocked in the head with bricks and hatchets and hammers. Get cut with pocket knives and razors and so forth. Run off to the foot of Beale, and some of them run into the river and drown. . . .

. . . the ambulance'd come and take 'em in. They'd all be in line, those ambulances, you wouldn't have to call 'em. They line up because they know what's gonna happen on Saturday night. They all gonna be in line and race at the bodies. If you wasn't dead, well, they'd have two drivers in there, and one driver take a needle and stick it in you, and you'd be dead before you reached the hospital. . . . That's the last of you. You automatically dead. No use you kill yourself because the ambulance driver done kill you. Aw, we used to have a rough kind of crowd.

(You see what sort of a man I have grown into as a result, but in order that you may be well informed about the times in which I lived, let me tell you that they were cruel. (Henry Vaughan))

NOAH LEWIS

Paris believes that he possesses me: what he holds is nothing but an airy delusion. (Euripides)

GUS CANNON

Bob Dennison, playin' a pipe. He wasn't playin' no jug. Bob Dennison from Nashville, Tennessee. Lived on that street where the Haymarket's at. That was Bob Dennison, he, poor boy, he's gone. And they brought it here, and I brought it here, and I see some them here coming talking 'bout they started it. They didn't do it. They didn't do it. I won't 'spute 'em.

Now I was playing some banjo with some kitchen mechanic down there, for the boys down there then. Up and down the country with my banjo. I been a ditch digger; I worked for Pritchett Brothers laying sewers. I'm a sewer digger—I dug one the other

day for a man they had a contract with. They say I'm too old to
dig no more, but for why, I'm used to doing it.

> (. . . *hope not being hope | until all ground for hope has | vanished.* . . .
> *(Marianne Moore)*)

Bill Wilbur

> . . . *she labored with love, with indefatigable industry, comforting
> herself modestly with the thought that the dressing-gown and the quilted
> blankets would clothe, warm, caress, and delight the magnificent*

GUS CANNON

Oblomov. For days, as he lay on the sofa in his room, he admired the way her bare elbows moved to and fro in the wake of the needle and the cotton. As in the old days at Oblomovka, he more than once dozed off to the regular sound. . . .

". . . That woman—what is she to you?"

"She's my wife," Oblomov said calmly. (Ivan Goncharov)

MEMPHIS WILLIE B. (BORUM)

You are nothing to me.

Come, my darling girls, | let us stop singing now | for soon it will be day. (Sappho)

ALABAMA

ED BELL

This worlde is full of variaunce | In everything, who taketh hede: | That feith and trust and all constaunce | Exiled ben, this is no drede; | And, save oonly in womanhede, | I can see no sikernesse. | But, for all that, yet, as I rede, | Bewar alway of doublenesse. (John Lydgate)

My mama didn't like me, | My papa give me away: | That's the very reason | I'm the rambling kind today.

BAREFOOT BILL

. . . even though I showed some favor | to those sweet looks and fair appearances | which proved so treacherous | and pierced me to the quick, | they've left me now | and failed me in my greatest need. | I'd better plough another field | and bang another coin | . . . And since I now must go | without assurance of returning | (I'm not without my faults, nor made | of tougher stuff than other men; | human life is an uncertain thing | and there's no respite from death; | also, I have far to go), | I now set forth this will. . . . (Francois Villon)

But let mee not upon my Love bestowe | What is not worth the giving. I doe owe | Somewhat to Dust: My Bodye's pamper'd care | Hungry Corruption and the Worms will share. | That mouldring Relick which in Earth must ly | Would prove a guift of horrour to thine Ey. (Bishop Henry King)

EDWARD THOMPSON

And I say to you: when someone goes someone remains. (César Vallejo)

A SURVEY OF SORTS: VARIOUS VOICES

CLIFFORD GIBSON

My dear's husband hates my life, | Fierce his attack, sly schemer. | Tight lipped, ill-famed, ignoble, | Vicious, mad scowl, like an ox, | Sometimes he's mute, good temper, | And sometimes he threatens me. (Dafydd ap Gwilym)

SUNNY BOY AND HIS PALS / TWO POOR BOYS

Two heavy horses and a slow carriage, that or something else. . . . (George Seferis)

JAYBIRD COLEMAN

I blow harmonica, but I don't try to blow like nobody but myself, you know. I mean, a lot of guys cross it. You can play it straight; you can cross it three times; you can cross it four times. . . . You know, you take ten keys and make forty out of them, take ten keys and make thirty, take ten keys and make twenty,—and you can play the ten keys. You cross it with your mouth, with your tongue. I can't show you how to cross it 'cause I got it in my mouth. Nobody can teach you how to blow —you just have to pick up on it. You can't be taught. One thing about it though: I think everybody should have their own style; you know what I mean—be themself. (Shaky Jake)

I sure would like to get one of Jaybird's old records so I could hear him again. He could make that harp talk. (Joe Coleman)

GEORGIA

CHARLIE LINCOLN

The next night the Prince came again, but she knew not of it. . . . The prince's attendant saw a palanquin . . . and said to His Highness, "Someone has already come—there is a palanquin." "Let us retire," said the Prince, and he went away . . . the Prince . . . did not write to her for a long time.

Yet at last: "Love and misery in various shapes / Pass through my mind and never rest." *She wished to answer, but was ashamed to explain herself, so only wrote:* "Let it be as you will, come or not, yet to part without bitter feeling would lighten my sorrow." *(Izumi Shikibu)*

DIRECTIONS: Add 1 cup boiling water . . . Stir until dissolved. Add 1 cup cold water. Chill until firm . . . Add 6 ice cubes . . . Stir until melted. (Standard Brands, Inc.)

His bony beird was kemmit and croppit, | Bot all with cale it was bedroppit, | And he was townishe, peirt and gukit. | He clappit fast, he kist and chukkit, | As with the glaikis he were ovirgane, | Yit be his feirris he wald have fukkit! | Ye brek my hart, my bony ane. (William Dunbar)

Dream love's pain: | Shocked: | Though reaching out | When no hand to touch (Ōtomo Yakamochi)

On a Christmas Day we were mushing our way over the Dawson trail. | Talk of your cold! through the parka's fold it stabbed like a driven nail. | If our eyes we'd close, then the lashes froze till sometimes we couldn't see; | It wasn't much fun, but the only one to whimper was Sam McGee. (Robert W. Service)

PEG LEG HOWELL

I stood on the corner, looked two blocks and a half / I didn't see
my rider but I'm sure I heard her laugh.

Lady Unluck, on the other hand | Clutches you to her loving heart; | She says she's in no hurry, | Sits on your bed and knits. (Heinrich Heine)

WILLIE BAKER

> *When he sleeps . . . stay there, rise not from your place   so that when he wakes he has to search for you. . . . (Mwana Kupona)*

BUMBLE BEE SLIM

> *The hye god, whan he hadde Adam maked, | And saugh him al allone, belly-naked, | God of his grete goodnesse seyde than, | "Lat us now make an help un-to this man | Lyk to him-self;" and thanne he made him Eve. (Geoffrey Chaucer)*

BLIND WILLIE McTELL

> *You too, who pride yourself that love's in flower— | Poor fool, no girl is constant for an hour | . . . "Once in a while," although her calls come fast, | Must be your rule: what's envied does not last. (Sextus Propertius)*

Now I'm gonna play you a blues that was made, back in the days of old, when blues first started being original. . . .

I'm talking about the days of years ago, count from nineteen and eight, on up, to the original years. Back in the years of, those days, blues have started to be original, and nineteen and fourteen: from then until the war time, people always had, times, from blues on up to original blues. Then on up to 1920: the changed blues. After then, there was more blues. After then, there come the jazz: blues. . . .

Oh I taken music up when I were: quite a child, but in the period of time I quit for eight years. After the eight years I went back to playing. . . . I continued my playing up until nineteen and twenty-seven, the eighteenth day of October, when I made records for the Victor Record people, and from then up until 1932 I played for the Victor people alone, by myself, but in the period of time, in 1929 I made records for the Columbia people, changing my name to Blind Samuel, and was the authorizer of this song, "Come Around to My House, Mama," "Cigarette Blues," and the "Atlanta Strut," and so on. And after then I worked with the Vocalion people of nineteen and thirty-three, taking up odd jobs, they paid me a small sum of money of fifty dollars a week, but they was getting all the records of blues that they can, which we call the alley. And after the period of time I picked up another job, with the Decca Record Company . . . they give me a small sum of money but get paid expense. And after the period of time I returned back to Augusta Georgia where they had moved the machine, where they have laid a gang of blues there, in the summer, in June of nineteen and thirty-six. And after the period of time I haven't made any more records, but I have lots to be released . . . in the meantime . . . I followed shows, different shows

around, medicine shows, carnivals, and all different types of little
funny shows, after a period of record making.

NORTH CAROLINA/VIRGINIA

BLIND BOY FULLER

> *I'd not wish my life longer | When she has no fuller life. . . . (Dafydd*
> *Nanmorr)*

My left side jumps, baby, and my flesh begin to crawl.

BLIND GARY DAVIS

There was a time when I went blind / . . . It was the darkest day
that I ever saw / It was a time when I went blind / I cried the day
I went blind. . . .

> *When through the North a fire shall rush | And rowle into the East, |*
> *And like a firie torrent brush | And sweepe up South, and West, | . . . O*
> *then it wilbe all too late | To say,* What shall I doe? *(Henry Vaughan)*

WILLIAM MOORE

> *I love securely, trusting powers divine, | And Cynthia the incomparable*
> *is mine. | I soar: the stars are not too high for me; | Henceforth, come*
> *dark, come daylight, mine is she. | No rival steals my well-vouched love*
> *away— | My glory, which shall see my hairs turn grey. (Sextus*
> *Propertius)*

ST. LOUIS

LONNIE JOHNSON

I worked all sorts of places—I worked at the Iroquois Theater for
a long time and I worked at Frank Pineri's place on Iberville and
Burgundy, oh God, I don't know *how* long—'bout four and a
half years or something like that. Strictly blues all the way—
on the violin. And I made several numbers on the piano—I used
to play piano for a while, but only blues, no popular songs. Then
I bought my guitar. I bought it in 1917. It's a beautiful instrument.
And at night, if you want to get the real effect of it, take a small
tub—you know, a small wash tub—fill it up with water, sit down
on the steps, and set that tub of water down. You set down there

and play it, and let that sound come through that water, and you talkin' about somethin' beautiful. . . .

So I tried to make it in Chicago, but I had to quit the music business. I worked for a firm making railroad ties in Galesburg, Illinois—that's right! Those ties weigh as much as me—180 pounds! So then I went to Peoria, Illinois—that's about sixty miles from Galesburg—and I work in a steel foundry there; play the blues at night. . . . That's true, I've done all kinds of work, even been a coal miner—oh, God, yes, I done everything! So right now I'm a janitor at the Ben Franklin Hotel. . . .

(Shamed, the world says, we poets! | And shamed the state of our craft! | The role of bard lacks honor; | It was once renowned, not scorned. . . . (Siôn Tudur))

CHARLIE JORDAN

Hard for one in need, bless her, | Long grief, to hold the tall dear: | I'll not have my slim-browed girl; | Her keeper won't allow it. . . . (Welsh lyric)

HI HENRY BROWN

They fought with God's cold— | And they could not and fell to the deck | (Crushed them) or water (and drowned them) or rolled | With the sea-romp over the wreck. | Night roared, with the heartbreak hearing a heart-broke rabble, | The woman's wailing, the crying of child without check. . . . (Gerard Manley Hopkins)

Jack Johnson wanted to get on board, | Captain said, "I ain't hauling no coal," | Fare thee, Titanic, fare thee well. . . . | When he heard about that mighty shock | Might-a seen the man done the eagle rock, | Fare thee, Titanic, fare thee well. (Leadbelly)

HENRY TOWNSEND

. . . I was followed | By Argus, a giant herdsman of ungoverned rage, | Who watched my every step with his ten thousand eyes. (Aeschylus)

I have never depended on the life of the blues singer as for support. I have always felt that I should do something else. . . . I drove a taxi for about twelve years, which is very educational for anybody —I mean dealing with the public, you know.

J. D. (JELLY JAW) SHORT

What I think about that makes the blues really good is when a fellow writes the blues and then writes it with a feeling, with a great harmony, and there's so many true words in the blues, of things that have happened to so many people, and that's why it makes the feeling in the blues.

I yoked a team of jade dragons to a phoenix-figured car | And waited for the wind to come, to soar up on my journey. | In the morning I started on my way from Ts'ang-wu; | In the evening I came to the Garden of Paradise. | . . . I watered my dragon steeds at the Pool of Heaven . . . | I . . . fly ever onward by night and by day | . . . look for a maiden below . . . | . . . the lovely daughter of the Lord of Sung | . . . the Lord of Yü's two princesses . . . | I . . . ordered Ling Fen to make divination for me. | He said . . . | "What woman seeking handsome mate could ever refuse you? | What place on earth does not boast some fragrant flower? . . ." | . . . I will go off wandering to look for a lady. . . . (Ch'ü Yüan)

BIG JOE WILLIAMS

Well you know that President Roosevelt, | He was awful fine; | Well he helped the crippled boys, | And almost healed the blind.

SOME PIANOS

WESLEY WALLACE

The train had been clattering along now for ten minutes and the little girl . . . whispered: "Mamma, I want to see. . . ."

The mother asked: "But what do you want to see? You can see everything, can't you?"

The little girl burst into tears: "I can't see the train."

Borlini let out a laugh, and the child's parents laughed too. . . . Only Aghios was touched. Only he felt and knew what sorrow there was in not being able to see oneself while traveling.

The pleasure of the journey would have been completely different if she had been able to see that great train with its engine as it slithered along the countryside like a swift, silent serpent. To see the landscape, the train and oneself at the same time—that really would have been traveling! (Italo Svevo)

BERT MAYS

(They say that Sasuke disliked seeing her laugh. I suppose he found it painful; since there is something poignant about a blind preson's laughter.) . . . To guide her, Sasuke would raise his left hand as high as her shoulder, and Shunkin would rest the palm of her right hand in his upturned palm. He seemed to be no more than a hand to her. (Tanizaki Junichirō)

LEROY CARR

I had the blues before sunrise, with tears standing in my eyes; /
It's such a miserable feeling, a feeling I do despise.

When I did, went to playing the real blues, I was gone, too, just gone. Know who learned me that? Nobody. It just come to me like anything else. Like you sit here and think about it. Maybe you go get something next door; come to you while you're resting. . . .

No matter how high a bird fly—in the elements—that bird's got to come down for food and water. (Scrapper Blackwell)

WALTER ROLAND

People said that a race of winged demons—the Tengu—lived in a certain valley of Kurama Mountain, and on nights when lightning flashes played through the clouds over this valley, they warned one another that the Tengu were holding their revels. And no man dared venture into that valley to spy on them, for the beak-nosed Tengu would scent out the stranger and set him swinging from the tallest treetop or else tear him to pieces. (Yoshikawa Eiji)

BLACK IVORY KING

The values of colors differ appreciably and have analogy to the differing values of other sensations. As sweet or pungent smells, as high and low notes, or major and minor chords, differ from each other by virtue of their different stimulation of the senses, so also red differs from green. . . . (George Santayana)

ROOSEVELT SYKES

I hate to think about another man snoring in my baby's face.

Bee not a Baker, if your head be of butter. (George Herbert)

LITTLE BROTHER MONTGOMERY

. . . I . . . was able to hear real people play—such as Son Framion and a guy named Friday Ford. There was another player that was called Papa Lord God and one named Vanderbilt Anderson . . . Leon Bromfield . . . and all those type of players. . . . And then I run up against Tommy Jackson—he was Tony Jackson's first cousin . . . he was a great musician. Sudan Washington was a great musician. Cooney Vaughns was one of the best piano players I ever heard and he was from Hattiesburg, Mississippi. They had one called Blind Homer—he was a juke piano player. Blind Jud—he was another. And there was Gus Pevsner, only he was a musicianer like . . . you know, musical, played by notes and things. . . .

Then so I came up in Arkansas, in Arkansas City and Eudora, round up in there. Lake Village—there I run up against a guy they called Burnt Face Jake: his name was Jake Facey but they called him Burnt Face Jake; he was a great piano player, had his own style of playing. . . . So in Lake Village I met Joe Martin: he died one Christmas I think, in 1923 or '22, or something like that. So I run across George Young—Son Young—he got killed at Waterproof, Louisiana; he was a great piano player. Walter Lewis—he was another one. I ran across another guy they called Skinny Head Pete—he was good. And also a boy they called Freddie

Coates in Greenville, Mississippi. I thought these guys were great. . . .

On up I learned a . . . blues from a great guy name of Loomis Gibson: we called it the "Loomis Gibson Blues" which is the name of it. . . .

When I got to Chicago in 1928 . . . I met quite a few piano players at that time coming into Chicago like I was, and some of them were already living there of course. Well there was fellas like Jerome Carrington, Jimmy Papa Yancey, Albert Ammons, Pine-top Smith, Robert Alexander, Clarence Jones—Ole Man Clarence we used to call him—and such fellas. Later on in years I run up against Bob Montgomery, another great piano player—I think he was some kin to Jump Jackson. . . .

> *(There were piano players all over the city, guys you'd never hear of again. (Jimmy Walker))*

There's a right way to play music and there's a wrong way. You can't just play the way you feel. . . . The music has to come from within, yes, but you have to play it right.

Lost John Hunter

> *. . . I heard a murmur, something gone wrong with the silence. . . .*
> *(Samuel Becket)*

Jesse James

> Speed. *But shall she marry him?*
> Launce. *No.*
> Speed. *How then? Shall he marry her?*
> Launce. *No, neither.*
> Speed. *What, are they broken?*
> Launce. *No; they are both as whole as a fish.*
> Speed. *Why then, how stands the matter with them?*
> Launce. *Marry, thus—when it stands well with him, it stands well with*
> *   her. (William Shakespear)*

Peetie Wheatstraw

> *Welcome, O welcome my illustrious Spouse; | Welcome as are the ends*
> *unto my Vowes: | I! far more welcome than the happy soile, | The Sea-*
> *scourg'd Merchant, after all his toile, | Salutes with tears of joy; when*
> *fires betray | The smokie chimneys of his Ithaca. | Where hast thou*
> *been so long from my embraces, | Poor pittyed Exile? (Robert Herrick)*

WALTER DAVIS

There was nobody at Ike-no-O who did not know about the nose of Zenchi Naigu. (Akutagawa Ryūnosuke)

SPECKLED RED

. . . they was real bad words, you see; I was playing in one of them turpentine jukes where it didn't matter. Anything I said there was all right in there, you see. I had to clean it up for the record, but it meaned the same thing. . . . In those days and in them places you could say some of them smelly words and don't think nothing of it, but it's a whole lots different now.

After I left Memphis I went all over the country. I played anywhere I could make a nickel. Wasn't making much. . . . 'Course back in them days you didn't need too much money, but you could make enough to get along. So I played around until 1939, when I come back to St. Louis. Left there, come back . . . and I been around there since 1941 about. I started playing at the Dixie Tavern—different joints, first one thing, then another. Then I quit. Quit for about ten years. Wasn't making nothing, so I went to work on Market, St. Louis—I got to be a shipping clerk, I didn't play nowhere.

(It probably goes to show that peace is not for us. I have never had a steady job since, though I have had easy seasons. (Ezra Pound))

Well now, . . . you know what I'm talking about. I don't know how to explain myself, but anyway, whatever it is, it's that. You know, it's got to be that.

You be good and I'll be good as I can.

CRIPPLE CLARENCE LOFTON

. . . but what I mean about this is when a musician—they all know one another—they all gets to a place and they sits down to a piano and they starts to barrelhousin'. And what I mean by barrelhousin'—barrelhousin' it mean store-porchin', and store-porchin' it mean one man be playin' a piano. . . . (Otis Spann)

CHICAGO

BIG BILL BROONZY

There was no one in the whole town willing to touch your wife, Caecilianus, gratis, while he was allowed; but, now you have set your

guards, there is a huge crowd of gallants. You are an ingenious person!
(Marcus Valerius Martialis)

Big Bill had been around a long time in Chicago when I come up
in '43, so he helped me to get my start. (Muddy Waters)

I played mostly in the streets for about three years . . . played on
Maxwell Street and places. And Big Bill took me up and then
Muddy Waters. (Little Walter)

And the first person I ran into playing here was Big Bill Broonzy
. . . So Big Bill he take me as his son and I played with him just
as long as I wanted to play. (J. B. Lenoir)

HOKUM BOYS : GEORGIA TOM (WITH JANE LUCAS)

O body swayed to music, O brightening glance, | How can we know the
dancer from the dance? (W. B. Yeats)

BIG BILL BROONZY

WASHBOARD SAM

Orphaned I | unshining | firefly (Kobayashi Issa)

Such wealth of buttocks would slow the walk of anyone. (Vallaṇa)

TAMPA RED

"Don't you fear God, Giaour? . . . Because, little Roumi, he who can sleep with a woman and does not, commits a great sin. My boy, if a woman calls you to share her bed and you don't go, your soul will be destroyed! That woman will sigh before God on judgement day, and that woman's sigh, whoever you may be and whatever your fine deeds, will cast you into Hell!" (Nikos Kazantzakis)

My theory of a song is that it should have some meaning.

After all, kids hear these things. I think anybody should be able to hear them. If some people get a joke out of them and have some fun with them, fine. But the words shouldn't force a joke on anybody who doesn't hear it.

JAZZ GILLUM

Come keen Iambicks, with your Badgers feet, | And Badger-like, bite till your teeth do meet. | Help ye tart Satyrists, to imp my rage, | With all the Scorpions that should whip this age. (John Cleveland)

SONNY BOY WILLIAMSON

Draw wine for me in the little flask   that makes a man stagger and sway | . . . When I am well wined I stand   demanding my keen-edged sword. . . . (Swahili song)

. . . I tell you who I was working with. Roosevelt Sykes. Working right on Indiana. And Sonny Boy Williamson was working just around the corner. So we would alternate on our intermission time and go round to the Plantation Club and keep him company and play with him, and on his intermission time he'd come round to the club where I was working at, a place called the Flame. So he just come round, and then he went back, went round the corner. He said, "Well, I'll see you after a while when you get off; come on round to the club." I say, "O.k." And about five minutes later a fella come round and say he's dead. And we thought he was kidding, you know? He had seventeen holes in his head with an ice pick. They ganged him. He was 'bout one of the finest fellas I know. (Lonnie Johnson)

(Powys, fair land and fruitful, | Fine taverns, sweet drinking-horns, |

A SURVEY OF SORTS: VARIOUS VOICES

It was a pleasant orchard | Till blue blade slew this wise lad. | Now it lacks, wretched widow, | Land of hawks, its nightingale. | Poor in bards, song degraded, | Is this land, hated by foes. | If grief must be, these three months, | Ah, why was loss no lighter, | When he met, cry of great rage, | A sword's edge. . . . (Dafydd ap Gwilym))

KOKOMO ARNOLD

From Ymir's . . . brains | were created | all storm-threatening clouds. . . .

The ancient one lives in the east | in the Wood of Iron | and there gives birth | to Fenrir's brood; | one of them . . . | will seize the sun. || He is gorged with the flesh | of the death-doomed | and with red blood he reddens | the dwellings of the gods; | sunlight of summers to come | will be black | and all weathers bad. . . .

The one who squats at the end of the sky | is known as engulfer of corpses, | a giant in eagle form; | they say from his wings | comes the wind | of this world. (Snorri Sturluson)

FLOYD COUNCIL

. . . behind us, moving more quickly, coming up and passing by, a crowd of souls, silent and devout, was gazing at us. Each was dark and hollow in the eyes, pallid in the face, and so wasted that the skin took its shape from the bones. I do not think Erisichthon was so dried up to utter rind by hunger, when he had most fear of it. (Dante Alighieri)

THE '40's AND '50's

ROBERT (JUNIOR) LOCKWOOD

One of those whom we call gentleman, who always carry some horn hanging at their backs, as though they would hunt during dinner, said: "I swear by God's body I would rather that my son should hang than study letters. For it becomes the sons of gentlemen to blow the horn nicely, and to hunt skilfully, and elegantly carry and train a hawk. But the study of letters should be left to the sons of rustics. . . ."

"You do not seem to me to think aright, good man," said I, "for if any foreigner were to come to the king, such as are ambassadors of princes, and an answer had to be given to him, your son if he were educated as you wish, could only blow his horn. . . ." (Richard Pace)

What is there to say?—I just make tunes, that's all.

TONY HOLLINS

I am prepared under my Constitutional duty to recommend the measures that a stricken nation in the midst of a stricken world may require.

These measures, or such other measures as the Congress may build out of its experience and wisdom, I shall seek, within my Constitutional authority, to bring to speedy adoption. (Franklin D. Roosevelt)

WRIGHT HOLMES

Baal went up into the heights of Saphon; | Baal viewed his girls: | He eyed Pidrai, Girl of Light, | Also Tallai, Girl of Rain. . . . (Ugaritic tablet)

JOHN HENRY BARBEE

I would not wish, my darling, | To live, lacking my fine girl. | From this pain that's upon me, | Gentle Morfudd, I shall die. (Dafydd ap Gwilym)

L. C. GREEN

Fatherless, sonless, homeless haunters. . . . (Edwin Muir)

MUDDY WATERS

Seven the maiden's kisses, | Seven birches by the grave, | Seven vespers and masses, | Seven sermons from the thrush, | Seven leaf-colored lyrics, | Seven nightingales and boughs, | Seven strokes of ecstasy, | Seven gems, seven lyrics, | Seven songs to slim Morfudd's | Firm flesh. . . . (Welsh lyric)

. . . I was just a boy and they put me to working right alongside the men. . . . Every man would be hollering, but you don't pay that no mind. Yeah, 'course I'd holler too. You might call them blues, but they was just made-up things. Like a fella be working or most likely some gal be working near you and you want to say something to 'em. So you holler it. Sing it. Or maybe to your mule or something or it's getting late and you wanna go home. I can't remember much of what I was singing now, 'cepting I do remember I was always singing, "I can't be satisfied. . . ."

HOWLIN' WOLF

Moreover the word of the Lord came to me, saying, Go and cry. . . . Therefore, hear. . . . : . . . weep sore for him that goeth away. . . . (Jeremiah)

MUDDY WATERS

JOHN LEE HOOKER

Among the animals the serpent was notable. Of all of them he had the most excellent qualities, in some of which he resembled man. Like man he stood upright upon two feet, and in height he was equal to the camel. . . . Envy made him meditate ways and means of bringing about the death of Adam . . . and he approached the woman, knowing that women are beguiled easily. (Louis Ginzberg)

And the Lord God said unto the serpent, Because thou hast done this, thou art cursed above all cattle, and above every beast of the field; upon thy belly shalt thou go, and dust shalt thou eat all the days of thy life: | And I will put enmity between thee and the woman, and between thy seed and her seed; it shall bruise thy head, and thou shalt bruise his heel. (Genesis: 3/14–15)

There's a lot of things that give you the blues, that give me the blues, that give any man the blues: it's somewhere down the line that you have been hurt some place.

SOMEWHERE TO END

SMOKY BABE

We sincerely believe coal is on the verge of becoming a great growth industry, especially in the utility market. (President Tarkington of Continental Oil Company)

BROTHER WILL HAIRSTON

After the final no there comes a yes | And on that yes the future world depends. | No was the night. (Wallace Stevens)

ROBERT PETE WILLIAMS

Music begin to follow me then. I been trying to stop playing, thinking 'bout preparing my soul for Jesus. . . . Just look to me like I can't put music down. Time I get hold of one guitar and I maybe sell it to somebody, well music just come back to me and worry me so, I just have to go back and buy me another guitar. . . . All the music I play I just hear in the air. You can hear the sound of it coming forth, sounding good.

Today I am old and grave; I recognize few, but I used to brandish a sharp spear bravely in a morning of cold ice. (Agallamh na Seanórach)

I got something to tell you baby / But I hate to tell you this / You

may not want to hear it / Some time I be walking along / Feel like
to me I'm gonna fall dead / I don't know, maybe my nerves bad /
'Cause I don't drink that much.

> *I see myself sometimes, an old man | Who has walked along with time
> as time's true servant, | That he's grown strange to me—who was once
> myself—. . . . (Edwin Muir)*

> *. . . the stranger and enemy, we've seen him in the mirror. (George
> Seferis)*

Me and my friends all sitting around, they can't help me and I
can't help them.

> *Ideal and dearly beloved voices | of those who are dead, or of those |
> who are lost to us like the dead. || Sometimes they speak to us in our
> dreams; | sometimes in thought the mind hears them. || And for a
> moment with their echo other echoes | return from the first poetry of our
> lives— | like music that extinguishes the far-off night. (C. P. Cavafy)*

A SURVEY OF SORTS: VARIOUS VOICES

ACKNOWLEDGEMENTS

To give credit, where due, passages in the preceding pages have, to the best of my memory, previously appeared as follows: George Allen and Unwin (L. Surmelian, *Daredevils of Sassoon*); Bollingen Foundation (Paul Valery, *The Art of Poetry;* Paul Radin, *African Folktales and Sculpture*); George Braziller (Robert Graves, *The Greek Myths*); *Boston Broadside; Blues Unlimited* (interviews by Pete Welding); Bowes and Bowes (Snorri Sturluson, *The Prose Edda*); The University of California Press (Ruth Finer Mintz, *Modern Hebrew Poetry;* Carlo L. Gilino, *Contemporary Italian Poetry;* Italo Svevo, *Short Sentimental Journey*); Cambridge University Press (A. J. Arberry, *Arabic Poetry*); Cassel and Co. (Paul Oliver, *Conversation with the Blues*); Jonathan Cape (Louis Zukofsky, *"A"*); J. M. Dent and Sons (Dylan Thomas, *Selected Letters*); Delmark Records (R. J. Koester, *Piney Woods Blues; The Dirty Dozens*); E. P. Dutton and Co. (Benedikt and Welwarth, *Modern French Theater*); Dover Publications (George Santayana, *The Sense of Beauty*); Faber and Faber (Wallace Stevens, *Collected Poems* and *Opus Posthumus;* W. H. Auden, *Essays in Criticism;* Nikos Kazantzakis, *Zorba the Greek*); Folkways Records *(Lightning Hopkins; Blind Willie Johnson; Furry Lewis; Barrelhouse Piano); Forbes Magazine;* Grove Press (Edwin Muir, *Collected Poems;* Eugene Ionesco, *Notes and Counter Notes;* Jean Genet, *Thief's Journal;* Samuel Becket, *Molloy*); Horizon Press (Martin Buber, *The Origin and Meaning of Hasidism*); Houghton Mifflin, Co. (Omori and Doi, *Diaries of Court Ladies of Old Japan*); Harvard University Press (D. H. H. Ingalls, *An Anthology of Sanskrit Court Poetry*); Harcourt Brace and World (C. P. Cavafy, *Complete Poems*); Kodansha International (Eric Sackheim, *The Silent Firefly*); Alfred A. Knopf (Yoshikawa Eiji, *The Heike Story;* Tanizaki Junichiro, *Seven Japanese Tales*); Little Brown and Co. *(The Fanny Farmer Cookbook);* Macmillan (J. P. Clancy, *Medieval Welsh Lyrics;* Greene and O'Connor, *A Golden Treasury of Irish Poetry;* Marianne Moore, *Collected Poems;* Dante Alighieri, *The Divine Comedy;* W. B. Yeats, *Collected Poems*); Melodeon Records (Library of Congress: *Blind Willie McTell*); New Directions (Ezra Pound, *Literary Essays; Pound/Joyce Letters and Essays;* Charles Olson, *Selected Writings;* W. C. Williams, *In the American Grain*); W. W. Norton (Edith Sitwell, *Alexander Pope*); *Origin* (Cesar Vallejo, "Poemas Humanos"); Peter Owen (Meyer Waxman, *Great Jewish Personalities*); October House (Ruth Whitman, *An Anthology of Modern Yiddish Poetry*); Oxford University Press (Lyndon Harries, *Swahili Poetry;* David Hawkes, *Ch'u Tz'u*); Oak Publications (Samuel Charters, *The Poetry of the Blues; The Bluesmen*); Orijin Jazz Library (Bernard Klatzko, re Charlie Patton); Princeton University Press (George Seferis, *Collected Poems*); Penguin Books (Leonard Forster, *German Verse;* F. G. Lorca, *Lorca;* Calvin Tomkins, *Ahead of the Game;* Leo Tolstoy, *Anna Karenina;* N. K. Sandars, *The Epic of Gilgamesh;* Ivan Goncharov, *Oblomov*); Random House (James Joyce, *Ulysses;* W. H. Auden, *Selected Shorter Poems*); Rinehart and Co. (Samuel Charters, *The Country Blues*); Scorpion Press (Paul Klee, *Some Poems by Paul Klee*); Schocken Books (Burnshaw, Carmi & Spicehandler, *The Modern Hebrew Poem Itself*); *Sing Out* (Julius Lester, interviews with Son House and Booker White); Standard Brands; Simon and Schuster (Louis Ginzberg, *The Legends of the Jews*); Takoma Records (Bukka White, *Mississippi Blues*); The Viking Press (James Joyce, *Collected Poems*); Vanguard Records (Bruce Jackson, *Skip James/Today!*); Western Reserve University Press (Makoto Ueda, *Literary and Art Theories in Japan*); and numerous other sources* which I regret I am no longer able to retrace; I apologize for any omissions or incorrect attributions.

*O my Lord, what shall I do with all this great material? When shall these thousand planks be a work of art . . . ? (Middle Irish epigram)